THE GENTLE
BARBARIAN

V. S. Pritchett

THE GENTLE BARBARIAN

The Life and Work of Turgenev

The Ecco Press
New York

Grateful acknowledgment is made to Penguin Books Ltd. for
permission to reprint brief excerpts from pages 94, 97, 105,
126, 142, 165, 169, 189, 220, 271, and 291 of Fathers and Sons
by Ivan Turgenev, translated by Rosemary Edmonds (Penguin
Classics, 1965). Copyright © 1965 by Rosemary Edmonds.

Library of Congress Cataloging in Publication Data
Pritchett, V.S. (Victor Sawdon), 1900-
The gentle barbarian.
Reprint. Originally published: New York:
Vintage Books 1978, © 1977.
Bibliography: p. 243
1. Turgenev, Ivan Sergeevich, 1818-1883.   2. Authors,
Russian—19th century—Biography.   I. Title.
[PG3435.P7] 1986   891.73'3   86-6238
ISBN 0-88001-120-3

Manufactured in the United States of America

For My Wife

*Tourguéneff le doux géant, l'aimable bar-
bare . . . nous charme, nous enguirlande—*

The Goncourt *Journals*

Acknowledgements

THERE has not yet been a definitive biography of Turgenev in any language. Much is mysterious and changeable in the life of a novelist who dazzled his friends by his conversation and his thousands of engaging letters. My own book is a portrait and, having no Russian, I have relied entirely on sources in English and French translation. I owe a considerable debt to Avrahm Yarmolinsky's brilliant *Turgenev: The Man, His Art and His Age,* to David Magarshack's capable *Life,* and for the crucial matter of Turgenev's relations with Pauline Viardot, to April Fitzlyon's *The Price of Genius.* These scholars and Henri Granjard and Alexandre Zviguilsky and their recent editions of Turgenev's correspondence with the Viardots have been invaluable and I thank them. My chief concern has been to enlarge the understanding of his superb short stories and novels and to explore the interplay of what is know about his life with his art. He was a deeply autobiographical writer.

I must thank the following translators on whom I have freely drawn, for enabling me to make my purpose clear: Constance Garnett; David Magarshack; Natalie Duddington; Rosemary Edmonds; Richard Freeborn; George Reavey; Leonard Schapiro; Robert Nichols; M. S. Mendel; and Isaiah Berlin both for his translation of *First Love* and his illuminating Romanes Lectures.

THE GENTLE
BARBARIAN

Chapter 1

Ivan Turgenev was born in the autumn of 1818 in Orel, a provincial capital some three hundred miles southwest of Moscow and halfway to Kiev. It was, in those days, a large town of distilleries, craftsmen in stone, glass, china and timber, and the centre of a rich agricultural trade in hemp, rye, wheat and tobacco, and famous for breeding horses and cattle. The merchants lived in dull stone houses two storeys high; there was a market-place stinking of rush mats and cabbage, there were bazaars which suggested the Orient. Nearby was the pillared mansion of the Governor with striped sentry boxes at the gates and the large private houses of the gentry, some of them with odd turrets on them. There was a promenade where the young trees were dying and scores of miserable taverns giving out clouds of tobacco smoke and the pervasive smells of spirits. On the outskirts were the tumbledown huts of the artisans, known by their sheepskin coats. At night most of them were drunk. Long before the industrial revolution reached Russia, Orel was reckoned to be a prosperous place. At sunrise all roads leading to Orel were crowded with long strings of wagons travelling to the market.

The Turgenevs had a fine house in Orel and another in Moscow. Ivan's mother, Varvara Petrovna, noted in French, the polite lan-

guage of her class, that the new baby was twenty-one inches long.
He was her second son. She was a very rich, trim but ugly young
woman, in her early thirties, fond of dress, six years older than her
husband, an almost penniless and handsome young cavalry officer
who had been forced by his relations to marry her for her money,
and after Ivan's birth he threw up his commission in the army.
When the end of the thaw made travel possible the following year,
he moved the family to his wife's enormous estate at Spasskoye.

The migrations of the gentry from their town houses to their
estates were remarkable processions as they went from post house to
post house over the bad roads of the monotonous countryside. The
family coach of the Turgenevs was a heavy vehicle drawn by a team
of six horses on the eighty-mile journey. A lackey sat on a mat on
the rear step holding on by a rope and was either spattered with mud
or choked by the clouds of dust. After the coach came a string of
inferior carriages and carts carrying luggage and servants. They
crossed between the low wooded hills of undulating country that
opened into ravines where small rivers ran out into marshland and
finally on to the endless steppe where the villages were poor. The
peasant huts with their roofs of rotting straw seemed to have been
trodden into the soil. In the woodland the huts were spacious and
were built of fir logs and roofed by boards. From what one knows
of Turgenev's father, the retired soldier who was both superstitious
and a sportsman, he would have counted the magpies for luck and
studied the edges of the woodlands for the first sight of snipe and
woodcock and kept his eye open for pretty women. His wife would
be watching the women working with long rakes in the fields, alert
to see if any of her serfs were idle. For Varvara Petrovna her vast
estate was a kingdom in itself; she owned all its villages and most
peasants in them, every horse, cow, pig, goose, even the nightingales
that sang in the trees.

What a hissing of marching geese, what a clatter in the rookeries,
what barking of dogs when the coach at last arrived at her mansion.
Her serf orchestra struck up a tune of welcome as the peremptory
mistress got out. What kneeling to the ground, what kissing of hands
for the privileged servants, what a ringing of bells from room to room
as orders were given, what excited trilling from the scores of cage
birds on the walls as the short, gypsyish mistress stared at her "subjects" as she called her forty house serfs, to detect who among them

had disobeyed her orders and what punishments she would award. The barking of the dogs was stopped at once. She could not bear it.

Spasskoye passed as one of the finest mansions of the province but was really a large, rambling manor house. It had an iron roof and was painted white and built mostly of timber. The central part to which verandahs gave a kind of elegance was two storeys high and, inside, a gallery of stone led to the two long low wings. The place gave the impression of being some enormous white owl that had spread its wings ready to swoop and hunt over the avenue of limes and the thirty acres of garden and park and far beyond. Attached to the house were the quarters of the house serfs, the ice house, the bath house, the house for smoking meat, the tannery, the workshops, the water well and even a mill for making wall-papers and the stationery on which Varvara Petrovna wrote her innumerable orders and comments. Most of the shoes and clothes—though not of the mistress —were made on the estate: with a *belle laide*'s passion for finery she sent to Moscow and even at times to Berlin or Paris for her own clothes. The estate produced all the food and drink it needed. In addition to the waiting servants, the house serfs included her serf doctor and her office clerks; like many landowners she had her own orchestra, singers and actors and as her sons grew there were nurses and valets and a procession of French and German governesses and tutors. She ran the place efficiently. Spasskoye was less a house than a self-sufficient feudal community, the estate was an empire numbering 5,000 "souls" and extended to thousands of acres and included twenty villages which she ruled as an absolute sovereign. Her retinue were indeed divided by rank and title. There was a Chamberlain; her personal maids were ladies-in-waiting and her private office had a dais on which she sat with her portrait behind her, ringing bells— she had a mania for bells—and gave orders and received deputations. None of her serfs could marry without her permission: many she ordered to marry. They were allowed to have children, but once the child was born it was sent away from the house. The police were not permitted to come to Spasskoye although she did soften a little towards the Chief of Police because he amused her—but he had to come to the back door.

In the finest rooms at Spasskoye the furniture was luxurious. The

---

chairs were in ebony, ornamented with bronze cupids leading lions by a chain of flowers, and were upholstered in yellow leather. There was an immense mirror—the marvel of the province. Guests were always coming and going, for Varvara Petrovna loved musical parties, masquerades and cards; and if she was giving grand dinners special food was sent for from Moscow three hundred miles away and arrived over the terrible roads by sledge in the winter or wagon in the summer, though usually in the winter the family moved to a house in Moscow until the thaw ended and travel was possible again. In the summer weeks she would go on a state progress to her villages and the long procession would take to the roads. Wagon-loads of pork and geese and other meats and drink for the journey went on ahead, followed by carriages and carts containing serving women, laundry maids, valets, butlers, clerks and the serf doctor, and finally in her own carriage the dominant Varvara Petrovna herself, with her unforgiving eye on everything.

All Ivan Turgenev's biographers and indeed Turgenev himself portray Varvara Petrovna as a domineering woman. She was governed by two passions: pride—as she admitted when she was dying —and *la rage:* the word "anger" is not strong enough.

Her handsome husband was a cooler, more elusive figure. He was an aristocrat of long line: his wife's family were, comparatively speaking, upstarts. The pedigree of the Turgenev family hung beside the portrait of his grandfather at Spasskoye and was an index to the fancy that they had descended from a Tartar chieftain of the Golden Horde. In that remote time they had given up the Mohammedan faith and one, indeed, became a martyr of the Orthodox Church. Two were killed in the Stenka Rozin revolt in the seventeenth century, others served under Peter the Great and the Empress Anna. They were a family of ruined soldiers. A great-grandfather had been taken prisoner by the Turks and the story was that he had escaped because his charm had beguiled one of the Sultan's wives—a tale close to the tastes of the master of Spasskoye who was noted for his love affairs at home and also, when he took his family on a grand European tour in 1822, in Paris. What was deadly to women was his fashionable feminine grace of manner. He was the cool, good-looking dandy, tall and powerful, an excellent horseman, and perhaps in recording Ivan's length as a baby, Varvara Petrovna was thinking of the height of the husband whom she adored, whom she had passionately pursued, and who did not love her at all. Once he had retired, still young, from the Army he left the management of the estate to her—he himself brought only a tiny place of 130 "souls" to the marriage—and settled to hunting in the fields and among the ladies.

Whether he knew it or not, Turgenev's intelligent but half-educated father was the victim of history. Like others of his class he spoke French in the house and was shaky in his Russian spelling. But not all the Turgenev tribe had been fighting men. One kinsman was the son of a director of Moscow University, another a State official working for the Russian government in Paris, a man of liberal intellect and an important contact in the Paris embassies. It was he certainly who advised the French Marquis de Custine when the Marquis went to Russia and published his notorious account of his journey in 1839, a book which infuriated Russian readers. This Turgenev kinsman had put the Marquis in touch with a Prince Kozlowski who told him that

> Russia, in the present age, is only 400 years removed from the invasion of barbarian tribes, whilst 14 centuries have elapsed since Western Europeans experienced the same crisis. A civilisation older by one thousand years, of course, places an immeasurable distance between the manners of nations. Long before the Tartar invasion Russia had received its rulers from Scandinavia and these had received in turn their tastes, their arts and their luxuries from the emperors and patriarchs of Constantinople.

The civilisation conquered by the Tartars and the saints and the rulers of the new dispensation had never heard of the chivalrous tradition of the West. The invaders remained Asiatic. Their monarchs were like Biblical Kings, they were patriarchs, and the Russian nation was not formed in the school of good faith and honour which had been so important and civilising in the history of the European mind. Indeed—

> The extreme despotism of the Russians was established in the very period when servitude ceased in Europe. Bondage became a constituent principle of society.

Turgenev's father was dead before Custine's ill-natured book appeared. He was certainly not a reading man. After his trip to France, Switzerland and Italy he returned to Spasskoye to live lazily to himself. He would have been about thirty-two when the tragic Decembrist revolt of 1825 marked the end of the hopes of reform and enlightenment which briefly followed the defeat of Napoleon. What the father thought about that revolt no one knows, but the fierce repression did paralyse the public spirit of the men of his generation. Reaction and dullness set in and he, like the rest of the gentry, was obliged to conform and to fade into private life on his estate—those little nations where inevitably women ruled and where the role of the men became futile.

In one of his very late stories, *First Love*, which tells of how a father and his young son fall in love with the same young woman, Ivan Turgenev draws a moving portrait of his father and, indeed, told friends that the story came directly from his own early youth. He had never seen, he said, a man more "elaborately serene."

> He took scarcely any interest in my education but never hurt my feelings; he respected my freedom; he displayed—if one can put it that way—a certain courtesy . . . only he never let me come at all close to him. I loved him . . . he seemed to me the ideal man—and God knows how passionately attached to him I should have been if I had not felt constantly the presence of his restraining hand. Yet he could, whenever he wished, with a single word, a single gesture, instantly make me feel complete trust in him . . . Sometimes a mood of gaiety would come over him and at such moments he was ready to play and romp with me . . . like a boy . . . Once, and only once, he caressed me with such tenderness that I nearly cried . . . I came to the conclusion that he cared nothing for me nor for family life; it was something very different he loved . . .

From his father's sayings, Turgenev took these words:

> "Take what you can yourself and don't let others get you into their hands; to belong to oneself, that is the whole thing in life". . . On another occasion, being at that time a youthful democrat, I embarked on a discussion of liberty . . . "Liberty," he repeated. "Do you know what really makes a man free?"
> "What?"
> "Will, your own will, and it gives power which is better than liberty. Know how to want, and you'll be free, and you'll be master too."

Before and above everything, my father wanted to live—and did live. Perhaps he had a premonition that he would not have long in which to make use of the "thing in life"; he died at forty-two.

And at the end of the story when the father is dying, he says to his son, words that Turgenev repeated in many of his stories throughout his life:

"My son," he wrote, "beware of the love of women; beware of that ecstasy—that slow poison."

The love the boy Turgenev had most to fear was his mother's love: he was the favourite son.

Varvara Petrovna's command of the passions, in all their manifestations, was inexhaustible. She was a round-shouldered woman with large, glaring black eyes under heavy brows, her forehead was wide and low, the skin of her face was coarse and pocked, her mouth large, sensual and cruel, her manner arrogant and capricious. She was as self-willed as a child, though like many ugly women she could be fascinating and charm her friends, and was very witty. Her history is pitiable. She was the child of violence in a family who had got much of their wealth by means little short of robbery. Compared with the Turgenevs the Lutovinovs were barbarians. The portraits of one or two of them hung on the walls of Spasskoye which Varvara Petrovna had inherited. They had flogged their way forward and Turgenev has described two or three of these ancestors. In the *Freeholder Usyanikov* there is one who grabbed a parcel of land from a neighbour and flogged him into agreement when the man threatened to take the crime to court. Another was a scoundrelly young Guards Officer and a thief who stole his father's money from the family chest where his bags of coins were kept. His portrait hung beside the picture of a young woman with her hair done in the high style of the eighteenth century. Beside it was the picture of an amiable young man whom Turgenev calls Rogatchov, who has a hole in the breast: the Guards Officer had seduced the young woman who was about to be married to Rogatchov and murdered him. The true story is worse than Turgenev made it: the girl was the murderer's sister. In the story called *The Brigadier*, the mother of Varvara Petrovna appears. The old lady was paralysed, yet in a fit of temper, she knocked her page boy unconscious and, frightened by what she had done, is said to have somehow got the boy to a chair, put a cushion over him, suffocated him and had him buried secretly.

This grandmother had been twice married. In her second marriage to a widower called Somov who had grown-up children, she turned against Varvara Petrovna who was the child of the first marriage. When the mother died the drunken stepfather not only beat the young girl but attempted to rape her. She escaped from the house with a nurse and walked twenty miles to an uncle's house at Spasskoye. All this is described in *The Turgenev Family* by Mme. Zhitova who, as an orphan baby, had been adopted by Varvara Petrovna in 1833. (Mysterious orphans appear again and again in the annals of the gentry families. Alexandre Zviguilsky, in *Ivan Turgenev: Nouvelle Correspondance*, dubiously suggests that Mme. Zhitova was a child born of an affair between Varvara Petrovna and a doctor, Andrei Bers, the father of Leo Tolstoy's future wife.) Varvara Petrovna once took the girl to see the stepfather's house which had become an empty ruin. Pictures still hung on the wall. In the hall was the bust of her Lutovinov father. They passed down an empty corridor and came to a door that was boarded up and when the child played with the handle, Varvara Petrovna dragged her away screaming:

"Don't touch it. There is a curse on that room."

The room was her stepfather's. When she calmed down she said to the girl:

"You don't know what it means to be an orphan: you are an orphan but you have a mother in me . . . to be an orphan without mother or father is hard, but to be an orphan in the sight of your own mother is horrible: that is what I suffered, my mother hated me."

As a young girl Varvara Petrovna had not been much happier at Spasskoye, for her uncle was irascible and stingy: she had the stubbornness of the injured and unloved and grew up to be a mannish young woman in the company of rough squires, and in his rages the uncle varied his fits of benevolence with drunken threats to throw her out of the house. He intended, she claimed, to disinherit her. His sudden death made her an heiress who, until she was thirty, was unable to get a man to look at her. Her tragedy was that when she did marry she adored the husband who had to be forced into the marriage.

Varvara Petrovna is one of those Russian Cinderellas who once they get their Prince avenge themselves for the wrongs of childhood and become tyrants. Mme. Zhitova was nevertheless devoted to her, found her generous and tender, and, while not denying her tyrannies, was inclined to pity her and say that her savage rule of her serfs was common form among some women of her class in the eighteenth century and that if rage was at the heart of her nature, she was really a country eccentric.

Mme. Zhitova's account of Varvara Petrovna's character begins when she was taken into the house. By then Ivan was sixteen and of the two brothers he is the peacemaker who tries to soften his mother's temper. In their boyhood she made both her sons feel the birch and indeed once when she was beating the older one she did it with such frenzy that she fainted and the naked boy had to call to the servant standing there, "Water, for Mama." Mme. Zhitova confirms that Turgenev's story of Varvara Petrovna and the dumb servant called *Mumu* is founded on fact, although Turgenev attributes it to his grandmother. In *Punin and Baburin* there is a scene which certainly occurred; Varvara Petrovna was in the habit of going out in the park in the afternoon to see that her serfs were working and one day she noticed a half-starved unsmiling youth in rags who was gaping at her and not putting his back into his job. His name was Yermil.

"I have no need of people with scowling faces like that," she said, for she required deferential smiles from her workers and ordered him to be sent off at once to a "Settlement." She often threatened servants with Siberia or prison. The sentenced man or woman had then to be led past her drawing-room window and to bow as he or she was taken off. Turgenev writes in the story:

Yermil stood without his cap, with downcast head, barefoot, with his boots tied up with a string behind his back; his face, turned towards the seignorial mansion, expressed not despair nor grief, nor even bewilderment, a stupid smile was frozen on his colourless lips, his eyes dry and half closed, looked stubbornly on the ground. My grandmother was apprised of his presence. She got up from her sofa, went with a faint rustle of her silken skirts to the window of the study and holding her golden rimmed double eye glass on the bridge of her nose, looked at the new exile.

Her clerk, the Baburin of the story, protested and she replied:

"That is of absolutely no consequence to me—among my subjects I am sovereign and answerable to no one, only I am not accustomed to have people criticising me in my presence and meddling in what is not their business . . . You too do not suit me. You are discharged." And turning to her steward she told him to pay off the clerk and get rid of him by dinner time. "Don't put me into a passion," she said. "What is Yermil waiting for? I have *seen* him. What more does he want?"

And, says Turgenev, she shook a handkerchief angrily out of the window.

After such a scene she would go back to her chair, her rage satisfied, and go on playing patience or reading the latest French novel. She despised Russian writing—except for a few lines of Pushkin.

Varvara Petrovna's husband seems to have behaved with formal indifference and amused himself with his love affairs or his shooting. Perhaps he too was afraid of the virago he had married, although it is said his concern was to preserve an illusion of decorum in the tormented house. He drifted into ill-health and a long illness. The two sons sat by his bedside when he died. Varvara Petrovna was away in Italy. Ivan was sixteen.

An early drawing of Turgenev in his boyhood before the tragic loss of his father—it appears in Yarmolinsky's *Life*—is of a decorous but slyly staring gnome-like little creature, with a large head too big for his body. The forehead is high and fine, the eyes are intently watchful and dead-still with mischief. He sits in a trance-like state as if memorising every inch of what he sees. He was noted for his precocious and unabashed remarks to distinguished guests which got him into trouble. He perhaps picked up banter from his mother. Children brought up under a tyranny and who are spoiled one moment and beaten the next are likely to be evasive and to lead a double life and lie their way out when in difficulty. He wandered about a large house that always had guests and hangers-on in it, and had some of the too-forward characteristics of the hotel-child of the restless European and American rich of later times. He knew very well that he and his older brother were the young masters; but in old age he said all he remembered was the birchings he got from his mother; and the cowed serfs and the severe German and French tutors. His ear for French or German was remarkable: he was a born mimic and with a gift for play-acting and fantasy. His real education, as was apt to happen to the children of the gentry, was given him by the servants. He listened to their stories, knew the barbarous wrongs his mother inflicted on them; starved of the despised Russian language in family life, he heard it continually from them.

Varvara Petrovna—who was an efficient ruler of her household—saw to it that her favourite serfs were taught to read and write, and one youth who had a taste for reading used to go off to the library secretly with Ivan to find a book. The library was not much more than a storeroom where the books were tied up in bundles that smelled of mice. They found an astonishing popular work called *Emblems and Symbols,* a sort of Russian *Iliad,* Turgenev called it, of fantastic verses about unicorns, kings, negroes, pyramids and snakes. There is a recollection of this discovery in *Punin and Baburin* when Punin

> shouted the verses out solemnly in a flowing outpour through his nose like a man intoxicated and beside himself with ecstasy . . . In this way we went through not only Lomonosov, Sumarokov and Kantemir . . . even Kheraskov's *Rossiada* . . . There is in it, among others, a mighty Tatar woman, a gigantic heroine: I have forgotten her name now but in those days my hands and feet turned cold, as soon as it was uttered. "Yes," Punin would say . . . Kheraskov he doesn't let one off easily."

The story of *Bunin and Baburin* was one of the things Turgenev wrote in the last years of his life and one is immediately struck by the minuteness of his observation and his feeling for solitude as a boy. To the child brought up in such a place Spasskoye was a timeless, boundless country: the immense gardens and distances of the estate would seem to be Russia itself; he would know few if any children of his own class and, if any did arrive, they would seem totally outlandish. His natural affections and play were with the children of serfs among whom he would be pleased yet irked by the sense of his own privilege. His childhood, as with so many rich children, was a training for the innocence of the rich who take private life to be the whole world. At a very early age and as the favourite, he found that he had two roles to play. The household was a sort of secret society containing the quarrels between a passionate mother and a cool husband and the infinite quarrels and intrigues of the hierarchy of tale-telling servants: he listened and he would try to keep the peace by charm and being funny. Watching was a necessity and an amusement. Very early he stared at faces and learned to read the moods and history that were built into them; and when, for self-preservation, he could get away he went out into hiding places in the gardens and the woods to watch the things of nature build *their* history, from minute to differing minute: to gaze at a leaf or a bird waiting for it to move, to listen to the differing sounds of his boots as he walked over leaves, over grass, through hemp fields, to notice every change of light and shadow and the movements of cloud in the sky as the moments of the morning or the afternoon passed.

> I raised my head and saw at the end of a delicate twig one of those large flies with emerald heads and long body and four transparent wings ... For a long while, more than an hour, I did not take my eyes off her. Soaked through and through with sunshine she did not stir, only from time to time turning her head from side to side and shaking her lifted wings—and that was all.

He had the eye of a naturalist; that is to say, there is no day-dreaming in it, no Wordsworthian moral content. He is already a collector of the events of the hour as it changes.

Chapter 2

WHEN they were nine or ten, the Turgenev brothers were put into a prep school in Moscow for a short time, then into a high school where they met mostly boys of their own class. At fifteen Ivan entered Moscow University, which was not much more than a secondary school to whom all, except serfs, were admitted. After a year or so there he advanced to Petersburg University with the fashionable intention of proceeding to the University of Berlin. This prosaic education was to fit young men of his class for high rank in the Tsarist civil service or life in the Army or at Court.

In Moscow Ivan drank his first draught of German idealism. The philosophy of Hegel turned young men of his generation to metaphysics and literature. At the prep school run by a cheerful old German, the students lived *en famille* and spelled out Schiller during the week, played forfeits or charades on Sundays and went in for passionate friendships. Later on in his stories Turgenev recalled these lofty attachments: in *Yakov Pasinkov*, for example, he tells of his feeling for Yakov, the ugly duckling of the school, who had sharply pulled him up for his very Russian habit of telling lies: he told them partly out of an impetuous bent for fantasy and also from a pleasure in swaggering, but he was always quick to repent of his exaggerations. He responded to Yakov's "goodness":

On his [Yakov's] lips the words "goodness," "truth," "life," "science," "love," however enthusiastically uttered, never rang with a false note. Without strain, without effort he stepped into the world of the ideal: his pure soul was ready to stand before the holy shrine of beauty.

The two were soon "soul in soul as the saying was." The language of romantic love had become the fashion under the German influence: it was a reaction from the correct, ironical, formal language of his mother's and father's generation. When Turgenev entered Moscow University the ideals of self-perfection and the sublime absorbed the students and became grandiloquent. His own mind had turned to poetry and there is one of his early attempts in a letter to his Uncle Nikolai, an affable gentleman who had settled on the family in Spasskoye in the easy-going Russian way, and who eased the difficult moments of life there. The poem is about the annual drama of the breaking up of the ice on the Moscow river in the thaw which always drew the crowd. These ice-floes "suddenly fly-bang!"—against the stone banks and are smashed to pieces.

> They swallow each other in the wrestling of the waters/
> The ice-floes are born of other ice-floes/
> A sea is born of another sea.

Once more, one notices, his eye moving from moment to moment.

His growing literary turn is seen in his reading. He has been "enraptured by reading Mirabeau" and the young linguist was soon moving into English literature: Shakespeare, Shelley and above all Byron whom he knows through Pushkin. Shakespeare and Pushkin became his lasting guides. There are no evocations of Moscow's gilded Asiatic steeples and gilded domes in Turgenev's wriing, but, as Gogol did, he was more likely to note oddities like the hundreds of crows perched on the crucifixes and cupolas. Life in Moscow was almost rustic. Alexandr Herzen, ten years older than Turgenev, and to whom one turns again and again for close social observation, says in *My Past and Thoughts* that the houses of the gentry were all huddled together and yet the inhabitants were not of a single type: they were specimens of everything in Russian history, living unhurried and easy-going lives. There

was a spaciousness of their own within them which we do not find
in the *petit-bourgeois* life of the West . . . the rank and file of this
society was composed of landowners not in the service or serving not
on their own account, but to pacify their relations, and of young
literary men and professors. There was a fluidity of relationships not
yet settled and of habits not reduced to a sluggish orderliness, a
freedom which is not found in the more ancient life of Europe
. . . the Slav laisser faire.

This Moscow lived by its dreams of Berlin and Paris. The talk
went on until two in the morning and since it was dangerous to
talk about politics, the subject had to be embalmed in literary
and philosophical argument. The Muscovites were far from the
formal Court life of Petersburg and the brisk coldness of official
manners.

All the same, "democratic" speculations were heard among the
older students and the professors who had been to Berlin, and
Turgenev, in his eager way, picked up one or two opinions that
caused him to be mocked as "the American"; the first sign of his
private horror of serfdom.

The boys came back to Spasskoye for the holidays and at fifteen
—Ivan told the Goncourts—he had his first mistress.

I was very young. I was a virgin and with the desires one has at the
age of 15. My mother had a pretty chambermaid who looked a little
silly but, you know, a silly look lends a certain grandeur to some faces.
It was rather a damp day, no a rainy day: one of those erotic days that
Daudet likes to describe. It began to drizzle. She took—mind you, I
was her master and she was my slave—she took hold of me by the hair
at the back of my head and said to me "Come." What followed was
the sensations we have all experienced. But the sweet clasp of my hair
accompanied by that single word—that still gives me a sensation of
happiness every time I think of it.

The incident would strike his mother as normal, indeed proper;
perhaps she arranged it. His inevitable love affairs would be under
her control in the manner of her generation. She distinguished
between sexual adventure and the far greater perils of love.

The boy had suddenly grown as tall as his father, indeed into a plumpish young giant with a long body and shortish legs which gave a sway to his walk. He had chestnut hair and large grave blue eyes, a bold nose. When his face was still the expression was of a young man self-absorbed, posing a little, and waiting. He had the fashionable lisp and he had some difficulty in getting his words out at first; the voice was gentle and caressing, but he was easily excited and then in talk and laughter the voice became high and shrill, even boisterous and he started pacing up and down the room like an actor carried away by his part.

In 1834 when he was sixteen, his mother pushed him on to Petersburg University, the proper place for a young nobleman and where she had good connections. He shared rooms with his older brother who was a cadet in the military college. His mother went off to Italy but presently there was the family tragedy. The father was dying at Spasskoye.

So much has been made of the powerful influence of his mother upon Turgenev's character that the father has come to seem a distant and negligent figure who let her run her family as she wished. This is not quite so. When he intervened his was the voice of authority and she had some awe of him. His distance had its spell. He was one of those fathers who have the disconcerting air of being a spectator in his own family. In this Ivan was very much his father's son; he too had grown into a restless spectator, his mind on his inner personal freedom. They went out shooting together: the father, though poorly educated himself, took an awkward interest in his son's education. Although he became a rationalist very early, Ivan was affected by the superstitions his father shared with the servants and one effect of seeing the agonies of his father's death was to convince Ivan for life that he would die of the disease of the bladder that killed his father.

It is tempting to trace Turgenev's life-long hypochondria to this event but when one considers the peculiar emotional conditions of life at Spasskoye, other influences pervade. Cholera moved from district to district among the peasants and the news of it besieged the minds of the landowners who shut themselves up in their houses when it was about. Varvara Petrovna feared it so much that she is said to have been borne round her grounds in a glass-enclosed chair when the plague came near. Spasskoye was a hothouse of imaginary symptoms and there was only a serf doctor living there to offer his crude remedies. Her temper brought on fainting fits and other disorders, and so strong was her will and imagination that she could act out any illness that suited her, with dramatic effect: it is not surprising that Ivan should have caught something of her morbidity.

Much more important was the effect of the father's death on Varvara Petrovna's attitude to her favourite son. She now turned greedily, almost amorously to him for the love she had not received from her husband. Her possessiveness increased and in the storms she created in the household he fell into the part of the soother, the peacemaker, the slave of her moods. When he was there—as Mme. Zhitova says—Varvara Petrovna forgot her violence, but at the same time, even he had to watch and calculate the moment when he could intercede. For she was capable of punishing the servants for whom he had tactfully spoken: it was a way of punishing him.

He went back to Petersburg to the familiar Arctic Venice with its enormous palaces, its wide, windy, dusty streets down which the cold winds of the Baltic blew; and where, when they were not blowing, the fog of the marshes on which Peter the Great had built the city made the air leaden. It was a city made for hypochondriacs, dangerous to the weak chest and the throat. Its famous staring white nights were hard on the nerves of the sleepless. The capital seemed, as Herzen said, a façade, a screen, an inhuman artifice.

One had to visualise behind the screen, soldiers under the rod, serfs under the lash, faces that betrayed a stifled moan, carts on their way to Siberia, convicts trudging in the same direction, shaven heads, branded faces, helmets, epaulettes and plumes.

What Petersburg really meant to Turgenev was that it was the stepping-stone to Berlin and Europe. In his *Reminiscences* he wrote:

I had long dreamed of that journey. I was convinced that in Russia one could acquire only a certain amount of elementary knowledge and that the source of true knowledge was to be found abroad. In those days there was not a single man among the professors and lecturers

at the University of Petersburg who could shake that conviction of mine; indeed they themselves were imbued with it . . .
The aim of our young men . . . reminded me of the search by the Slavs for chieftains from the overseas Varangians.

There was no order in Russia. Everything he knew about his country disgusted him. He was for "plunging headlong into the German sea," as soon as he could. He was ready for the Greek and German classics. And in his third year he showed Pletnyov, his professor, a laborious attempt to write a Russian *Manfred*: a play called *Steno* in iambic pentameter in the required Italian setting—"a perfectly preposterous work." The professor invited him to his flat and made gentle fun of it and he met a little literary society and caught sight of Pushkin, the demi-god, at the theatre.

I remember his small, dark face, his African lips, the gleam of his large teeth, his pendent side-whiskers, his dark, jaundiced eyes beneath a high forehead, almost without eyebrows and his curly hair.

Not long after the poet was dead, killed in a duel, and he saw him lying in his coffin. He does not mention that his distant Turgenev kinsman was one of the only two persons permitted by the Tsar to escort the body by sleigh to his grave at Pakov.

The times were bad for literature. Writers were still suffering from the effects of the repression that had begun twelve years before, after the aristocratic revolt. There was no free press—indeed to start a new paper or journal was forbidden—no public opinion, no personal freedom. The only outlet lay in private conversation in small gatherings and even then conversation was restrained. Turgenev gives an account of an evening at Pletnyov's flat—most people lived in flats in Petersburg—and gives one or two exact thumbnail sketches of the forgotten writers who gathered there.

To begin with, the notorious Skobelev, author of Kremnev, afterwards commandant of the St Petersburg fortress . . . with some of his fingers missing, with a clever, somewhat crumpled, wrinkled, typical soldier's face and a soldier's far from naive mannerisms—a man who had knocked about the world in short.

There was an editor, "an equerry in the uniform of a gendarme," and Guber, translator of *Faust,* an officer in the Transport Department, with tousled side-whiskers which were, in those days, taken to be a mild assertion of liberal tendencies; and a shy, listening poet, dressed in a long-skirted, double-breasted frock coat, a short waistcoat with a watch chain of blue glass beads and a necktie with a bow, whose very ordinary Russian face suggested the self-educated artisan or house-serf.

At nineteen, Turgenev, with his handful of unpublished poems, was the shy listener and so conventional in his tastes that he saw nothing beyond a crude joke in Gogol's *The Government Inspector* which had been put on because it gave the Tsar himself a chance for one of his loud guffaws at lines like: "You're taking bribes not according to your rank."

In his years at Petersburg Turgenev read widely and showed more signs of turning to academic life than of distinction as a poet. His mind was set on enlightenment in Berlin, and where he had no difficulty in persuading his mother to let him go.

The day of departure came. The whole family went to Kazan cathedral to pray for him. With him went his valet Porfiry, a serf of his own age who was in fact his half-brother, the son of Turgenev's father by a maid at Spasskoye. There were tears at the parting. The mother made him swear not to gamble, and as she was carried back to her carriage she fainted. His brother saw him on to the steamer for Lübeck. "I plunged," Turgenev wrote in famous words, "into the German sea which was to purify me and when I emerged from the waves I discovered myself a Westerner." The first venture towards expatriation had begun.

And there was a literal plunge into the sea. Not long after the steamer left harbour and was still close to land it caught fire. It carried 280 passengers and 28 carriages, for before the railway age well-off Russians always took their carriages with them on the European tour. Turgenev had already forgotten his promise to his mother and was winning at cards when the cry of "Fire" went up and the ship listed, throwing the tables and his money across the saloon. Like most of the passengers, with the exception of the Danish sailors, the women and children and a Russian ambassador, the young man lost his head. In old age Turgenev gave his version of the affair and he turned it all into a frightening farce. There was a general who shouted, "We must send a courier to the Emperor." Another gentleman, who was travelling with an easel and a portrait in oils, jabbed it through the eyes, ears and nose and mouth with his umbrella; a German brewer was in tears and called out to a sailor "Captain! Captain," who replied, "I am the Captain. What do you want?" Seeing the water reddened by the flames, Ivan writes: "I said to myself, 'So that's where I shall die and at the age of 19.'" He says he rushed to the ship's side, pretending that he was going to commit suicide, for he could not swim. From what one knows of him this may be true, for he was given to half-comic theatrical fits of extravagance. The story is confusing. One moment he is bravely clambering across the roofs of the burning carriages on the deck, the next he is hanging by a rope over the ship's side and a fat woman jumps on top of him and they both tumble into a life-boat. He mentions a tall man, another general, who pushes a woman aside and jumps onto a boat which has capsized. There is really far too much detail in the report: it is written to settle the gossip about his absurd and cowardly behaviour that dogged him all his life.

He got ashore safely in the company of a Mme. Tyutchev and her children—she was the wife of the poet—and somehow got them to Berlin by road and there he seems to have begun a long love affair with her.

Unluckily a few weeks after the fire, malicious gossip about his antics on the steamer spread to the drawing-rooms of Petersburg: the fat young giant with the shrill voice had pushed past all the women screaming, "Save me. I am the only son of my mother." The anecdote got into the papers. Rather too pedantically Turgenev pointed out that since his mother had two sons he could not have said these words that had brought ridicule on him—but he did say it was natural for a green youth to be terrified of being burned alive or drowned. The story took on so thoroughly—Dostoevsky used it years later in the caricature of Turgenev that appears in *The Possessed*, a novel noteable for its pillorying of many literary figures—that it got to Varvara Petrovna, who wrote angrily that it was indeed not his fault that he was called *le gros monsieur*, but to have made such a spectacle of himself had marked him as a ridiculous coward. Hence, in old age, his attempt to tell "the true story" of his panic and the appearance of another possible *gros monsieur*, the tall general in the story. A reckless story teller himself, Turgenev invited malice in return for his witticisms. One possible witness is missing from the story: Porfiry, the half-brother and the serf-valet whom he took to Berlin—but perhaps he was not on the steamer and had been sent on by another route. But good came out of the disaster from Varvara Petrovna's point of view when later on her son told his mother of the affair with Mme Tyutchev. A passing love affair with an intelligent married woman years older than himself, she wrote, was—as the French had taught her—just the thing to form a young man.

In Berlin, Turgenev and Porfiry settled into a modest flat. Porfiry was a clever boy who had inherited the Turgenev habits of over-eating and chasing girls. The two young men lived like school boys together rather than as master and servant. They sat about playing cards; they organised rat hunts and Turgenev wrote Porfiry's love letters for him. He was also determined to force his mother to set Porfiry free; he sent him to a medical school in Berlin and when he eventually returned to Spasskoye he became her house-doctor, expert in calming her with his chief remedy—laurel drops. But she refused to give him his freedom and Porfiry himself refused it while she was alive; like many of the serfs he suspected that emancipation was a doubtful advantage and he enjoyed his power over the old lady.

Young Russians who went to Berlin for a larger education than they could get in Russia—"that immense and sombre figure, motionless and masked like the Sphinx"—carried their Russia with them. They fell into two main groups: the politicals who thought of nothing but drastic social change, and the metaphysicals who were under the full influence of German idealism. In *My Past and Thoughts,* Herzen says both parties were endlessly trying to "get out of the Chinese shoes of German manufacture in which Russia had hobbled for 150 years and though they may have caused painful corns they have not crippled their bones."

Turgenev was at an age for rushing into more "soul-in-soul" friendships, and he found them in two very different men: the aesthete philosopher Stankevich—a few years older than himself—and the young Bakunin. Herzen gives one of his terse, detailed portraits of Stankevich:

Stankevich, also one of the *idle* people who accomplish *nothing* . . . had made a profound study of German philosophy, which appealed to his aesthetic sense: endowed with exceptional abilities, he drew a large circle of friends into his favourite pursuit. This circle was extremely remarkable: from it came a regular legion of *savants*, writers and professors, among whom were Belinsky, Bakunin and Granovsky . . . Sickly in constitution and gentle in character, a poet and a dreamer, Stankevich was naturally bound to prefer contemplation and abstract thought to living and purely practical questions; his artistic idealism suited him; it was "the crown of victory" set on the pale, youthful brow that bore the imprint of death. The others had too much physical vigour and too little poetical feeling to remain long absorbed in speculative thought without passing on into life. An exclusively speculative tendency is utterly opposed to the Russian temperament, and we shall soon see how the *Russian spirit* transformed Hegel's teaching and how the vitality of our nature asserted itself . . .

And he goes on to say how the scholarly, scientific jargon of the Germans was unsuited to the leading characteristic of the Russian language which has extraordinary ease in expressing

. . . abstract ideas, the lyrical emotions of the heart, "life's mouse-like flittings," the cry of indignation, sparkling mischief and shaking passion.

a sentence that conveys the kind of language that was forming in Turgenev's mind and enabled him to become eventually a master of Russian prose.

Bakunin, though deep in the same beliefs, was beginning to emerge and turn to politics.

What was it touched these men? . . . They had no thought, no care for their social position, for their personal advantage or for security; their whole life, all their efforts were bent on the public good, regardless of all personal profit . . . The interests of truth, the interests of learning, the interests of art, *humanitas*, swallowed up everything.

Turgenev himself evoked this period of his life when he came to write his first novel, *Rudin*, in which Stankevich—as Pokrovsky and Bakunin (as Rudin), are drawn from life. Stankevich had, Turgenev says, the magnetism of the saint. Self-perfection was the business of life and he rejected all political commitment. He deplored Turgenev's frivolity and reproached him for telling lies.

Bakunin was four years older than Turgenev. In *Rudin*, Turgenev writes of his domineering and flamboyant character:

> As we listened to Rudin [i.e., Bakunin], we felt for the first time as if we had grasped the general principle of the universe, as if a veil had been lifted at last. Even if admitting he was not uttering an original thought—what of that? Order and harmony seemed to be established in all we knew . . . he had a prodigious memory and what an effect he had on young people. (The young) must have generalisations, conclusions, incorrect if you like but still conclusions. A perfectly sincere man never suits them. Try and tell young people you cannot give them the whole truth and they will not listen to you.

The friendship of Bakunin and Turgenev was a friendship of blue-eyed Slavonic giants. The Berliners were amazed by the sight of the two dandies, Turgenev in his green swallow-tail coat and Bakunin in his lavender one, as they sat in the cafés, went to concerts and theatres and appeared in the fashionable salons, united by the teachings of Hegel. Turgenev was under the spell of Bakunin's eloquence: on Bakunin's side there was the passion for domination and also—since he was forming a lifetime's genius for living at other people's expense—a lavish if disinterested enjoyment of Turgenev's money.

Bakunin's dominance, in these two years, had an additional grace: he was the ruler and protector of three sisters. Turgenev had fallen in love with the plainest one; Stankevich and the critic Belinsky with the other two. The story is an odd one. Bakunin was the eldest of ten children born to a fairly wealthy landowner in the sleepy province of Tver and had organised his brothers and sisters into a kind of conspiracy of sensibility against the father he detested. He loved his sisters jealously and when they grew up he meddled in their love affairs or marriages, in order to keep his hold on them; indeed it is thought that failure in this was the private source of his turn to wild political conspiracy and to Anarchism. There is a strong suspicion that he was impotent and he was certainly a stern supervisor of Turgenev's sexual morals. Herzen ironically reports Bakunin as saying to Turgenev in the proper language of the period:

> "Let us go and plunge into the gulf of real life; let us fling ourselves on the waves and pick up a pretty actress."

It sounds like a cry of exasperation at Turgenev's wandering thoughts. Unhappily for their friendship Turgenev had fallen in love in a philosophical way with the sister to whom Bakunin was most attached and there was another difficulty in this: Hegelians believed that ideal love reached its most delicate manifestations in the brotherly and sisterly affections, which in this case had a disturbingly incestuous, though innocent, significance for Bakunin. What Turgenev afterwards called Bakunin's "diplomatic habits" came at once into play. He concealed his violent jealousy by drawing Turgenev out, listening to his accounts of his feelings, analysing them, introducing doubts on the highest principles. He gave his sister the same analytical treatment. If Turgenev was an idealist at the time, he was also a hedonist and he began to find Tatyana's conversation, and his own, when they all spent a summer at Tver, too metaphysical. The first shock in his friendship with Bakunin came when he discovered that Bakunin had read his love letters, full of extravagant phrases in German and he had to listen to Bakunin's talking like a father to him. The second shock was the discovery that Tatyana had really fallen in love with him. Turgenev had been deluded by his bookishness and was dutifully reliving the painful story of *Eugene Onegin* in the compulsive fashion of his generation. He cooled. He remembered Stankevich's warning against "the lie in the soul," and learned how difficult it is to get out of such a situation without cruelty and guilt. Tatyana became ill, he hesitated for a long time and then broke with her in exalted German—it sounded more heartfelt in a foreign language—and the letter contained a psychological insight into this kind of platonic love which could have been put with more tact:

> It is for you alone that I wished to be a poet, for you with whom my soul is bound up in such an ineffably wonderful way that I almost do not feel the need to see you.

So Pushkin's *Eugene Onegin* was brought up to date. Tatyana's laugh was bitter. Turgenev's shame at his proneness to juvenile self-deception turned to anger with himself and her. A long time passed before the guilt—and the resentment of a feeling so uncalled for—worked its way out of him. Bakunin despised Turgenev, told him he himself had now stopped living in his imagination and was now living "in a more realistic manner," and borrowed more money from him. The friendship was over. There is a double guilt—the one expressed in Turgenev's story, *A Correspondence*, written a few years after:

> Falsehood walked hand in hand with us because it poisoned our best feelings, because everything in us was artificial and stained.

Worse. There was the Russian disease:

> We Russians have set ourselves no other task but the cultivation of our own personality and habits of self consciousness distort the very striving for truth.

It is noticeable that even in such an intimate "confession" he enlarges it by invoking the ever shadowy figure of Russianness. To be a Russian is a fate.

———

From these happy, heady years in Berlin, these gifted young men who lazily despised the stolid Berliners as they drank up their philosophy eventually emerged and chose their different directions. Bakunin, the dynamo, never lost his habit of meddling and intrigue but now carried it flamboyantly into revolutionary politics and in a few years would be shackled to a wall in an Austrian prison, under sentence of death and, with a mixture of luck and cunning, would escape in middle age from Siberia. The petty destroyer of other people's love affairs became the anarchist and enthusiast for the destruction of society. The gentle Stankevich went off to Rome and died, very young, of tuberculosis. His death affected Turgenev deeply, for Stankevich's conversations, his contemplative idealism, had had a lasting influence on him. Turgenev was the slowest to find his way. Rich and lazy—lazy and hesitant in disposition, but not in intellect—he had read enormously in English, French and German literature and in the Greek and Roman classics and was likely to become, and indeed did become, the most cultivated Russian in Europe; but he was lost in the Romantic dream, writing his lyrical poetry which was no better than anyone else's and was half-inclined to take to academic life. He knew he had brains enough to master that with his eyes closed. He was wavering, as he wavered when he listened to the Russian Hegelians who had moved towards politics in a theoretical way, believing that the hopes of the French Revolution were still alive; one day he would be carried away by them, the next day he was the sceptic. He was an apolitical young poet with one passionate political conviction: the son of the despotic owner of five thousand serfs was convinced that serfdom was a cruel and corrupting form of slavery and was at the root of Russian inertia and backwardness. The one gain from "the plunge into the German sea" was, he said, that he had become a Westerner for good. Peter the Great, who, in the eighteenth century, had forcibly introduced administrative reforms and the need for science, was Turgenev's hero; and he rejected for good the doctrines of the Slavophils, who held that the traditional religions and peasant culture of Russia and the Tsar who ruled it should stay withdrawn from the corrupting taint of Western ideas.

He had been home once or twice in the Berlin days. He had travelled for a year in France, Italy and Switzerland. He had marched over the Alps, alone, thinking of himself as Manfred. He had been comically drunk on German wines and had fallen briefly for girls in German inns. On his first return to Spasskoye in 1839 he ran into two domestic dramas. For one a superstitious serfwoman was responsible. She had been fumigating a sick cow in the stable by burning herbs on a shoe and burying the shoe under the floor. The place went up like tinder and Spasskoye caught fire. Most of the fine furniture went and, apart from the stone gallery corridor, there was only a wing left. Varvara Petrovna watched it all from an armchair on the lawn, surrounded by what could be rescued. One of her personal maids, a German girl called Anna, rescued a chest containing 20,000 roubles from a serf who was going off with it: the brother Nikolai courageously rescued the bedridden nurse who had helped Varvara Petrovna escape from her stepfather when she was a girl. Nikolai was the hero and he and the strong-minded German maid presently became lovers and the secret was soon out. Unlike Ivan, Nikolai was a serious lover; that was intolerable to Varvara Petrovna who had no objections to her sons going to bed with servants—she would simply send their babies away—but she told Nikolai firmly to remember the duties of his rank and not to be carried away by the empty *"promesses des passions: elles évanouissent . . ."* The tortured Nikolai married Anna secretly. Varvara Petrovna raged when she eventually discovered this and cut him off. He had by this time become a civil servant and for years she left him to struggle on a poor clerk's income and refused to see him or his wife or their children. Ivan did all he could, as usual, for reconciliation, but the sixty-year-old mother was obdurate. Nikolai lived in misery on his pay for many years but when he was the father of three, she did at last put on one of her staged scenes. She agreed to go to Petersburg, to look at the three children—but in the street outside his house. She stared at them and went off asking for their pictures to be sent to Spasskoye. Reconciliation? No. When the pictures arrived she took them to her room and smashed them.

For years no one could persuade her to receive her eldest son or his wife. Even when, in a terrible year, the three children died, she was unmoved. But with Ivan her relationship took an exalted, passionate and curious turn. In her letters to him when he was in Berlin or Petersburg, and in her diary, strange words have been found. She wrote in the disconnected, sentimental way of a naïve school girl who is in love, or in the flirtatious manner of a worldly old woman. Mme. Zhitova says she once sat down before Ivan's picture and wrote in her diary:

> To my son Jean. . . . Jean is the very sun of my life. I see only him and when his image fades, I am blind and don't know where I am. A mother's heart is never deceived, my instinct, Jean, is stronger than reason in me.

In her letters, Yarmolinsky tells us in his biography, there are strange phrases where she addresses him as *"ma chère fille, ma Jeannette . . .vous êtes ma favourite . . .* ssh, for heaven's sake, let nobody hear it!" She even calls herself his "most tender father and friend . . . I

alone conceived you, all that I am you are." And she writes of a
Queen Bee being dried by the drones: "She stretched her legs with
an air of dignity, played the coquette, feigned extreme fatigue. Oh
woman, you are the same in all creation, living to please and to be
admired." And then, sternly, to her son—"You are an egoist of
egoists. I know your character better than you know yourself . . . I
prophesy that you will not be loved by your wife. You will not love
the woman but only your own pleasure." Slyly she wheedled the
story of his love affairs from him.

But these intimacies, after he had finished with Berlin, were
uneasy. She had sent dozens of letters to him while he was away: he
had replied to very few of them. Indeed Nikolai had said "Ivan only
writes when he wants money." (This was true: he had run through
20,000 roubles in these student years and when she sent him money
to buy her gloves or hats, he had pocketed it and forgotten to send
them.) When she heard he was writing poetry she was scornful.
There was worse. In Petersburg he had written one or two critical
articles for a review. This was nothing short of a descent into "clerk-
ing" as she called it and not an occupation for a gentleman. It was
like becoming one of the serf-clerks on her estate or some cheap
foreign tutor. She despised Russian writers and when he persuaded
her to read Gogol's *Dead Souls* she had to agree it was "frightfully
amusing," but very improper: the impropriety lay in making fun of
the gentry. She wanted Ivan to marry a woman of his own class and
either to become important as a State official or to be a *comme-il-faut*
man about town, doing nothing. She did not mind which. She
thought his opinions about serfdom were puerile. In the meantime
she flirted and quarrelled with him by turns. She despised his tender
heart and if he annoyed her she could always threaten to beat or
humiliate one of the serf boys or girls, so as to get even with him.
If he did not bow to her she announced, with frank sadism, that she
would take it out on others.

Turgenev now returned to the idea that his philosophical studies
might equip him for a professorship. The mother gave in, for the
time being. He went back to Petersburg and sat for his exams and
passed easily. He had only now to write a dissertation. And here he
gave up. It was too simple to become a professor: one had merely
to memorise the acceptable ideas of other people, and the end of the
love affair with Tatyana had turned him against German idealism.

He seems to have celebrated that apostasy by coming down to Spasskoye and getting a child by one of the seamstresses there. Varvara Petrovna was afraid that Ivan would follow the example of Nikolai and to stop that she agreed to have the child in the house, for Ivan soon went back to the capital and the child, called Pelagea —her name was later changed to Paulinette—was a useful item of emotional blackmail. When Ivan seemed to be obedient the little girl was brought from the servants' quarters into the drawing-room; when he was not, she was sent back to the servants and he was thereby punished.

The only means Varvara Petrovna now had of ruling her sons was to keep them short of money. Nikolai had been totally cut out; now Ivan was taught a lesson, if not as severely. To placate his mother he took a job in the Ministry of the Interior. His chief—who may have had more influence on him than has been noticed—was Vladimir Dahl, a schoolmasterly writer of Danish origin who had written a standard work, *A Reasoned Dictionary of the Living Great Russian Language* in four volumes, but he was also a writer of anecdotes or sketches in the "natural" or documentary style. Ivan had entered the office to appease his mother, but really in order to spend his time writing long narrative poems of his own. His official task was to write a report on the needs of Russian agriculture. He knew that his report would lead to nothing: it was an exercise and would simply be filed away with dozens of others and be forgotten. He made the safe conventional criticisms of serfdom as other officials had done: one had to be careful not to say serfdom should be *abolished.* One simply lost the subject by going into speculations about reform. It was obvious to Dahl that the young dilettante was a useless civil servant whose work could not be relied on and that he was using the office for doing his own writing and, when he was not doing that, going off into Society to play the dandified drawing-room poet. Yet, from the point of view of the artist, no experience is lost. Writing the report was a help in due time when he came to writing the views of Lavretsky in *A Nest of Gentlefolk,* many, many years later. There is a passage from the report (quoted by David Magarshack in his *Life)* which makes the dangerous comparison of the genuine aristocracy of the free Norman Knights of England with the Russian nobility who were mere servants of the Tsar.

It was 1843. He was twenty-five, and it was a decisive year for

---

Turgenev. At his own expense he published the narrative poem *Parasha* he had been writing in office hours, and he came under a lasting influence: he met the great critic Belinsky.

In a very few years, when he became famous, Turgenev grew to detest his poetry and did his best to keep it from the public eye and raged when anyone mentioned it. It was, he said, second-rate and like "dirty tepid water." Yet *Parasha* marks a turning point: Belinsky wrote a long article praising the poem. *Parasha* is a closed book to those of us who cannot read Russian; nearly 100 years later Prince Mirsky in his *History of Russian Literature* says it is not contemptible. Belinsky was older than Turgenev but, like him, had passed through the same phase of German idealism and had become the father of "commitment" in Russian literature, which, for better or worse, has lasted with intervals until the present day, and one can understand what had pleased the critic. It was a long narrative story placed firmly in Russian life. Instead of Italianising his people, Turgenev has taken his pair of young lovers from Pushkin's *Eugene Onegin* and has turned them into simple, puzzled young Russians of his generation. The hero is a scornful, careless young gentleman —another Lensky, or Turgenev himself; the heroine Tatyana is a simple, natural, devoted girl. They marry happily and are lost in the dullness of provincial life. The tone is now lyrical, now bantering and ironical. Gracefully Turgenev seems to be mocking his own disconcerting feelings about Tatyana Bakunin, particularly—as David Magarshack says, in the line:

"I do not like ecstatic young ladies . . . I dislike their pale round faces"

and also his own weakness for aristocratic society. Even Varvara Petrovna, who was proud of the copy he sent her and even more proud that like a gentleman, he had paid for its publication and was therefore not a scribbler, enjoyed its light conversational tone and especially its descriptions of country life.

"We country folk," she said, "love everything real. Your Parasha poem or story smells of wild strawberries."

She also picked up a social hint from the line: "*Kvas* was never served in the best houses" and banned the vulgar drink from Spasskoye—a pretty compliment. In her happy moments she was an engaging child and one can guess, in this respect, what Turgenev's talents owed to her.

The next step in Turgenev's liberation came that summer when Belinsky became his friend and father-figure. There is a long and brilliant picture of him in Turgenev's *Literary Reminiscences*, one of the best portraits which the master portrait painter ever wrote. Belinsky was already famous as a harassed and pugnacious journalist. He was the son of a doctor, his grandfather a priest—a class despised by the gentry—and since he came from Moscow he was a figure of ridicule in official Petersburg where he seemed as grotesque in his almost childish way as Gogol was. A shock of fair hair fell over his face, his nose was flattened, one of his shoulder blades stood out strangely, he was hollow-chested and he had a terrible consumptive cough and he had the habit of walking with a downcast head close to the walls of the street so that someone once said they had seen wolves like that in the forest, but only when they were chased by dogs. But he could be an enchanting talker, though when there were Slavophils present in a diplomatic or in a fashionable salon, he would break into roaring taunts and temper. Turgenev was captivated by his blue eyes which had golden sparks in them when he was excited.

Belinsky was a poor man and earned his living by reviewing books and there was always a rush for his paper. He was obliged to review everything that was published, piles of stuff from cookery books upwards; but the attraction of his hurried writing lay in the sly way he had of slipping in his serious opinions on the state of Russia in the repressive reign of the Emperor Nicholas, in his cunning at getting round the severe censorship. His political commitment did not blunt his perceptions of the values of art—as happened ten years later among the didactic critics of the next generation. In speaking of Belinsky as a "committed" artist, Turgenev is also giving us the views he himself stuck to all his life:

> he was much too intelligent, he had too much common sense to deny art, to fail to understand not only its great significance, but also its very naturalness, its physiological necessity. Belinsky recognised in art one of the fundamental manifestations of the human personality, one

---

of the laws of our nature, a law whose validity was proved by our daily experience. He did not admit of life only for life's sake; it was not for nothing that he was an idealist. Everything had to serve one principle, art as well as science, but in its own special way. The truly childish and, besides, not new but "warmed-up" explanation of art as an imitation of nature he would have deemed worthy of neither a reply nor of his attention . . . Art, I repeat, was for Belinsky as much a legitimate sphere of human activity, as science, as society, as the State . . . From art he demanded truth, vital, living truth.

Turgenev had published *Parasha* at a bad time for writers; the censorship quibbled over every opinion and took a sadistic pleasure in annoying writers about their prose style. One of the censors was jovial. He used to say he did not "want to cross out a single letter in an article; all he wanted to do "was to destroy its spirit."

The censor said to me one day, looking with feeling into my eyes: "You don't want me to cross anything out. But just think: if I don't cross anything out I may lose 3000 roubles a year and if I do—who cares?"

There was bribery everywhere; serfdom; the army in the saddle; no courts of justice; the number of admissions to the universities had been reduced to three hundred; serious books could not be brought in from abroad; denunciations on all sides. What could be done?

"Well," said Turgenev, "you went to see Belinsky."

The friendship was long and there is no doubt Turgenev and his friends helped Belinsky with money. The fact that Belinsky thought nothing of the rest of his poetry, and when the first of the *Sportsman's Sketches* appeared he was only a little more tolerant, did not affect the affection of the two men. Turgenev went to Salzbrunn and Paris with him but like many ardent Westerners, Belinsky was bored by Europe when he saw it, had not the slightest interest in European history and could speak no foreign language. Paris revolted him as it was to revolt Tolstoy. Belinsky used to call Turgenev "the gamin," but what impressed him about "the gamin" was that he was an educated man.

Belinsky's friendship is a sign that there was a change in Turgenev's character. He had come from Berlin snobbish, scornful and foppish and he was beginning to find by self-effacement his real powers.

Chapter 3

Wнат Turgenev needed in order to outgrow the dilettante self was not only a change of mind but, above all, a deepening of his power to feel. He had not yet known the force of passion.

In November of 1843 Pauline Viardot-Garcia, the Spanish singer, came from Paris to Petersburg to sing the part of Rosina in *Il Barbiere di Seviglia* at the magnificent opera house which had been remodelled and which could hold an audience of three thousand people. Italian opera had not been heard there for a generation and the season aroused wild enthusiasm. It was a triumph for the young singer and for her middle-aged husband who was her impresario. She had succeeded in London but had been edged out of the Paris opera by the established prima donnas.

The event was not one that a poet and young man of fashion could miss but Turgenev was in a bad way for money because his mother now refused to pay off his heavy debts and kept him to a very small allowance. She had been amused by *Parasha* as a personal present but she was not going to do anything for a common scribbler who dragged the family name into the papers. He could earn very little by his occasional writing, but he somehow got a cheap seat at the opera and saw on the stage a slight young married woman of twenty-two, three years younger than himself, with no figure and almost ugly to look at. She had black hair, a wide mouth, a heavy underlip that seemed continuous with her chin and a very long neck. The effect was of sullenness in a strong, gypsyish way, the hooded eyes were large and black, the pupils lifting in one of those asserting Spanish stares of mockery and pride; yet the stare would break into sudden vivacity, warmth and enticing smiles. And then the voice!

Musset, who had known Pauline Garcia and had been in love with her when she was seventeen, said the voice had "the velvetness of the peach and youth," and had written a poem in which the first verse runs:

> Oui femme, tel est votre empire;
> Vous avez ce fatal pouvoir
> De nous jeter par un sourire
> Dans l'ivresse ou le désespoir.

But the last verse contains the lines:

> Mais toute puissance sur terre
> Meurt quand l'abus en est trop grand,
> Et qui sait souffrir et se taire
> S'éloigne de vous en pleurant.

The extravagant words of Heine about her voice are well-known:

Her ugliness is of a kind that is noble and, if I might almost say beautiful, such as sometimes enchanted and inspired the great lion-painter Delacroix. . . The Garcia recalls to your mind not so much the civilised beauty and tame grace of our European homeland, as the terrible splendour of an exotic wilderness and during some moments of her impassionated performance, especially when she opens wide her large mouth with its dazzling white teeth and smiles with such savage sweetness and delightful ferocity, you feel as though the monstrous plants and animals of India and Africa were about to appear before your eyes as though giant palms festooned with thousands of blossoming lianas were shooting up—and you would not be surprised to see a leopard or a giraffe or even a herd of young elephants stampede across the stage.

Musset was more precise. Recalling the resemblance of her voice to the voice of her famous sister, La Malibran, he said there was "the same timbre, clear, resonant, audacious; that Spanish *coup de gosier"* which has something, at the same time, so harsh and so sweet in it that it reminded him of the taste of wild fruit.

Heine's grotesque images magnify the reality. Pauline Viardot was an exotic: her inheritance came from the Triana. The strictly dedicated young artist, who had been brought up in cultivated circles in Paris, had race in her. She had the fine carriage of Spanish women; she sparkled in repose. Many other writers speak of something noble in her plain masculine face; in her portraits which are, of course, idealised, there is something else: authority. Such a strange figure must instantly have brought back to Turgenev the half-barbarous spell of his plain mother. Love at first sight, Jane Austen said, was a sign of giddiness: Turgenev certainly had the reputation of giddiness in Petersburg. But with him, love at first sight seems to have been a recognition of an earlier image printed in the heart.

If the voice of Pauline Viardot was part primitive and a gift of nature, it was exquisitely schooled beyond the rough spontaneity of popular Andalusian singing. An exacting musical culture had produced it: Pauline was born into a family who had been musicians for three generations. Her father, Manuel del Popolo Garcia, had been born in Seville in 1775; her grandfather had been a gypsy and as a child had been one of the harsh, shrill choristers of Seville cathedral and had become very quickly a professional singer and composer. Manuel Garcia's wife is said to have been an actress with all the hard-headedness of the theatre in her. There had been nothing for a poor ambitious man like Manuel in Spain and, being enormously energetic, subject to strong impulses, and having the gifts of a showman, he had moved the family in a business-like way to Paris. There he soon made a reputation as a tenor and pushed on to Italy, where he sought out Rossini who wrote for him the part of Almaviva in *Il Barbiere di Seviglia:* the opera in which Turgenev first heard Pauline was almost the Garcia family's property. Her father and her famous sister, La Malibran, had made their names in it.

In considering the character of Pauline one has to look more closely at the influence of this elder sister's life and fame. She was much older than Pauline, who was a child when her sister was already celebrated in Europe and America. In her scholarly life of Pauline Viardot and her indispensable account of her relationship with Turgenev, *The Price of Genius,* published in 1964, to which all writers on Turgenev owe a debt, April Fitzlyon tells us that La Malibran became the incarnation, the goddess of the Romantic movement. Every poet worshipped her. Beautiful and of great independence of spirit she had caused an upheaval in the Garcia family by quarrelling with her father and marrying Malibran, an American banker, when they were in New York. Manuel had been unrelenting and even cruel in the training he had given his daughter and she had married Malibran to get away from him. She was not cast down by the failure of her marriage—her husband went bankrupt at once and became unimportant in her life—she eventually divorced him and after many love affairs married a gifted Belgian violinist. The extraordinary girl was not only a singer but a talented painter and a daring horsewoman.

One early adventure of the Garcia family—of which Pauline and all of them were proud—occurred when Manuel, having done well in New York, dragged his family to Mexico, where again they made a small fortune and decided to go back to France. On the rough and dangerous journey from Mexico City to Vera Cruz they were attacked by brigands who soon disposed of the frightened escort of soldiers and robbed the party of everything. Although Pauline was frightened—she was only seven—she used to say in old age "all this was terribly beautiful, I liked it." And apparently, the excited and cheerful Garcias laughed all the way to Vera Cruz afterwards.

Pauline had scarcely known her marvellous and tragic sister. La Malibran was killed at the age of twenty-eight in a riding accident when she went to sing in Manchester. The father was more tender with Pauline. She would have preferred to have been a pianist and was very accomplished, but singing was the family tradition and she was persuaded by her sister's fame to emulate her. To La Malibran singing had come by nature, she had an unmatched ease and range of voice and could move from tragedy to comedy without effort. She was indeed lazy. Not so Pauline: she worked at whatever she was doing (the family said), "like an ant." By temperament she was an intellectual; she applied her will and very good mind to her task of acquiring range by will and this quality was to have a special appeal to Turgenev's deep regard for critical intellect. Throughout her life, music critics were amazed by a singer who studied the literary texts

of the operas she sang in. There are two more aspects of her character as an artist: the story of her sister's life warned her against a
reckless marriage and the Bohemian love affairs that had followed.
Pauline was no rebel. And there was the influence of her shrewd
mother who embodied the cautious business sense of a family of
geniuses who put their art first.

When Turgenev was carried away by Pauline's voice in Petersburg
he was listening to an achieved artist who had worked hard as he had
not and, who although three years younger than himself, was already
an idol. She was well-educated. She was a quick linguist. She was
married and a mother. Her French husband, Louis Viardot, was in
his forties. He was the capable and honourable son of a respectable
judge and, in addition to being her impresario, had a modest reputation as a translator, a writer of travel books and studies of European
painting.

There was nothing reckless in this marriage, even though Pauline's husband was in his forties, twenty-one years older than herself;
she respected him, she relied on him absolutely but was not in love.
The curious and sensible marriage had been arranged by George
Sand, who had known the Garcias and Louis Viardot for years: and
it can be said, at any rate, to have satisfied George Sand's ruling
maternal passion. More than once, after her own unhappy marriage,
she had been attracted to young women and in the young Pauline
she saw a girl whose independence as an artist of growing powers
would need protection from the dangerous temptations and illusions
from which she herself had suffered in her own early scandalous days.
In middle age, however, George Sand's motives were never quite
simple: her jealousy was aroused when she heard Musset, one of her
own disastrous and discarded lovers, was courting the girl, who,
luckily, was disgusted by his drinking and his libertine life; but that
would still leave her open to folly. George Sand worshipped the artist
in Pauline and indeed was using her as a model for the ideal artist-
heroine of her longest and most famous novel, *Consuelo:* Pauline
always said that the portrait perfectly described what she herself
was like and wished morally to be, although the wild adventures of
the ᴗook were romantic invention.

Louis Viardot might be thought a comic middle-aged figure: he
was short, he had a large nose which was a gift to caricaturists, he
looked as if he were going to tip over; people found him dull, inclined

to fuss and a pedant. (In one of his *Prose Poems*, "The Egoist," Turgenev is thought to have portrayed him as the imperturbable right-thinking man.) He was a decent man of principle. If public opinion in France or, indeed abroad, was to be considered—he shared the Republican and anti-clerical opinions of George Sand and particularly of Lerroux the Radical politician who had been her lover; but Pauline's mind was in her art. She knew he lacked the engaging, child-like qualities; if she did not love him she respected him and, with the utmost dignity and consideration, he loved her deeply. She had never loved anyone except her father and, perhaps, in Louis she saw a father reborn. It was noticed that she often called him "Papa."

Turgenev went night after night to hear the singer. He pushed into his friends' boxes—he couldn't afford one of his own—and he shouted his admiration. His gentleness and shyness vanished as his shrill voice screamed applause, his mad behaviour was the joke of the season. There is nothing like the sight of a giant who is out of his mind. There was no performance without it. People told Pauline that the noisy ass with the long chestnut hair was a young landowner, a good shot and a feeble poet. The young singer had the pretty tactics of fame at her finger tips: an admirer who was far richer than Turgenev had given her a huge bearskin which was spread on the floor of her dressing-room and there she sat like an idol and four of her admirers were allowed the privilege of sitting at a proper distance on the paws. It was a long time before Turgenev was allowed to join her privileged admirers in her dressing-room and win his right to a paw. Once there, the quick, serious charm, the wit and his power of telling and acting amusing untrue stories came back to him. His French and German were perfect. But surrounded as she was by more important admirers, Pauline took little notice of him.

Turgenev had to be content to concentrate on Louis Viardot, who, like himself, was often pushed into the background and, in the classic fashion of such triangular beginnings, it was the men who became friends first. Writing his books of travel and art, managing the opera company and Pauline's career, seeing to it that she would indeed be another Malibran, developing her distinct personality and style—these were the lasting preoccupations of Louis Viardot's busy life. But once business was over, Louis Viardot saw a flattering and aspiring young writer with whom he had a quite unexpected taste in common. It was decisive. Louis was fanatical to the point of comedy as a sportsman: he loved slaughter, as Pauline once said. He loved shooting birds in season and out. The sportsmen of Spasskoye and of Courtavenel in France, where Louis had bought a converted medieval chateau and estate, had a subject less strenuous than a love of music.

And there was more than that. The man of forty and the young man of twenty-five had other things in common. Pauline's Spanish spell had also caught Louis. He had written a book on Spain and had translated *Don Quixote*—not very well, they say. There was also the bond of politics: the two men were rationalists and democrats. Viardot was even thought to be politically dubious by the Russian secret police. The pair were at one in their hatred of serfdom. Louis was much taken by the clever young man and saw he could be congenial and useful. He saw that Pauline could clinch her popular success by singing a few Russian songs and that Turgenev was the man to teach her something of the language. Certainly they all met for this useful purpose, in the Viardots' apartment in Petersburg.

Pauline herself was captivated by the mixture of Oriental barbarity and polish in Court Society in Petersburg where everyone spoke French. She was persuaded to sing some Spanish gypsy songs to Russian gypsies: both parties were convinced that Russia and Spain had far more in common than they had with Western Europeans and in this their instinct was right. It is an irony that Turgenev, the Westerner who believed the future of Russia lay in learning from Europe, should have been brought to his one great and lasting passion by what looks like an atavism: her Spanishness had its Islamic roots; his own, remote though they might be, had something of this too. The Andalusian wit and feeling that underlay her French upbringing responded to his lazy, open Russianness. There was more than the buried image of his mother in Pauline, more than the attraction of a common love of music and the belief in the supremacy of art, more even than the conventional attractions of a handsome man for a plain woman, or of a young Quixote for a young woman who was set on the practical matters of her career.

The Viardots left Russia. The following year they came back to Petersburg and then went on to Moscow, where Turgenev took his mother to hear Pauline sing. His mother had heard the gossip about his absurd behaviour. She was annoyed. She did not mind him going

---

to bed with serf girls or having an older mistress of his own class—
he had been having an affair with a miller's wife when he was out
shooting near Petersburg just before meeting Pauline—but to dangle
so seriously after a foreign actress killed any chance of the marriage
his mother had hoped he would make. After hearing the singer she
sulked, but came away saying "It must be admitted the damn gypsy
sings well."

The embittered, ill and ageing sovereign of Spasskoye was at this
period of her life, showing her own ever-increasing powers as an
actress. She had, as we know, broken with her son Nikolai because
of his disgraceful marriage; cutting Ivan's allowance to next to nothing had not prevented him from stooping to literature and accepting
an invitation from the Viardots to visit them in France. (He went,
on the pretext that he had to see a doctor about his eyes.) She could
not stand the company of her brother-in-law who had come to live
in the house and got rid of him. Worse: the old gentleman had
married and very happily. In spite of everything, she longed for the
sons who would not obey her and she put on fantastic and malevo-
lent scenes. One year she announced that there would be no Easter
Festival—an appalling sacrilege in the eyes of her peasants and her
neighbours. She ordered the priest to stop the ringing of the church
bells and though the servants laid the great table in the hall with the
Sèvres porcelain and had set out the bright red eggs, the lamb made
of butter and the Easter cake, she made them clear it all away
untouched.

In another scene she sent for the priest to hear her confession, but
when he got there she called for her house serfs to be assembled and
told the priest she wanted to be confessed publicly. The priest
protested that this was against the laws of the church but she
shouted and threatened till the terrified man gave in.

The most powerful scene occurred on the date of Ivan's birthday,
a sacred day for her. She ordered him to come home. Budding
orange trees were placed in tubs on the verandahs, the cherry trees
were brought out of the forcing sheds. A great feast with the foods
Ivan loved was laid out on the tables in the stone gallery, the flags
of the Lutovinovs and Turgenevs were hoisted over the house and
she had a signpost erected on the road on which the words *Ils*

---

reviendront were painted. Neither son came, and retiring to her room she announced that she was dying. She called for Ivan's portrait and called out, *"Adieu,* Jean. *Adieu,* Nikolai. *Adieu, mes enfants."* As the household wept she ordered them to bring in the icon of the Holy Virgin of Vladimir. She lay on her bed imitating the death rattle with her favourites kneeling at her bedside—they knew it was all a farce—and obliged the forty servants from the highest to the lowest to come in and kiss her hand in farewell. When this was done she suddenly called out in a stentorian voice to Polyakov, her chief servant: "Bring some paper." Her box of loose sheets for making strange notes was at her bedside and when it was given to her, she wrote down:

> Tomorrow the following culprits must appear in front of my window and sweep the yard. You were overjoyed that I was dying. You were drinking and celebrating a name day and your mistress dying!

The next day the drinkers, from the principal servants downwards, were made to put on smocks with circles and crosses on their backs and clean out the yards and gardens with brooms and shovels in sight of her terrifying window.

In the following year—in 1846, according to Mme. Zhitova—Ivan did come home to ask her to recognise his brother's marriage and to give him money. She stormed and refused. They got on to the subject of serfdom. Mme. Zhitova says she heard a conversation. It could have been matched, in this period, in landowners' houses in Ireland or in the American South.

> "So my people are badly treated! What more do they need? They are very well fed, shod and clothed, they are even paid wages. Just tell me how many serfs do receive wages?"
> "I did not say that they starve and are not well-clothed," began Ivan Serfevitch cautiously, stammering a little, "but they tremble before you."
> "What of it?"
> "Listen mama, couldn't you now, this minute, if you wanted, exile any one of them?"
> "Of course I could."

"Even from a mere whim?"

"Of course."

"Then that proves what I have always told you. They are not people —they are things."

"Then according to you they ought to be freed?"

"No, why? I don't say that, the time hasn't come yet."

"And won't come."

"Yes it will come, it will come soon," cried Ivan Sergevich passionately in the rather shrill voice he used when excited and he walked quickly round the room.

"Sit down, your walking about worries me," his mother said.

"I see you are quite mad."

The Viardots' third season in Petersburg lasted until the spring of 1845 and they returned to France. Turgenev resigned from his post in the Civil Service on the excuse that he was having serious trouble with his eyes and accepted an invitation to stay with the Viardots at Courtavenel. There are signs that Pauline had lost her indifference and was falling in love against her will, and Turgenev spoke of this time as "the happiest time of my life." From any other man these words would indicate that he had conquered, that the love was returned and fulfilled; but one notices that when he became the master of the love story, he is far more sensitive to the beginnings of love than to its fulfilment, to the sensation of being—to use one of his titles—"on the eve" of love, of standing elated as he waits for the wave to curl and fall. The spring—and also the autumn—mean more to him than high summer.

He went back to Petersburg and had some small successes writing for *The Contemporary,* a new review which was making an impression, and was distraught at being unable to see her. At last, in 1847, he borrowed money and went to Paris again and the Viardots let the penniless writer stay on at Courtavenel whether they were away or not. They were often away for months on end, as Pauline travelled from success to success all over Europe. If, as some believe, they ever became lovers, it was in the next three years and if they did not, it was the time when what has been called "a loving friendship" sparkled and crystallised.

Courtavenel was a strange and spacious house. It was close to Rozay-en-Brie and lay in dull but good shooting country, convenient for Paris. Louis Viardot had bought it from a Baron. It had two faces.

The older face dated from the sixteenth century and had towers, a moat and a drawbridge; the modern one suggested bourgeois wealth and respectability, just the place for a prosperous family who entertained largely and would soon acquire a town house in the rue de Douai in Montmartre where they would go in the winter. When the Viardots went off they left behind them Pauline's mother and her in-laws, her little girl and her governess, and a crowd of servants and gardeners, guests and visitors continued to come and go. When Dickens stayed there with the Viardots he complained that there was a general air of transience about the place; it was like a railway junction where people were changing trains, but to Turgenev such a life had all the easy-going openness of life in a Russian country house, without the provincial stagnation. The lonely young man who had not been able to stand life with his mother at Spasskoye had found a home and a cheerful family. He became a great friend of Mme. Garcia, Pauline's mother, who was affectionate and full of salty Spanish proverbs. Pauline wrote letters to her mother and occasionally to him and they were read and re-read aloud; and he wrote amusing letters on his own and the family's behalf and showed them to her mother before he sent them so that she could add postscripts of her own.

It is on the letters that Turgenev wrote to Pauline at this period —and indeed all his life—that we have chiefly to rely for our conjectures about their mysterious relationship and especially for our sight of his character. He wrote to her constantly about what he was doing, the people he met and especially about his reading and about her music and her performances, for he followed every report of them. Our trouble is that although she made time to write to him in her distracted life, only a handful of her letters have survived. He longed for them; occasionally some—to judge by his replies—were delightful for a lover to receive; but there is not a sensual or even an extravagant word of feeling in the few we have. She chattered away but is reticent and no more than affectionate.

The question of Turgenev's relationship with Pauline and the changes in it are important. It was the opinion of a large number of his Russian contemporaries that his love for her was fatal to his talent, for it was an obsession that took him away from Russia and damaged his understanding of his own country. It was also their opinion that she enslaved him and reduced him to the state of her *cavalier servant* and that he became the humiliated figure in a *ménage à trois,* and that his love was not a strength but a sign of his chronic weakness of will, at the root of his pessimism and his melancholy.

Turgenev called Courtavenel "the cradle of his fame." There at the age of twenty-eight he felt that *épanouissement de l'être* which gave him his first important subjects. His letters of this time are the happy letters of a mind finding itself and growing. It is a cultivated mind. It is endlessly curious. It is spirited and critical: the letters are brilliant, changeable, discursive talk, all personality. One can see that Pauline Viardot was drawn to him by not only his gaiety and his serious interest in her art, but his ease as a natural teacher. He was flattering, but the flattery was instructed. For example, he told her she had not quite mastered tragic parts where her talent would eventually lie—Iphigenia would suit her, but Goethe was "a shade calm" because "Thank God you come from the Midi—still there is something composed in your character."

Turgenev read everything rapidly and with excitement. He tells her that he has picked up a book by a fool called Daumer who holds the theory that Primitive Judaic Christianity was simply the cult of Moloch revived. A silly theory, but there *is* a terrible side to Christianity: the bloody, disheartening, anti-human side of a religion which set out to be a religion of love and charity. It is painful to read of the flagellation, the processions, worship of relics, the autos-da-fé, the hatred of life, the horror of women, all those wounds and all that talk of blood.

Under her husband's influence Turgenev's conversation was peppered with bits of Spanish. Pauline, of course, knew the language well. Turgenev took Spanish lessons at Courtavenel and was soon reading Calderón. Of Calderón's *Devoción de la Cruz* he says he is the greatest Catholic dramatic poet since Shakespeare—like him, the most humane and the most anti-Christian: He has

> *cette foi immuable, triomphante, sans l'ombre d'un doute ou même d'une réflexion: Il vous écrase à force de grandeur et de majesté, malgré tout ce que cette doctrine a de répulsif et d'atroce. Ce néant de tout ce qui constitue la dignité de l'homme devant la volonté divine, l'indiff-érence profonde pour tout ce que nous appelons vertu ou vice avec laquelle la Grâce se répand sur son élu—est encore un triomphe pour*

*l'esprit humain, car l'être qui proclame ainsi avec tant d'audace son
propre néant, s'élève par cela même à l'égal de cette Divinité fantasque,
dont il se reconnaît être le jouet.*

He has moved on to Calderón's *La Vida Es Sueño* with its wild
energy, its profound and sombre disdain for life, its astonishing
boldness of thought, set side by side with Catholic fanaticism at its
most inflexible. Calderón's Segismund is the Spanish Hamlet. That
life is a dream will be both context and impulse when Turgenev
found his genius in poetic realism and already we see him forming
his theory of the contrasting characters of Hamlet and Don Quixote.
But a Hamlet who marks the difference between the South and the
North. Hamlet is the more reflective, subtle and philosophic; the
character of Segismund is simple, naked and as penetrating as a
dagger: one fails to act through irresolution, doubt and brooding: the
other acts—for his southern blood drives him to do so—but even as
he acts he knows that life is only a dream. (The lover is subtly trying
to stir her southern blood and draw out her Spanishness.)

Contemporary literature, he reflects, is in a state of transition. It
is eclectic and reflects no more than the scattered sentiments of their
author. There is no great dominant movement—perhaps industrial-
ism will take the place of literature; perhaps *that* will liberate and
regenerate mankind. So perhaps the real poets are the Americans
who will cut a path through Panama and invent a transatlantic
electric telegraph. (Once the social revolution has been achieved a
new literature will be born!) He doesn't suppose that a spirit as
discriminating, simple, straight-forward and serious as hers is has
much patience with the stories of Diderot: he is too full of paradox
and fireworks, though sometimes he has new and bold ideas. It is by
his *Encyclopaedia* he will live and by his devotion to freedom.
(There will be more than a touch of Diderot in the construction of
Turgenev's stories.)

Louis Viardot has asked him to arrange his library. There is a list
of books read: M. Ott's *History* is the work of a Catholic Democrat
—something against nature: that idea merely produces monsters.
There are other nauseating books on history in the library: Rolteck,
for example, with his flat, emphatic style but there are the spirited
letters of Lady Mary Wortley Montagu; an absurd Spanish novel;
Bausset's *Napoleon,* the book of a born lackey; a dull translation of

Virgil's *Eclogues,* not exactly a marvel in the original. He has started on the *Koran* but despite its good sense he knows it will all lead sooner or later to the usual Oriental flatulence.

But he knows that what she will most want is news of the theatre, what he is doing and the small events of life in Paris where he goes to buy the papers for critiques of her performances and to stroll in the Tuileries and to watch the pretty children and their staid nurses and enjoy the crisp autumn air. Autumn on a fine day is rather like Louis XIV in old age. He expects she'll laugh at that idea. "Well, go on laughing to show your teeth."

Another day he goes to the woods at Ville d'Avray:

L'impression que la nature fait sur l'homme est étrange. Il y a dans cette impression un fonds d'amertume fraîche comme tous les odeurs des champs, un peu de mélancholie sereine comme dans les chants d'oiseaux

and adds that he adores the reality, the changes, the dangers, the habits, the passing beauty of life. While he is rearranging Louis Viardot's library the servant is polishing, washing, tidying, sweeping, waxing from morning to night. One night as he goes up to bed he hears two deep sighs that passed in a puff of air close to him. It froze him. Suppose the next moment a hand had touched him: he would have screamed like an eagle. (Question: Are the blind afraid of ghosts?) He lists the sounds he heard one night as he stood by the drawbridge: the throb of the blood in his ears, the rustle of leaves, the four crickets in the courtyard, fish rising in the moat, a dull sound from the road, the ping of a mosquito. He goes out to look at the stars and writes what will become one of the certainties of his life:

Cette chose indifférente, impérieuse, vorace, égoiste, envahissante, c'est la vie, la nature . . .

Still, tell Louis there are a lot of quail about and shooting begins on the 25th. There is a plague of orange tawneys *(rougets).* In an hour her aunt has caught *"cinquante, cincuenta, fünfzig,* fifty," on her face and neck. He's scratching himself with both hands. They're all waiting for Mlle. Berthe's arrival, *para dar a comer a los bichos* ("to give the bugs a meal"), as Don Pablo says, as a useful diversion. M.

Fougeux arrives, the king of bores. Turgenev goes rowing and puffing around the moat with him. The moat needs dredging. Fougeux is a man who speaks only in clichés and quotations. Over and over again he says "Nature is only a vast garden." God!

One night he has a long fantastic flying dream. He is walking along a road lined with poplars and is obliged to sing the line *"À la voix de la mère"* a hundred times before he will be allowed to get home. He meets a white figure who calls himself his brother and who turns him into a bird. He finds he has a long beak like a pelican and off they fly:

> I can remember it still, not simply in the head, *but* if I can so express myself, with my whole body.

They fly over the sea and below he sees enormous fish with black heads and he knows he has to dive for them because they are his food. A secret horror stops him. The sun suddenly rises and burns like a furnace. And so on. (Perhaps he was dreaming about his mother, his brother and the carp lying deep in the fish pond at Spasskoye. Many times in his later writings he evokes gross sinister fishes rising out of the deep water to threaten him. A great many years later, in a gloomy period of his life, he put this dream into a rhapsodic fantasy called *Phantoms:* it has little merit but suggests an erotic excitement or the frustration and fear of it.)

From her exhausting tours and the applause of audiences in London, Germany and Austria, the singer and her husband returned at intervals to Courtavenel to rest. They had taken in the young Gounod and Turgenev was for a time a little jealous of Pauline's interest in his work: there was some local gossip—George Sand indeed wrote to Pauline asking if he were "a good man"—but the friendship seems to have been strictly musical in its interests, though when Gounod suddenly married, his wife made trouble when Louis and Pauline sent her a bracelet.

On Sundays Turgenev would go off shooting with Louis or would go for charming walks with Pauline. They lay under the trees talking or reading books aloud or in the house he would go through the works she was studying. If there were parties Turgenev danced with her; he was an excellent dancer. On ordinary evenings, the family of aunts sat about reading, knitting and sewing, and an uncle taught Pauline's rather spoiled little daughter Spanish, Gounod worked on a musical score, and Turgenev told stories.

Then Louis and Pauline were off again and every few days he was writing to her. The letters begin, Bonjour or Dear Madame Viardot, and there were friendly messages to Viardot. To hers, Viardot often added a postscript. Nothing could have been more correct; but by 1848, his letters often end in ardent phrases in German. She is his "dearest Angel." Again "Thank you a thousand, thousand times for . . . you know why . . . you the best and dearest of women . . . what happiness you gave me then . . ." And "Give me your kind and delicate hands so that I can press and kiss them a long time . . . Whatever a man can think, feel and say, I say it and feel it now."

Her hands were beautiful and he worshipped them all his life. In a letter sent to her in 1849 he said in German:

> All day I have been lost in a magical dream. Everything, everything, all the past, all that has been poured irresistibly and spontaneously into my soul . . . I am whole . . . I belong body and soul to my dear Queen. God bless you a thousand times.

In July '49 at Courtavenel he went off to a village fête, studied the faces and watched the sweating dancers. He passed the next day alone and wrote to her in German:

> I cannot tell you how much I have thought of you every day, when I got back to the house I cried out your name in ecstasy and opened my arms with longing for you. You must have heard and seen me!

There is a line in one letter in which, once only, he addresses her as *"du."* From this and from the paragraphs in German some biographers have thought that Pauline and he had become physically lovers and that German was used to hide the fact from her husband who is said not to have known the language. This is most unlikely: Louis had been many times to Germany; as a capable translator in a bilingual family, he must at least have picked up some German in the course of his business and indeed from Pauline's singing. German is more likely to be "a tender little language" between intimate friends and Turgenev, the polyglot, liked to spice his letters with foreign words for he could not use more than a word or two of Russian to her. Perhaps in using German he was simply using the romantic language of the sublime he had learned in Berlin when he was nineteen. Expressions of love are at once more extravagant and frequent in a foreign tongue and, for that reason, have the harmless sense of theatrical fantasy or flattery: platonic love affairs live by words and not deeds. George Sand wrote with the same exaltation in her novels; and young women of the period would expect no less from a correspondent, especially from the Russian "openness." There is no sign that Pauline ever replied to Turgenev in such terms.

It is impossible to say more about the nature of this love for the moment; but there is strong reason to suspect that Pauline, duty or no duty, "hot southern blood" (as she once or twice said) or not, was one of those gifted young women who do not feel physical passion until later in life and have something mannish in their nature. And what about the guilt Turgenev may have felt in being in love with the wife of a generous friend? This is also a mystery: there is only a slight sign of this embarrassment in his stories.

In their biographies, Yarmolinsky, Magarshack and April Fitzlyon differ considerably in their interpretation. Yarmolinsky is vivid, engaging and ironical in the disabused manner of the nineteen-twenties and regards the love affair as purely platonic on both sides, a deep *amitié amoureuse,* which would go a long way to explaining why Turgenev never gave it up and why Louis Viardot tolerated it. (Louis was to become the father of four children.) Magarshack asserts that Pauline did become Turgenev's mistress and that the affair came quickly to an end because she gave him up for Ary Scheffer, the painter, who often came to Courtavenel and that when she and Turgenev were reconciled she was unfaithful to him and her husband again. He also accepts the common gossip that her second daughter, Didie, and her son Paul were probably Turgenev's children. Neither of these writers has closely considered the character of Pauline and all the evidence as searchingly as April Fitzlyon has done. She believes that Pauline did fall seriously in love with Turgenev and indeed felt passion for the first time; that it is just possible they were briefly lovers, though to neither of them was physical love important—indeed Pauline may have been put off by a dislike of "conjugal duty"—and that, in any case, she put her art before personal relationships always and is well-known to have disapproved of the Bohemian morals of her profession. Far from having been her lover, Ary Scheffer—a man as old as her husband and a stern moralist—would be the counsellor who prevented her from leaving her husband for Turgenev and made her control her heart by her will which was certainly very strong. She says it is indeed just possible in the case of the son that Turgenev was the father, but it is unlikely and there is no evidence. And that although Turgenev made bitter remarks in the vicissitudes of his attachment to her and in his masochistic way said that he lived under her heel as many of his incredulous friends thought, he endured what he did endure because he was in love with his own chivalrous love.

In this situation Louis Viardot behaved with dignity and concealed the pain he must have felt. He was passionately in love with his wife and was no cynic: he remained friends with Turgenev all his life, although some thought their attitude to each other formal.

The situation indeed changed, as we shall see.

Whatever went on at Courtavenel in those early years there is no doubt that Louis and his wife must have regarded Turgenev affectionately as an extraordinary and exotic case. Viardot himself, as a traveller and one who had felt the Spanish spell of his wife, must have felt the Russian spell of Turgenev. They must have been astounded by the story of his barbarous experience at Spasskoye, and have been amazed that the giant had grown to be grave and gentle, as well as gifted. And Louis must have recognised a wit and a mind far richer than his own. The Viardots felt concern for his talent and both pointed to the dangers of idleness to a man who was rich enough to do nothing. Pauline was no amateur: she was an artist and a professional and it can never have entered her head that Turgenev, who was incapable of managing money or any practical matter, could replace her husband. One can see by their kindness, and especially Louis Viardot's, that although they saw his distinction and originality, their feeling must have been protective. Viardot had no small vanity in his own taste and exercised an almost fatherly right to give sound advice to the feckless aristocrat and was aware of having two artists on his hands whom he could keep in order. He was a rational man but quietly firm in requiring moral behaviour and decorum.

There is a line in *A Month in the Country,* the play that Turgenev began to write before he left Courtavenel and which in many respects is drawn on his situation as a lover. Rakitin, the lover, is made to say at the crisis of the play:

"It is time to put an end to these morbid, consumptive relations."

Consumptive? Or self-consuming? It strikes one that those words must have been actually spoken at Courtavenel not by Turgenev but by Viardot. They have his manner.

There comes a moment, in one of the last letters Turgenev was to write from Courtavenel, when he adds a sentence in German:

What is the matter with Viardot? Is he upset because I am living here?

Chapter 4

TURGENEV was all personality but he did not pour everything away in talk at Courtavenel. He began to write and indeed earned a little money. He had before him the example of a young woman who sacrificed her personal feeling for her art. And there was the industry, even the literary influence, of Louis Viardot himself, who saw that Turgenev's talents would have to struggle against his expectations of great wealth and ease. The methodical slaughterer had written a book about his holidays with the gun. When he and Turgenev went out shooting near Rozay-en-Brie the dull country brought his memories of the ravines, the marshes, the oak woods of Spasskoye to life. He discovered that, Westerner though he was, he carried an ineffaceable Russia inside him; the Russia of his boyhood and young manhood became all the clearer in detail and stronger in meaning for being distant. Distance also freed him of the direct rancours of politics. He sat down to write prose, the first of *The Sportsman's Sketches*. He was proud to write to Pauline that he had sent off packets of manuscript to *The Contemporary* in Russia and the editor and the readers asked for more.

When he became a writer of stories Turgenev was obliged to find some way of disguising himself and of distributing his character among the people he created. In *The Sportsman's Sketches* he had to be, with his natural modesty, what he had been—an anonymous amateur of his sport, coming casually upon the country people of the private nation he had been brought up in. The people and woods of Orel and Kaluga were his educators as a writer.

He goes out apparently with nothing in his head except the simple happiness of the outdoor life and the love of nature. He walks or rides for miles, sleeps in the hay of any old hut. The day alone is the containing shape and the formlessness of the day is exactly suited to the eye that picks out the portrait of a human being as he picks out a snipe or a woodcock. One notices at once how he is neither an essayist nor a documentary reporter: a simple, reflective, poetic feeling sustains him. In the well-known opening sketch the enquirer's canvas may show through, but as in Maria Edgeworth's Irish writings (which, surprisingly, he had read), he sees a peasantry as they are.

> The peasantry of Orlov is not tall, is bent in figure, sullen and suspicious in his looks; he lives in wretched little hovels of aspen wood, labours as a serf in the fields and engages in no kind of trading, is miserably fed and wears slippers of bast: the rent-paying peasant of Kaluga lives in a roomy cottage of pinewood, he is tall, bold and cheerful in his looks, neat and clean of countenance; he carries on a trade in grease and tar and on holidays he wears boots. The village of Orlov province (we are speaking now of the eastern part of the province), is usually situated in the midst of ploughed fields, near a water course which has been converted into a filthy pool. Except for a few ever-accommodating willows and two or three gaunt birch-trees, you do not see a tree for a mile around: hut is huddled against hut, their roofs covered with rotting thatch.

We see the landowner Polutykin drawn from life as everyone else is: "An enthusiastic sportsman and it follows, an excellent fellow," who was always trying to marry rich heiresses and when turned down, would "shower offerings of sour peaches and other raw produce from his garden upon the young lady's relatives." We see two of Polutykin's peasants: one is Khor—the polecat—a practical, sly, long-headed fellow who could easily buy his freedom but pretends he can't afford it. Kalinych, his closest friend, is an enthusiastic dreamer "who could charm away haemorrhages, fits, madness and worms; his bees always did well; he had a light hand." Kalinych does poorly on his plot because Polutykin insists on dragging him out shooting every day. This opening sketch also recalls the plain manner of Cobbett and contains one very Cobbettish statement about "the pedlars or eagles"—men who sell scythes to the peasants at mowing times and often exploit them. When the landowners took over the trade from these pedlars the peasants were angry: they missed the pleasure of bargaining and trickery; for "the eagles" also went round the villages to buy up rags for the paper-mills and their visits excited the women who sold every bit of rag they could lay hands on, even their husbands' clothes and their own petticoats. "The eagles" tried to get "hemp" off the women, but the men stopped that: getting "hemp" on the side was their own little racket.

This first sketch which was published in *The Contemporary* was a success. In the next one, *Yermolai and the Miller's Wife*, Turgenev grows into the artist's power of secreting himself in the scene and among the people, so that while he stands waiting for the snipe to come down to the dark edge of the forest we get fragments of Yermolai's vagabond life in the woods. He was required by his owner to bring two brace of grouse and partridge once a month. He was out all day and night and could always do a good fifty miles without realising it, sleeping in trees, roofs, bridges and barns. He often lost his gun, his dog or his clothes; was often threatened for one thing or another. Odd in an expert hunter, he had not the patience to train a dog but he was superb in catching crayfish in his hands, in scenting game, snaring quails, training hawks, in capturing the nightingales by imitating their notes. After an evening's shooting the sportsman and Yermolai camp by a fire near a mill and the miller's wife comes out to see them, bringing tea, potatoes, bread and eggs.

> A mist had risen from the river; there was no wind at all; from all round came the cry of the corncrake and faint sounds from the mill wheels of drops that dripped from the paddles and water gurgling through the bars of the lock.

And Turgenev eavesdrops on a desultory conversation between Yermolai and the miller's wife. We have grasped Turgenev's mastery of the miniature portrait, now we see his mastery of natural dialogue:

"And how are your pigs doing?" asked Yermolai.

"They're alive."

"You ought to make me a present of a sucking pig."

The miller's wife was silent for a while and then she sighed.

"Who is it you're with?" she asked.

"A gentleman from Kostomarovo."

Yermolai threw a few pine twigs on the fire, they all caught at once and a thick white smoke came puffing into his face.

"Why didn't your husband let us into the cottage?"

"He's afraid."

"Afraid! The fat old tub. Arina Timofeyevna, my darling, bring me a little glass of spirits."

The miller's wife rose and vanished into the darkness.

Yermolai began to sing in an undertone

> "When I went to see my sweetheart
> I wore out all my shoes."

Arina returned with a small flask and a glass.

Yermolai got up, crossed himself, and drank it off at a draught.

"Good" was his comment.

The miller's wife sat down again on the tub.

"Well, Arina Timofeyevna, are you still ill?"

"Yes."

"What is it?"

"My cough troubles me at night."

"The gentleman's asleep, it seems," said Yermolai.

"Don't go to a doctor, Arina, it will be worse if you do."

"Well, I'm not going."

"But come and pay me a visit."

Arina hung down her head dejectedly.

"I will drive my wife out for the occasion," continued Yermolai. "Upon my word I will."

"You had better wake the gentleman, Yermolai Petrovitch—you see the potatoes are done."

"Oh, let him snore," said Yermolai.

One can guess from this dialogue that Turgenev has been trying to write plays. Two generations later Cheklov will learn the lesson from him.

And now, untroubled by the formal unity required by a story, Turgenev goes off at a tangent and "explains" that he knows the miller's wife was once lady's maid to the wife of a landowner called

Zvyerkoff and a terrible story is revealed. It is in fact—though he does not say so here—very close to the awful story of Varvara Petrovna's savage behaviour when her own lady's maid and favourite got married and was pregnant. The miller's wife had been carrying on with Zvyerkoff's footman. Zvyerkoff dramatises himself in the Russian way:

> My indignation broke out then. I am like that. I don't like half measures! Petrushka was not to blame. We might flog him, but in my opinion he was not to blame. Arina . . . well, well, well, what more's to be said? I gave orders, of course, that the girl's hair should be cut off; she should be dressed in sackcloth and sent into the country. My wife was deprived of an excellent lady's maid . . . There, there, now you can judge the thing for yourself—you know what my wife is . . . yes, yes, yes, indeed! . . . an angel. She had grown attached to Arina and Arina knew it and had the face to . . . Eh? no, tell me . . . Oh? And what's the use of talking about it? . . . I, indeed—I— in particular felt hurt, wounded for a long time by the ingratitude of the girl . . . You may feed the wolf as you will, he has always a hankering for the woods . . .

And what happened to Petrushka? He was not flogged but he was sent into the army—the serf's chief dread.

The wild ducks fly over. Yermolai and the sportsman Turgenev fall asleep in the hay.

In *The Bailiff* and *Bir Yurk* the violence and corruption of serfdom are outspokenly the subjects: but in *Lgov* serfdom has its farcical aspects. The enormous impression which the sketches made as they came out over the years springs from Turgenev's art in portraying the peasants as feeling people, making even the humblest of them to appear to have a sort of self-preserving genius; they are incurably human and are so known to us in voice and habit that it is a shock when we remember "These are slaves." The silent power of Turgenev's sketches comes from the fact that his art is liberating the people he describes; each one is more alive and human than his "situation" as part of the problem of serfdom. To call them a "problem" dehumanises them. Turgenev reveals people living in their natures.

When we get to *The Singers* and *Byezhin Prairie* which were written later there is a sudden swell of feeling and power as the writer becomes assured and extends the skills of his art. He is writing now of the peasants alone—the landowners are dropped —and particularly of the two pastimes they excel in—their singing matches and their story-telling—"they really are musical in our part of the country: the village of Sergievskoe on the Orel highroad is deservedly noted throughout Russia for its harmonious chorus singing."

In the dirty little inn at the top of the ravine two rival singers draw lots and the booth-keeper begins.

> Half-shutting his eyes, he began singing in a high falsetto. He had a fairly sweet and pleasant voice though rather hoarse: he played with his voice like a woodlark, twisting and turning it in incessant roulades and trills up and down the scale, continually returning to the highest notes, which he held prolonged with special care . . . he was a Russian *tenore di grazia, ténor léger*

finishing up in a whirl of flourishes and trills. He is followed by Yakov called the Turk, a ladler in a paper factory, an artist in every sense of the word: he covered his face with his hand and when he uncovered it and began to sing his face was as pale as a dead man's:

> The first sound of his voice was faint and unequal and seemed not to come from his chest, but to be wafted from somewhere afar off, as though it had been floated by chance into the room. A strange effect was produced on all of us by this trembling resonant note; we glanced at one another, and Nikolas Ivanitch's wife seemed to draw herself up. The first note was followed by another, bolder and prolonged, but still obviously quivering, like a harp string when suddenly struck by a stray finger it throbs in a last swiftly dying tremble; the second was followed by a third and gradually gaining fire and breadth the strain swelled into a pathetic melody. "Not one little path ran into the field" . . . I have seldom, I must confess, heard a voice like it; it was slightly hoarse and not perfectly true; there was something morbid about it at first . . .

Yet a spirit of truth and fire, a Russian spirit was in it and it went straight to the heart. Tears came to the eyes of the drinkers in the inn. Turgenev continues:

———

in every sound of his voice one seemed to feel something dear and akin to us, something of the breadth and space, as though the familiar steppes were unfolding before our eyes into an endless distance.

(One can see how in the drawing-room of Courtavenel when she perhaps had sung *cante hondo* to him, Pauline Viardot would bring an echo of Russia back to him, not only as a cultivated grace but as, something primitive. Music was their bond.)

The singers sit down to get rotten drunk and the sportsman goes home in the evening and here Turgenev shows he can create dramatic emotion and then return to the ordinary voices of everyday life. He walks off down the hill from Kolotovka in the evening haze:

> When all at once from somewhere far away in the plain came a boy's clear voice:
> "Antropka! Antropka—a—a!" he shouted in obstinate and tearful desperation, with long, long drawing out of the last syllable.

Thirty times at least he repeated that shout when suddenly:

> from the farthest end of the plain, as though from another world, there floated a scarcely audible reply "Wha—a—at?"
> The boy's voice shouted back at once with gleeful exasperation: "Come here, devil, wood imp."
> "What fo—or?" replied the other after a long interval.
> "Because dad wants to thrash you."
> The second voice did not call back again and the boy fell to shouting "Antropka" once more. His cries, fainter and less and less frequent still floated to my ears, when it had grown completely dark and I had turned the corner of the wood which skirts my village and lies over three miles from Kolotovka . . . "Antropka—a—a" was still audible in the air, filled with the shadows of the night.

That note about the distance of Kolotovka, in its careful way, places a day of powerful feeling in its common locality—the master's touch.

In *Byezhin Prairie* the writer is seen once more enlarging his art and deepening his feeling. The sportsman has lost his way home and as the summer night comes on he stumbles into a group of peasant boys who are sitting round a fire in the ravine. At this hot time of the year they have the job of galloping horses out to graze because in the daytime the flies drive the animals mad. They are shy of the sportsman and his dog but let him sit with them. He says nothing. He simply watches and listens. The night darkens and between the sudden, quickly fading blazes of light from the fire he sees a head of one of the horses for a second or two.

> It stared with intent blank eyes upon us, nipped hastily at the long grass and drawing back again vanished instantly . . . The dark unclouded sky stood inconceivable, immense, triumphant above us in all its mysterious majesty. One felt a sweet oppression at one's heart.

The boys had stopped talking, but began again when they had forgotten the sportsman was there. They started talking of ghosts, the *domovoy* who came at night and made the mill-wheels turn in the paper factory and who scared them by giving a cough; or the *russalka*, the witch who had a voice as shrill as a toad's and who wanted to be tickled; of a man who drowned in the river; of Trishka, the marvel, whom no one can catch. If he is in prison he asks for a bowl of water and dives into it and vanishes; put chains on him —he claps his hands and they fall off. There is talk of the water pit where some thieves drowned a forester who cries out still from the water. Pavel, one of the boys, goes off to draw water from the river and comes back saying he has heard the water spirit calling him from under the stream. So the boys go on frightening themselves and trying to brazen it out until one by one they fall asleep. Once more, Turgenev plays with his skill to catch the moments as they drop by.

> The moon at last had risen: I did not notice it at first: it was such a tiny crescent.

How naturally he catches the moment between noticing and not noticing. This, one says, is where his art lies; not simply in seeing, but in the waywardness and the timelessness of seeing. Seeing is like light and shadow, playing over what is seen. Things seen are exact yet they flow away or are retrieved: the past and the present mingle in a clear stream. There are two masters of seeing in Russian literature: Tolstoy and Turgenev. Tolstoy sees exactly as if he were an animal or a bird: and what he sees is still and settled for good. He has the pride of the eye. Turgenev is also exact but without that decisive pride: what he sees is already changing. In one of his letters he quotes with admiration an image of Byron's "the music of the face"—the movement from note to note, the disappearance of the thing seen in time as it passes.

The brief tales told by the boys in their natural, half-scared language are not simply a collection of peasant superstitions, they are part of their boyhood on that particular night—on another night, in another place, the boys would be different. On another night they would not have been stopped (as they were once or twice on *this* night) by the cry of a heron or by their dog getting up and suddenly barking and rushing into the woods with Pavel after him to catch a frightened horse. This was after Pavel went to fetch water from the river and came back saying he had heard his name called by the drowned boy from the water. An omen? Yes, an omen. The sportsman left the boys just before daybreak. All were asleep except Pavel who half rose and gazed intently at him. He nodded and the sportsman walked homeward along the bank of the river, shrouded with smoky mist and then came

> torrents of young hot sunlight, crimson at first and later brilliantly red, brilliantly golden. Everything began quivering into life, awakening, singing, resounding, chattering

and after he had gone a mile or two, the horses rushed by, chased by the boys.

> I have, unfortunately, to add that in that same year Pavlusha died. He did not drown; he was killed in falling from a horse. A pity, for he was a fine lad!

The last sentence is a mistake, but the casual note of Pavel's death is not perfunctory: it recalls the omen, it restores the story to the chances in the life of every day, the sense of the acceptance of life and of death. In an account of the death of a woodcutter, Turgenev writes:

> How wonderfully a Russian peasant dies! The temper in which he meets his end cannot be called indifference or stolidity; he dies as though he were performing a solemn rite, coolly and simply.

It has been objected that Turgenev confined himself to the serfs who lived on his mother's estates and, even there, that he knew only the house serfs intimately and from the immediate master-and-man point of view. He was the outsider and the country gentleman. This judgment is too sweeping, as many incidents in the *Sketches* show, and, in any case, a writer's talent has a right to itself. If he was born an outsider, he also *chose* to be an outsider or scrutinising spectator who was in the classical tradition he inherited from his love of Pushkin: from the outside he can summarily penetrate the inside—by his images and sentences—and see his truth. This power of "telling the truth" grew and when he attempts the subjective he is less successful and falls into sentimentality. There is one story in the *Sketches*, "The Tryst," in which he tries to evoke a peasant girl's feelings about love, where we see this happening and in which he falls into the falsity of the non-peasant writer writing about peasants from the inside.

Chapter 5

D URING these three years in France, Turgenev was not always at Courtavenel. When he got money for his *Sketches* or when he could borrow from Mme. Garcia, he stayed in Paris and he also managed to run up debts to the tune of 6,000 roubles, on his expectations. (It may be that this troubled the precise Louis Viardot more than anything else.) In 1848 he had a flat near the Palais Royal and then moved to a cheaper place at the corner of the Boulevard des Italiens and the rue de la Paix and was working on two plays: *A Provincial Lady* and *A Month in the Country.* Pauline Viardot had turned his mind to the theatre. Like most of the Russian gentry in Paris, he was there to despise the French. The Russians met to shout out their souls through the night at the house of the rich Annenkov, the perpetual traveller, talker and fat lazy gourmet, who amused himself by analysing the characters of his friends who borrowed money from him. Turgenev disliked the formal sameness of the city, but he loved the food; he shared the general Russian opinion that the Paris of Louis Philippe was "unbeautiful"—Herzen called France "the cuspidor of Europe." And Belinsky, who died that year, called Paris meaningless. Throughout the nineteenth century only Gogol seems to have been captivated by Europe, but for him Europe had meant Rome. Turgenev, more instructed than most, understood their nostalgia for the timeless, empty distances of the Russian landscape and the dilapidated condition of Russian life. Russia was feudal, but, at least, it was not middle-class. It was not packed with the characters of Balzac's novels which nauseated him. The Latins, he explained eventually to the Goncourts, are men of *"la loi"* but in Russia *"la loi ne se cristallise pas."* The Russians are thieves and yet even a man who confesses to twenty thefts if it is shown that he was in need or hungry will be acquitted. But:

> *vous êtes de la loi, de l'honneur, nous tout autocratisé que nous soyons, nous sommes moins conventionnels, nous sommes des hommes de l'humanité.*

And another time he said the Russians were a race of liars in life because they have been slaves so long but in art they love truth and reality.

In February of that year he followed the Viardots to Brussels to hear Pauline sing and there one morning the hall porter woke him up and shouted "France has become a Republic": the riot-spotted reign of the bourgeois king, Louis Philippe, had come to an end. He took the train to Paris at once. Crowds were in the streets. News of revolution in Poland, Italy and Germany was coming in. The wretchedly paid factory workers in Paris were demonstrating. George Sand was editing *Le Bulletin de la République:* socialism had almost arrived. But by the time of the bloody "June days" the middle classes had triumphed: the Republic was dead and Louis Napoleon was nosing his way towards the throne. Turgenev wrote to Pauline Viardot, who had gone on to Hamburg and Berlin to take the part of Valentine in *The Huguenots,* describing the disturbances in the Paris streets, and was struck by the now half-festive, indifferent, expectant state of the crowds. He was amused by the cigar pedlars. He questioned the workers when they marched on to the Constituent Assembly. They were waiting, the workers said. But he couldn't for the life of him, he said, find out what the workers wanted or what side they took. Was history an act of God, accident, irony or fatality? He was asking the same question about his impossible love for Pauline Viardot.

Twenty years later, he put down in his *Reminiscences* a remarkable account of the insurrection in June: *My Mates Sent Me!* He always said that he was a physical coward; but if he hated and feared violence his eyes were not cowardly. They were alive to every change of scene and mood. A column of the National Guard, occupying one side of the Boulevard, turned to face a barricade. The day was hot:

In spite of the arrival of such a considerable number of people everything grew much quieter around; voices were hushed, bursts of laughter became less frequent and shorter; it was as though a haze had fallen over the sounds. An empty space suddenly appeared between the barricade and the National Guard, with two or three small, slightly spinning columns of dust whirling along over it and —looking round apprehensively, a little black and white dog walked about on thin legs in it. Suddenly—it was difficult to say whether from the front or from behind, from above or below— there came a short, loud report; it was more like the sound of an iron bar falling heavily on the ground than a shot and immediately after this sound there came a strange, breathless silence. Everything seemed to grow tense with suspense—and suddenly over my head there came an unbearable loud rattle and roar, like the instantaneous tearing of a huge canvas. That was the insurgents firing through the Venetian blinds of the top floor of the Jouvin factory they had occupied.

He bolted with some of the crowd to a side turning, catching sight as he ran of a man on all fours in front of the barricade, a man in a cap with a red pompom and the black and white dog spinning in the dust. He reached a small barricade in one of the back streets where a boy of twelve was pulling faces and waving a Turkish sword and a fat national guardsman white as a sheet ran stumbling past, moaning, with blood dripping from his sleeve.

Herwegh, the German poet, had fled from the fighting in Baden-Baden and was hiding in the flat above Turgenev's and a workman had come across Paris, risking his life, to tell Herwegh where his baby son was. Turgenev gave the man something to eat and thanked him and offered him money. He refused it. Turgenev asked his name. He refused to give it.

There is no need for you to know my name. To tell you the truth what I did I didn't do for you. My mates sent me. Good bye.

Turgenev's comment tells us everything about his humanity as a man and his truthfulness as a writer:

> It was impossible not to admire the old man's action and the uncon-
> scious, almost majestic complicity with which he accomplished it. It
> evidently never occurred to him that he was doing anything extraordi-
> nary, that he was sacrificing himself. But it is impossible not to admire
> the people who sent him, either, those who at the height of the
> desperate fighting, could remember the worry and anxiety of a "bour-
> geois" they did not know and took care to set his mind at rest. It is
> true that 22 years later men like these set Paris on fire and shot their
> hostages; but he who has even a little knowledge of the human heart
> will not be shocked by these contradictions.

Herzen was in Paris at the time and the effect of the revolution of '48 on him was to put an end to the political illusions he shared with the Russian Romantics. It had destroyed their dream. As E.H. Carr pointed out in *The Romantic Exiles,* the Romantic movement had come thirty years late to Russia. Up till now they had believed that the ideas of the French Revolution were still a force in Europe: the events of '48 had shown them that, above all in France, it was no longer a force. Napoleon had killed the Revolution for good; money and the *petit-bourgeoisie* were in power. Herzen understood that the views of the Russian revolutionaries like himself had been out of date. There had always been a deep strain of original scepti-cism in him and now it had become bitter and pungent. He ridiculed the absurd antics of the out-of-date conspirators in Paris. Yet he said he wished that he had died with a rifle in his hands on the barricades, for at least he "would have carried with him to the grave two or three convictions."

Turgenev saw the Herzen family every day. They lived in the Champs-Élysées, close to the Arc de Triomphe which had just been finished, and Turgenev read poetry to Natalie Herzen's daughters and distracted them all by his mimicry and play-acting, even alarmed them by his bursts of light-headedness and left them depressed. Once he dressed up in Natalie's velvet cape and pretended to be a madwoman, another time he sat on the window-sill, pretending to be a cockerel and screaming in a high voice "Cock-a-doodle-do." In one of his comic fits he pulled down a curtain and stood himself in a corner with a dunce's hat on his head. Afterwards he fell into silent brooding and Natalie Herzen, who was on the verge of a miserable love affair with Herwegh, tried to draw him out on the subject of love. Perhaps Turgenev's failure to respond to her attempts to find out the truth about his relations with Pauline and Louis Viardot—a matter of exemplary interest to her, for her Herwegh was married—caused her to turn against Turgenev: she said he gave her the sensation of being in a damp, musty, empty house.

Were his antics and his moods of depression the symptoms of the sickness of an impossible love?

The cholera terrified him; it was the Russian plague following him to Europe, eating its way from street to street. Presently he had a fever and he bolted out of Paris to the Ville d'Avray and there slowly the fever abated. His capacity to create the symptoms of illness—bladder trouble is one, for example—seems to be at one with his genius for fantasy and to his general sensibility. One of his beliefs was that he had a thinner skull than other men.

He recovered and went to Courtavenel. The Viardots had left for a long series of engagements in England which they disliked but where Pauline always had enthusiastic audiences, so he went off to Hyères to convalesce, and he wrote to "the most loved, dearest and only woman" asking for every detail of her performances and chattered about his journey—thirty-six hours to Lyons in a crowded compartment with a French grocer who boasted that he himself had killed seventeen insurgents in the street.

> *"Ah! voyez-vous," disait-il, ce n'était pas long, on leur criait: "à genoux, gredins," ils se débattaient—mais paouf, un coup de crosse dans la nuque, paouf! une balle à bout portant entre les deux sourcils—et drig, drig, drig—les voilà qui gigotaient sur le pavé."*

The grocer was a fat man, a regular at the Opéra Comique. Turgenev went down the Rhône by steamer to Avignon and then on to Hyères. In his letters the ardent German phrases to "my dear beloved angel" and "to the whole of your dear being" from her "old and faithful lover who loves you," continue.

At the heart of his troubles was the knowledge that his long stay in France must come to an end. His *Sketches* were a success and he knew that his presence in Russia was indispensable to him as a writer. On the other hand, Russian officials kept an eye on Russian exiles and were especially sensitive at this moment, for after the revolutions of '48 any Russian who was in touch with the revolutionaries like Herzen and Bakunin, as Turgenev had been, were under suspicion. Pauline Viardot had allowed Bakunin to use her Paris address for his letters and Turgenev had been warned by friends that he had better wait until the political climate became milder, yet, if he stayed on, the Russian government might go as far as cancelling his passport and sequestrating the money he eventually expected from the Spasskoye estate. This had nearly happened years before to Herzen, who had, however, cleverly made arrangements with the Rothschilds to get his fortune out of Russia before the ban fell, but Herzen was now an exile for life. Her control of money was Varvara Petrovna's weapon against her sons. Turgenev wavered; he wrote to Pauline:

> Russia can wait—that immense and sombre figure motionless and masked like the Sphinx of Oedipus. She will gulp me down later. I can see her coarse, inert look fixed on me with gloomy attention, as befits eyes of stone. Set your mind at ease Sphinx. I shall return to you and you can devour me at your leisure if I do not solve your riddle for yet a little while.

The powerful image—Oedipal indeed—showed how strong and ineluctable his involvement with the Russian situation was. It amounted to a passion. But the Sphinx did not wait. His mother was very ill, slowly dying of dropsy. At Courtavenel there may have been a decisive incident—perhaps with Viardot. Changing his mind from week to week, so that the Viardots in London did not know exactly when he went, weeping and his head burning, he packed up his things in misery and on a night in June 1852 he took the boat from Le Havre to Petersburg, looking gloomily at the sea and holding his precious dog Diane on his knees. At the last moment he left his bedside rug to Pauline, asking her to put it in the little salon where she worked, so that she would remember him every day. (It is a Sterne-like gesture yet, unlike most Russians, Turgenev hated Sterne!) "Farewell," he wrote, "my dear kind family, my only family, the ones I love more than anyone in the world. I embrace you all . . . Come for the last time into my arms so that I can hold you against my heart." The flat coast of Finland came up. The sky was pale: *"C'est le Nord."* And he quotes lines from a song of Gounod's *Vallon, "D'ici je vois la vie"* and *"Repose-toi, mon âme."*

> *Que me veux-tu avec ton Vallon avec ta tristesse pénétrante, avec les accents émouvants. Laisse-moi un peu en repos, laisse-moi regarder en avant—les cordes que tu fais vibrer sont douleureusement rendues depuis quelques temps. Laisse-les se reposer, se taire.*

Pauline said they were all broken by his going but knew that his family affairs had forced him to go. Louis added a postscript—as he sometimes did to Pauline's letters—saying he hoped Turgenev would eventually return and come back *indépendant* with a well-settled vocation when he had settled his affairs and told him to get out of Petersburg quickly because of the cholera.

Two years after this parting, Viardot wrote to say that there was a nice little farm going near Courtavenel if Turgenev was interested: on Viardot's side the parting seems to have quietened any private suspicions Louis may have felt or spoken.

For a time the known letters of Pauline to Turgenev were tender; in one, either in Andalusian merriment or perhaps at his request, she enclosed clippings from her fingernails and told him how she had rearranged the furniture in her little salon. He said he wished he were the carpet under her feet and sent her a lock of hair.

But the family troubles in his mother's house in Moscow were appalling. He got there to find her physically helpless, but in a state of unbelievable malignancy in the worst traditions of the Lutovinovs. She sat in her drawing-room playing patience, putting off Ivan's pleas for his brother and himself by raging about Nikolai and Ivan's "gypsy" and rambling on about her favourite blends of tea. Her mind was consumed with thinking up tricks and vengeances. She had, for example, agreed at last to recognise her eldest son's marriage, but on condition that he give up his job in the Service and settle on a small farm which had belonged to the Turgenev family. In a frightful scene, notable for its alternating scheming silences and sudden euphoria, she drew up a deed of gift giving this little property to the two sons, but they saw she had consulted no lawyer and the deed was not worth the paper it was written on. Not only that, she had given secret orders to her bailiffs of this estate and her own, to sell all the stock and corn stored in the barns quickly and to send all the money to Moscow. There would not be a single grain of corn for the new sowing; she was giving them empty land, without horses or cattle and with no money to farm it. The brothers had to tell their mother to her face, as calmly as they could, that she was cheating them, but neither the tears of Nikolai who was nearly out of his mind or all Ivan's calm reasoning could change her mind. They had to tell her that they would never see her again. Her reply was to smash Ivan's picture on her writing table and throw it on the floor. Ivan gave Nikolai and his German wife the small farm at Turgenevo, and they all went to live there. Ivan had a broken-down room in a disused paper mill on the place.

Mme. Zhitova—the "orphan"—acted as a go-between when Varvara Petrovna moved from Moscow to Spasskoye, twelve miles from Turgenevo and although she does not mention it, it seems from Turgenev's letters that he thought their half-sister has become a grasping hypocrite. And there was a private agony for Ivan: when he was in the Moscow house he saw an eight-year-old girl living with the servants. She was Pelagea, his own child by the serf woman who had looked after the linen and had been sent away to Petersburg where she worked as a serving woman. He had had no further contact with her.

It tells us much about the atmosphere of the Moscow house and Turgenev's state of shock that he thought it necessary to get a maid to take Pelagea into the street so that he might look at her and talk to her. It tells us more about him that he was moved to confess his story at once to Pauline. He had convinced himself, in their curiously "staged," even artificial relationship, that the Viardots were his "only real family" as if he and she were characters in a play. He wrote to tell her of the shock the discovery of his daughter had been. At the meeting in the street, he said, he saw before him a child who was exactly like himself when he was a boy of eight. She had his face: the sight of it accused him and mocked him. What shocked him was that he could divine nothing of the mother whom he had merely used and of whom he had absolutely no recollection. One wonders if this could possibly be true: he could remember well one or two touching details of his affairs with other serf women. He said:

71

Oh my God, how I would have loved a child who brought back to me the memory of a woman I had loved.

It was the remorse of the man who saw he too was guilty of the evils of serfdom. He feared what would happen to the child after his mother died. He wanted her to be brought up free. Should he put her in a convent? He begged Pauline for advice, he appealed to her heart and said he would follow it to the letter. He could not return the unwanted child to her mother, who had lovers in Petersburg.

Between the lines one reads the fervour, the leap-into-the-air of the wild hope that the Viardots would take the little girl in. The child might save him from what he most feared—that in absence Pauline would forget him. The other letters that went between Moscow and Courtavenel are missing and one can only guess at what was thought and said, but the astonishing thing is that the Viardots did agree to take Pelagea and bring her up with their own daughter. It is particularly astonishing because Pauline herself was mostly an absent mother and had at this time little maternal feeling and that Louis Viardot, at the age of fifty, was often irritated by his own daughter, who was spoiled by Mme. Garcia and the aunts. But Louis Viardot was a humane and enlightened man and he would be moved by this gesture against serfdom. He considered himself the close paternal friend of the talented young writer. The child of a friend would be no burden and might be a mollifying companion to his own difficult daughter. And there is another aspect: the Viardot family had its own "orphan," a half-nephew, Joaquin Ruiz Garcia, the son of Manuel Garcia's illegitimate daughter born of an affair he had had before his marriage, and who passed as a "cousin" in the family.

Turgenev's gratitude was eloquent. He renamed the child Paulinette and, once again, with theatrical feeling, declared that Pauline would henceforth be her "mother"; that the child should be "their" daughter. The play was like the fancy of a child and there was indeed something, as Pauline said of him afterwards, naïve and child-like in the dilettante of Petersburg. The matter was quickly settled, for the Viardots understood the terrible stories he had told them of his mother's rule. Turgenev found a French woman who was returning to Paris, put Paulinette in her care and set them on the road to Stettin in Poland. He travelled with them for three days by diligence and studied the child's character. She showed herself to be intelligent if tough and forward, for she had had her way with the old serf women who had brought her up and treated her as an amusing toy. She loved music, she said; but she had seen "many evil things." She told him for example that she didn't feel sorry for anyone—no one had felt pity for her. But suppose, he had asked, if she saw someone suffering? To that the child said "What about it? The only person I'm sorry for is myself." And added that although she was only little she knew what the world was like: "I've seen everything," she said. He told Pauline that, like himself, the child had sulky moods. Still, he was confident that her life as a free person in a civilised house where she was loved would transform the little savage.

Four years passed before she saw her father again and she *had* been transformed, but not as all had foreseen. Music bored her. She did not like her new mother and she quarrelled jealously with Pauline's Louise. And she grew up to be watchful and knowing about what went on in the Viardot family.

Soon after the quarrel with their mother about the estate, Turgenev left Moscow for Petersburg and Varvara Petrovna left for Spasskoye. When she got there she heard that her sons had secretly been there to collect their things. She screamed at her butler, "How dared you let them in."

"We could not refuse them," the trembling butler said, "They are our masters."

"Masters! Masters! I am the only mistress of this place," she said, and snatching a riding whip she slashed him across the face.

She did not stay long at Spasskoye. Her illness got worse and the procession started back over the rough roads to Moscow, where her doctor said she was suffering not only from dropsy but from consumption. She was slowly dying and sat in silence. No one dared mention her sons to her. She was preparing herself for death, but her vitality kept her alive longer than anyone thought possible. She wrote a note to be given to her sons after her death which ordered them to give her butler and Porfiry, the serf doctor, their freedom and sums of money.

When at last the death agony began, Nikolai came to her side. She stroked his head and murmured Ivan's name—but the news had not reached him. She had ordered her orchestra to play dance music in the next room as she died.

Afterwards, a note was found in her diary. It said: "My mother! My children! Forgive me. And you Lord forgive me for pride, that deadly sin, was always my sin."

"God save us," Turgenev wrote to Pauline, "from a death like that." It horrified him. Even in the years when he had made excuses about coming home to see his mother, even when he persisted in his love for "that gypsy," she had ruled him from a distance. Now he had no ruler or only an imagined ruler in Pauline.

He was suddenly rich. The huge estate was equally divided between his brother Nikolai, a man who was to show himself as practical and as careful to improve his capital as Turgenev was careless. Ivan's share was 30,000 acres of which Spasskoye alone had 3,000 and he had the large income of 25,000 roubles a year. He righted some wrongs at once: he freed all his household serfs. With the others he had his difficulties, but in putting them on an annual rent, instead of sticking to the old system of making them work half the week for him without wages, he showed that he was not a serf-owner, but a landowner who had, like Lavretsky in *A Nest of Gentlefolk*, a serious interest in the land. But Turgenev, though he might see the importance of this, was temperamentally unfitted for the role of master. Viardot wrote to advise him to install a manager and he did so: a friend and writer called Tyutchev and his family were put in charge. It was soon noticed that they spread all over the house at Spasskoye. The neighbors said that Turgenev gave the impression of being a lodger: so he was because, restless like his mother, he was often up in Moscow and above all Petersburg on his literary business. He was bored by provincial life. He still longed for Courtavenel and spoke of going there in two years and he was avid for the letters that took fifteen days to reach him. He blessed the Viardots again and again for their goodness to his daughter. Scrupulously he sent money for her pension to Louis Viardot. He had recovered from the misery of the parting. There was something, he said, that goes straight to the heart in being on one's native soil, among people who talk your own language and who, good or bad, are made of the same clay as oneself. Things might go badly, but at least one was in one's natural element. His only trouble was that he was thirty-two. His youth had gone. Seven years had passed since he had been taken to see her—he wrote to Pauline—for the first time.

In Petersburg he took an expensive and handsome flat where he kept a valet and a cook and, once more, was the gourmet and dandy with a monocle on its ribbon, entertaining his friends and going from drawing-room to drawing-room. The chestnut-haired young man was becoming prematurely grey and the grave blue-eyed gaze of the man of the world brought the women buzzing round him to hear his witticisms and his laughter. He had always charmed society, but now *The Sportsman's Sketches*—though not yet published in book form—had made him a celebrity. The unsuccessful poet had vanished. He had become the dangerous writer, the hope of the young enemies of serfdom. He had moved to minor successes in the theatre. He had written three plays: *The Bachelor,* which had short runs in Petersburg and Moscow, despite a poor second Act; the long *A Month in the Country;* and a witty one-act piece, *A Provincial Lady.* The last was a great success in Petersburg. He had caught influenza but went to the packed theatre and murmured Pauline's name for luck as the curtain went up. He found the acting of the young première detestable, but at the end the applause was so loud and sustained that he lost his head and ran out of the theatre.

But the censor refused to pass *A Month in the Country* because of its "immorality"; it would have been permitted if Rakitin had been shown to be in love with a widow, but not with a married woman. The play is usually taken to be based on Turgenev's relationship with Pauline and does seem to be a partial transfiguration of it, but the differences are obvious. The story has been transferred to Russian provincial life in which the characters are trapped by the boredom Turgenev hated. Pauline was not a bored provincial woman on the verge of middle age; Turgenev was not an idler; there was no young girl in rivalry with Pauline. The only possible portraits are the young man with whom Natalya has fallen in love: he is a sort of Gounod but without the temperament. The farming husband might be Viardot. It was always Turgenev's habit to start with models from real life and, as many writers do, to transfer them to other scenes or to add bits of other people and aspects of himself to them. No doubt, for Turgenev's ear and memory were quick, some of the lines of the play may have been spoken at Courtavenel but one notices how the burden of the play is borne by Rakitin-Turgenev rather than by Pauline-Natalya. It does contain Natalya's mockery of Rakitin's poetic talk of Nature, which Pauline may have spoken, but it is the bitter, analytical Turgenev who warns the new young lover in words that his own father might have used.

> Love, whether happy or unhappy is a real calamity if you give yourself up wholly to it. You wait! I don't suppose you know yet how those delicate hands can torture you, with what tender solicitude they can tear your heart to pieces. You will find out how much blazing hatred is hidden beneath the most ardent of love . . . You will find out what it means to belong to a petticoat, what it means to be enslaved, to be infected and how shameful and weary such slavery is.

The play was not performed in Russia until the seventies—thirty years on—perhaps because of the novelising longueurs of the original version—and it charmed an audience who looked back upon the graces of the forties with nostalgia. The success was also due to the brilliant young actress Savina, who when she read it felt the part of the young girl Vera was far more important than the part of Natalya and, by this insight, brought the play to life. She was at that time unaware of any autobiographical sources there might be. We can agree that in Rakitin, Turgenev was mocking himself. From the point of view of Turgenev's novels it is interesting that he has found his future setting: the Russian country house, the future classic scene of the Russian novel; and that the comedy is as ordered as a dance and sparkles like a poem. It foreshadows the mastery of poetic realism in the love stories to which he was about to turn.

The Russian Sphinx looked stonily at his success. The revolution of '48 had made the police and censors watchful. They were watching for Turgenev to make the small careless error. Their chance came the following year in 1852: the great Gogol died suddenly at the age of forty-three. The censor had not forgotten that the Tsar, in a moment of levity, had allowed *The Government Inspector* and *Dead Souls* to ridicule the official classes; Gogol himself had recanted and had come to regard his great works as scandalous. Just as Tolstoy was to denounce his own work after his conversion, so Gogol repudiated everything he had written except a huge and wearisome volume of moralising letters he had written to a pious aristocratic lady. Gogol had even attacked the readers and critics who praised him and left Russia for years of travel in Europe and the Holy Land. His feeble health had been ruined by gluttony which he abandoned for diets that starved him. His morbid secretiveness had become religious mania and eccentricity was verging on madness, and just before his death he burned the second part of *Dead Souls:* he had gone out of his mind in trying to kill his own fantastic comic spirit.

The censors were now determined to have their revenge and to suppress eulogies of the early Gogol. Turgenev had been to see the sick man a few months before his death and wrote a portrait of him in his *Literary Reminiscences.* He noted the famous comic nose which gave Gogol his cunning fox-like look, the puffy lips, the bad teeth; but he said the tired eyes of the great artist and poet sparkled. It was tragic to hear the old fox now praising the censorship and saying it developed the acumen or patience of authors! In his account of Gogol's reading of *The Government Inspector* there is a passage which reveals as much of Gogol as of Turgenev the raconteur:

> With what puzzled and astonished expression did Gogol utter the phrase of the Mayor about the two rats (at the very beginning of the play)—"They came, they sniffed and they went away." He even looked up at us slowly, as though asking for an explanation of such an astonishing performance.

Different as the two men were, they were masters of timing and were united in their habit of marvelling at the sight of small things.

Indignant at the silence of the Press at Gogol's death, Turgenev sent an ardent, personal eulogy to a Petersburg paper: this was brave in the climate of the time. His letter contained one very dangerous thought, "Only thoughtless and short-sighted people do not feel the presence of a living flame in everything uttered by him." Officials do not like being called short-sighted. The Petersburg censor banned the letter. The last thing the censor wanted to see fanned was "a living flame." At this, and counting on the traditional jealousy be-

tween the Petersburg and Moscow censors, Turgenev easily got the
Moscow censor to pass the letter. When the Tsar heard, he sacked
the Moscow man and ordered the author of *The Sportsman's
Sketches* to be arrested for "manifest disobedience," the fundamental, everlasting Russian sin. When a time-serving University Chan-
cellor called Gogol "a servile writer," Turgenev wrote a letter to a
friend: "Sitting up to their necks in shit these people have under-
taken to eat it to the full." The police intercepted the letter. Turgenev was sent to jail for a month and then to exile on his estate and
remained under police supervision until 1856—although *The Sportsman's Sketches* slipped by in the meantime without hindrance in
volume form! One more censor was sacked.

From prison he got a letter out secretly to the Viardots and said
he was treated decently. He walked up and down for exercise 416
times a day and reckoned that he covered two kilometers. It wasn't
exactly cheerful, but his room was large, he had books. He could
write and indeed he wrote one of his most famous reminiscent tales,
Mumu, "a true story," the account of his mother's cruel treatment
of a dumb servant whose only love was for his dog. She ordered him
to get rid of it because she could not stand its barking; the servants
conspire to help him, but when this fails, he is forced to go off and
drown it. For Turgenev, *Mumu* is dumb Russia. The servant leaves
the house for good and walks twenty miles to his own village, but
with "an invincible purpose, a desperate and yet joyous determina-
tion . . . his eyes fixed greedily straight before him." Passion has been
born: the passion for his own freedom.

Crowds came to visit Turgenev in jail on the first day. That was
soon stopped but the ladies hung about outside to catch sight of him.
Excellent food was sent in. He made the governor drunk and got him
to join in a toast to Robespierre and amused himself by looking over
the dossiers of suspects or arrested men which were left lying about
in the governor's office. But his smuggled letter to Pauline became
less light-hearted:

> The saddest thing of it all is that it is a final Goodbye to all hope of
> travelling abroad: it is true that I had never deluded myself on that
> score. I knew well that when I left you it would be for a long time,
> perhaps forever. I am left with only one desire: that I shall be allowed
> to travel where I like in Russia.

There was another reason for his despair. He had heard that Pauline was again pregnant. If he had had any mad dream that he and she would be united, this marked the fortifying of her marriage. The child was a daughter, Didie, and in time Pauline had a third daughter called Marianne and a son Paul. If the friendship continued, he would always be, as he put it, on the edge of another man's nest. The letters that passed between them had always been formally addressed, but now the private ecstasies in German are dropped.

His arrest, the short imprisonment and the two years of exile on his estate to which he was sentenced, and subsequent police supervision, were a lasting shock to a man who put his freedom first. It was a shock of disgust and it certainly put an end to a plan he had to travel across Russia. He was not allowed to go more than forty miles from Spasskoye. It is true that the arrest added to his fame as the author of *A Sportsman's Sketches:* he became the most promising writer in Russia, for Tolstoy had not yet appeared and Dostoevsky had written only *Poor Folk* and *The Double* and in two years would be silenced by his long exile in Siberia.

The separation from the Viardots was excellent for the writer if it was wretched for the man. Turgenev realised in Spasskoye that in the nine years since he had first met Pauline he had become a different man and that the house had changed. He still had his room with its screens by the bedside—they were decorated with a mosaic in wood crudely copied by Varvara Petrovna's orders by a serf-workman from an album she had brought back from Sorrento—there was a large ikon in one corner and a leather armchair, relics of his mother's life and his writing tables by the window looking out on his avenue of limes. Everything had aged. The housekeeper, who used to lavish raspberry jam on him, had shrivelled. The high-heeled and ribboned goat-skin slippers of the butler still creaked, but his legs were like sticks inside his yellow breeches and his face had shrunk into a sort of little fist. All the man's teeth had gone. The boys on the estate had suddenly become men. In the garden he gazed with wonder at the birches, the maples and an oak sapling he had planted. How tall they were; how fine his avenues of limes. The birds—birds appear in nearly all his stories—the orioles, the nightingales, the doves, the woodpecker and the cuckoo filled him with tenderness, but the house smelled musty although he was fond of the ancestral furniture, the old chests and their brass plates, the fly-blown glass lustres, the white armchairs with oval backs. He had simple home-made stuff in the room where he worked. The green blinds had turned yellow and threw off a soft light on the ceiling.

> Memories of childhood flooding back upon me—wherever I went, whatever I looked at, they surged on all sides, distinct, to the smallest detail, and, as it were, immovable in their clearly defined outlines . . . then I gradually turned away from the past and all that was left was a sort of drowsy heaviness in my heart.

He looked at his books. There was his *Candide* of 1770, newspapers and periodicals of that year: his Mirabeau—*The Triumphant Chameleon*—and his great-grandmother's French grammar and books he had bought abroad. *Faust,* for example, which he knew once by heart, a poor edition of 1828.

At Spasskoye he passed as a clever, lazy man who played chess and draughts and games of Preference. He entertained his neighbours and was bored. The only diversions were days of shooting. People tried to marry him off as we can guess from his story *The Two Friends,* for he was a catch. Letters from Pauline became rarer. He writes to her: no music, no friends—not even neighbours. The Tyutchevs are excellent people but we do not live in the same world. What have I left? Work and memories but if the former is to become possible and the latter less bitter I must have letters from you with news of your happiness and the breath of sunshine and poetry that they bring. My life is dripping away like a tap.

Music was what he missed most. Mme. Tyutchev could be pushed to the piano but her husband had no music in him. The daughter could only thump. He went to the houses of his neighbours but these parties turned into sing-songs and charades. In his story *The Two Friends* there is a comic account of a young lady who is urged by her father to sing "that Italian piece where you go patter-patter like peas." The girl's shrill voice breaks into howls and "from certain nasal sounds it could be surmised that she was singing in Italian." The charades led to clowning and Turgenev, always an actor in his mad moods, could easily act a hare sniffing and munching, passing its paws over its face, pricking up its ears and bounding off. (He had clowned at the Herzens, one remembers, when he was under stress in Paris in 1848.)

The stream of letters that had crawled across Europe from the Viardots in the early days of his absence had begun to dry up. He complained that Pauline told him less and less about herself: he and she, he felt, were only in touch by their fingertips. "The affections wilt when the chances of meeting again are almost nil." He himself had little to tell her. He told her about his shooting and tempted Viardot with the numbers of birds shot. There were messages from her, not altogether assuring, about Paulinette.

Despite the dangers of seeing autobiography even in novelists in whom the autobiographical strain is strong, one can see a likely fragment of it in his short story in letters, *A Correspondence*, which he had begun to write far earlier. The end looks as if it had been tacked on. It is in many ways, biographically speaking, an addition to his self-accusation about the jilting of Tatyana Bakunin and may go back further to one of those love-affairs in Berlin which Herzen taunted him about. There appears to be an oblique reference to Pauline who appears here as a ballet dancer:

> One could not even call the girl a beauty: I have only to close my eyes and at once the theatre is before me, the almost empty stage, representing the heart of a forest . . . and she running in from one wing on the right. . . and from that fatal moment I belonged to her like a dog. . .

And:

> I never anticipated that I should come to hanging about rehearsals, bored and frozen, behind the scenes, breathing in the smut and grime of the theatre, making friends with all sorts of unexpected persons. Making friends did I say?—cringing slavishly upon them. I never anticipated that I should carry a ballet-dancer's shawl, buy her new gloves, clean her old ones with breadcrumbs. . .

But when he says that love is not a free union of souls as the German professors had somehow taught him, but a state in which one person is slave and the other master—"Ah, we're great hands, we Russians, at making such a finish"—the bitterness he felt at Spasskoye is plain.

In the April of 1853 Turgenev read in the newspapers and heard from friends that the Viardots were again in Petersburg. He was pained that she had not written to tell him of this journey. A bad omen. Then he heard that Louis Viardot had taken seriously ill and had been sent back to France. She was on her own and was coming to give performances in Moscow. His hopes blazed up. He was in exile and was forbidden to travel but he took a gamble and travelled there secretly on a false passport. It is known that either she had a cold or feigned one, cancelled her performances for a few days, and that they met. What happened between them or what was said is unknown. April Fitzlyon suggests that there was a struggle between duty and love in Pauline's mind and that duty probably won. In *The Price of Genius*, she quotes a confession to the German conductor, Julius Rietz, written at a later date:

> What interior happiness one has each time that willpower has gained a victory over passion, over instinct! It breaks you, but the knowledge of having raised yourself a step towards good sustains us and gives us sometimes the strength to resist cruel sufferings. When one wishes to, one can always find antidotes—yes, alas, one finds them.

But what were the antidotes? Casual love affairs? Surely not—she disapproved of the escapades of her friends. Her family? The taste for fine houses? The social excitements of fame and applause? Concern for money? Hers was a fiercely competitive life.

Although she is likely to have admired his recklessness in coming to Moscow, she would be angrily aware of the political embarrassment she would be put into. Her life was public and gossip would be damaging to her and certainly would get back to Viardot. There may have been no struggle with her heart at all, for what was much on her mind at this time was that there were signs that she had begun to strain her voice. A letter written by Turgenev when he got back to Spasskoye suggests that the singer was agitated and displeased. Perhaps she was worried about Viardot's health? Turgenev said that her two letters from Moscow and Petersburg were "laconic," but—being given to thinking in confusing images—he added that the second *a l'air d'un torrent qui tombe, chaque mot est tout impatient de ne pas être le dernier.*

Her letter sounded as though it had been a series of unfinished exclamations. And, with irony, he said he hoped that when the whirlwind in which she was living had died down she would give a more detailed account of what she was doing. He then turns to his health, as usual, and says it is going *"clopin-clopant"* like a hare that has been "peppered in what hunters call its 'sac' '': he has the idea that he is suffering from a trifle known as cancer of the intestine.

After this meeting their relationship came virtually to an end on her side. In two years she gave birth to her third daughter.

Turgenev distracted himself with a love affair with a serf-girl called Feotiska. According to Isaac Pavlovsky's *Souvenirs sur Tourguéneff*, which is interesting on the customs of the country, Turgenev had a relation, a young beauty of sixteen who managed a small estate of her own. She was taken aback when Turgenev offered to buy her personal maid from her. She haggled and stuck out for the high price of 700 roubles—25 or 30 roubles was the usual price. The girl—Feotiska—was thin, dark and plain: her sad eyes seem to have attracted him. He paid the price demanded and she was in tears when he took her to Spasskoye. He felt so strongly at the time that he made serious attempts to educate her, but she hated that and broke into violent rages. She bore him a son—his second illegitimate child—but he believed that he was not the father of it and got rid of her by marrying her off to a petty official. The child was put into an orphanage and he was never afterwards able to trace it. Fatherhood, one can see, was not one of Turgenev's gifts.

Whether he told Pauline about Feotiska is not known. He probably would not have thought such sexual affairs important enough, though, in a naïve way, he did tell her about his passing flirtations. Perhaps he hoped they would cause what Balzac used to call a "profitable jealousy." They did, for Pauline was possessive of the man she did not want and her temper was roused. The coolness after Moscow had obviously some connection with a letter from him telling her that he had thought of marrying another girl, a cousin called Olga Turgenev, a pretty and witty little blonde girl of nineteen. For a month she had turned his head, but it all came to nothing. When Pauline was angered by this he pointed out that she had had the first news from himself.

Chapter 6

ALTHOUGH Courtavenel had been "the cradle of his fame," getting away from the presence of Pauline and the "consumptive relationship" was a release for the hidden novelist. As early as 1847 he had written a story about his days as a student, *Andrey Kolosov*, a kind of prose *Parasha*, which Dostoevsky had called a landmark. It attacks the romantic sickness from which he was recovering, "the faint-hearted creatures who from dullness or weakness go on playing the cracked strings of their flabby and sentimental hearts." The narrator is one of these: he is the weak young hero-worshipper of the ruthless student Kolosov, known as "the extraordinary man"—a theme which will recur again and again in Turgenev's writing: the preoccupation with the need of an exemplar or leader which was felt by educated young Russians in the next two decades. The story has also another aspect, not often considered by admirers of his sensitive and poetic writings; Turgenev's gift for the raw sardonic comedy of vulgar or shabby genteel life in which Gogol and Dickens are his masters. The "unpresentable persons" belong to the low families who scheme to make a "catch" for their oppressed daughters and they are a welcome relief. They also set the story in perspective and his management of perspective is Turgenev's distinctive gift. The passing effect of a minor character, the awful

Shtchitov, who is compared to "the unswept floor of a Russian restaurant," is to send up the unheroic narrator who, on the wave of imitative sentimentality, tries to take on the poor girl whom the "extraordinary" Kolosov has grown bored with. Turgenev's point is: Better the ruthless man who throws the girl over than the sentimentalist who broods on "the sacredness of love" and who will be a muddler and, inevitably, turn into a cad and leave a trail of mess and snuffles behind him. The comedy is not harsh and sour. Turgenev is the dispassionate observer of youth in the years when one feeling so naturally changes into its opposite. The scene in which the narrator declares his love for the jilted girl—and in which it is clear that he has really been unconsciously in love with Kolosov and not with her—is done in the manner from which Chekhov learned in the next generation:

> I almost shouted: "I love you. I want to marry you. I want to be your champion, your friend. I don't ask for love. Till tomorrow." With these words I rushed out of the room. In the passage [her father] met me, and not only showed no surprise at my visit but positively, with an agreeable smile, offered me an apple. . . "Take the apple, it is a nice apple. Really!" Mechanically I took the apple at last and drove all the way home with it in my hand.

The ludicrous incident, like some discordant musical note, does not belittle the girl's misery in love, as mere wit or humourousness would do, but makes us respect its pathos.

There was no established tradition of story telling or novel writing in Russian literature. Turgenev is a founder and innovator: the great novels of the nineteenth century were in the future—he was at the beginning of that awakening which was to run parallel with the awakening of the Russian peoples themselves. Behind him there were fables and the superb narrative of Pushkin's *Eugene Onegin*: that *did* offer to the coming Russian novelists the model love story, but it was done in verse. It was important in forming the classical cast of Turgenev's genius and was a source of his kind of poetic realism. But neither he nor any of the Russian novelists had the equivalent of Defoe, Richardson, Smollett, Sterne, Fielding, Scott or the early Dickens before them. Russian culture in the eighteenth century had been bred in France and was an interest of the educated classes only. Turgenev regarded Pushkin as a master because Pushkin sought to replace French influence by the influence of the German and the English—by Goethe and Shakespeare. From Pushkin he learned how to give an ironical picture of society, the art of miniature and its opposite, spontaneous improvisation.

Turgenev was only slightly drawn to French models. Diderot and Mérimée amused him because they were writers of novellas. Balzac he detested: "a mere ethnographer," he said. After Pushkin, Gogol was a tempting genius, but Gogol's realism broke into poetic and chaotic fantasy: he dived into comic disorder and the grotesque; his language was almost malignly rich, his imagination was so secretive, devious and conniving that it spread, so to say, into the underground of character and situation. But Turgenev's temperament was for the classical and concise: where Gogol was involved and satirical at once, Turgenev was the spectator—his work before anything else was shaped and lyrical. He sought to tell the observable truth; Gogol went on into sly wild journeys of fancy beyond it and, of course, in the end, went over the precipice into piety and metaphysical remorse.

Turgenev's other contemporary was Lermontov, who was killed in a duel. He was a violent and Romantic Byron; there was no violence, no man of ruthless action in Turgenev and no taste for danger and romantic *actes gratuites* and dramatic pungency. But he did see in Lermontov a drastic talent made for the novella of 30,000 words. The Lermontov influence is strong in two early Turgenev stories: *The Jew*, the laconic and horrifying tale of a wretched spy who uses his daughter as bait to soldiers waiting for battle and is hanged; and in *The Duellist*, the tale of a young officer's half love-affair with the dour regimental killer who is watching for one more chance of an affair of honour, the direct influence of Lermontov is strong; indeed these two stories are so well done that one suspects the Lutovinov strain in Turgenev was not quite extinguished and, in life, survived in the gentlemanly killing of birds.

But the central preoccupation, well-rooted in Turgenev's mind, was with establishing the idea of civilisation—which he eventually spelled out letter by letter—and the autonomy of art in a country that, for him, had been barbarous or inert for centuries; the belief in these values, he observed, often took too hopefully the wrong road and led the unwary or the innocent into delusions and self-deception, but as values they stood firm. Under the despotic system in Russia the hopeful were easily frustrated and, if they lacked will, easily became resigned or drifted back, when youth had passed, into futility and went to pieces. For fifty years the question of the emancipation of the serfs had been argued but it drifted: the drift had come to be regarded as a state of grace. As an intellectual, Turgenev knew the pleasant futility of endless speculative talk and, in this connection, it is interesting to compare the Russian situation with the Spanish of the nineteenth century, the situation of a country hostile to the West and stagnant and, which, after 1898, produced a group of writers one of whose themes was *abulia,* the lack of will. As a novelist he knew his part was to see the Russian situation in terms of living men and women and what they represented, truthfully. It was easy to write essays about ideas; it would be easy, had he been a German, to write a tutorial *Bildingsroman;* but as a Russian and in his country, he had to innovate and invent a new art.

———

At Spasskoye in the fifties he tried first of all a very long reminiscent novel about the Lutovinovs, but it became shapeless and he gave it up. He also tried his hand at plain realism in *The Inn,* a story of peasant greed: it fails because it is photographic. He did better in *A Backwater,* a tragedy of provincial isolation. He had little power of invention but, as many writers of talent do, he got round this by turning his defects to advantage and discovered the hidden logic and drama of mood. A trivial word spoken when the company are for a moment silent will have the grace effect of a bell-like echo later on in the story. At once the structure of the story is sonata-like, one is left with the reverberations of a note hanging in the air after it has been struck on the key.

Looking at the life around him he at last sees that the gentry have become prolific in a type that he calls the superfluous or unnecessary man, a race of failing Hamlets. Superfluous men haunted Russian fiction for more than a generation and Turgenev will eventually arrive at the conclusion that there is a continual struggle between Don Quixote and Hamlet in the Russian temper, and saw this conflict in himself. The first of his Hamlets appears in *The Hamlet of the Shchigrovsky District.* (It was eventually published as one of his pieces of marksmanship among the landowners of *The Sports-*

———

man's Sketches and it is brilliant farce.) Yet we are made to feel sympathy for the nameless, ridiculous self-styled Hamlet who appears in it, a man who feels himself to be inferior to governors, princes, officials, even to the local police. The melancholy of Turgenev does not thwart his comic gifts: the opening account of the male house party in a provincial mansion is pure Gogol:

> these well-disposed people were engaged in importantly sorting their cards and casting sideward glances at newcomers without moving their heads: also five or six district officials with round tummies, puffy sticky little hands and modestly immobile feet. These gentlemen spoke in soft voices, regaled everyone with timid smiles, held their cards close to their shirt-fronts and, when playing trumps, did not thump them down on the table but, on the contrary, let them drop with a floating motion on to the green cloth and, as they gathered in their winnings, produced a slight but very decorous and polite creaking sound.

The excellence in this story lies in the way Turgenev conveys that everyone in the party is aware of everyone else: the party moves, the eyes glance, the vapid thoughts are telegraphed with meaningless content round the room. We are only at the beginning of Turgenev's curious liquid gift which became eventually supreme in Proust. When the story breaks into the vegetable Hamlet's confession of his burning incompetence in growing up, in marrying, his troubles as a landowner and a widower, and as a widower who can't even be sad, our laughter is still there, but we are half-ashamed of it.

In *A Correspondence* the broadness has gone and is replaced by a serious attempt to analyse moral failure. *A Correspondence* can be read as a savaging of his own failure in love—and at times it cuts to the bone—but enlarged by a Russian context. There are traces of Diderot and although a story told in letters has an old-fashioned air to us, it is never flat and, with his experience as a failed playwright behind him, he knows at what point to make a break and dramatically build up tension. A man and a woman who have been unhappily in love with other lovers, discuss their situation and expose their characters and one can read into the man's words an exposition of Turgenev's own compulsive leaning to the *amitié amoureuse*. But the Russia of his generation comes in:

We Russians have set ourselves no other task in life but the cultivation of our own personalities—and so we get again one monster the more in the world, one more of those worthless creatures in whom habits of self-consciousness distort the very striving for truth.

They are morbid, perpetual, self-paralysed psychologists.

The woman in the correspondence replies with an indignant protest that the intelligent young Russian girl is destroyed by the fickleness of young men who are futile because they are without a firm role in society. There are no male heroes: it is the women who, at least, grow up and become strong.

Self-mockery or self-castigation, as he called it, runs through Turgenev's stories of this period and reaches its climax in *The Diary of a Superfluous Man*. This type, with the absurd name of Tchulkaturin, is born useless, a supernumerary, the "fifth wheel" of the cart or the "fifth horse" in the team, who shambles along and does not pull. The diarist is dying and looks back on his life with a self-pity that does not pervade because Turgenev is writing bitter comedy: the comedy of a man who misreads not only his own feelings, but indulges in pretentious false emotions and is wrong about everyone else. There is a farcical Gogol-like party: he provokes a duel with his rival in love, a visiting Prince. He hopes the duel will make an heroic impression. Instead it outrages the whole town who now regard the feeble fellow as a jealous, bloodthirsty monster, even a madman: "It is needless to say that the Ozhogin's doors were closed against me. Kirilla Matveitch even sent me back a bit of pencil I had left in the house."

"How much happiness a man can extract from the contemplation of his own unhappiness," the diarist writes. Turgenev is attacking himself and his own self-pity and even in the pathetic scene of the diarist's death, savaging his own fear of death. The story is an alarming piece of hilarious clowning by the sad actor, as well as a comic picture of what life is like among the top officials in one of the thousands of provincial towns in stagnant Russia. The brief portraits—small things like the girl whose eyes are either raised high or are lowered as a device to hide an awful squint—these are brilliant. And from a short-story writer's point of view, the timing and spacing of episodes is perfect. It is certain now that Turgenev is a master of his craft and there lies our pleasure in what might otherwise have weighed us down as a moral diagnosis. Still we are a little irked by the overtones of languid, poetic madness. When Gogol or, later on, Dostoevsky presented such scenes they gave themselves to them with more energy: even the weak or meek characters of Dostoevsky have some inner stubbornness in their passive natures.

Looking back on these stories written in his early thirties one understands why his friend Annenkov begged Turgenev to "stop taking a voluptuous pleasure in himself," that is "in your authorship and to do without the sudden appearance of odd fellows of whom you are too fond" and that he should not be so coquettish about the miseries and contradictions of life. His people should "appear unostentatiously without suspecting that anyone is looking at him." Turgenev himself was tiring of his skills and his wit. He had always feared the amateur in himself. He wrote in a letter:

> I have done enough of extracting the triple essence from human character, of pouring it into small bottles. "Sniff it, gentle reader, uncork it and sniff it. It has the Russian bouquet, hasn't it?" Enough, enough. But the question is, am I capable of doing something great and calm, am I going to succeed with clear simple outlines? That I don't know and I shan't know until I try. But believe me you will hear something new from me or you will hear nothing. For that reason I am almost glad of my winter seclusion. I shall have time to collect myself; and above all in solitude one is away from things, literary and journalistic especially. I shall become somebody only when the *littérateur* is destroyed in me.

At the time of the Olga Turgenev affair he had been visiting the Aksakovs on their estate. The father was a shy and kindly man— the memoirs he eventually wrote are exquisite accounts of Russian life in the earlier generation and are classics. The son was a fanatic Slavophil and Turgenev enjoyed violent arguments with him—bits of him crop up in many of Turgenev's portraits of the Slavophils. He returned to Spasskoye and got down to writing *Rudin,* a novel which would be a final attempt to dispose of the illusions of his youth and to complete his portrait of the superfluous or supernumerary man who had been deprived of purpose by the Russian situation. By an irony of history the moment was well-chosen, for the Crimean War started in 1854. Turgenev was torn by the fact that the West had declared against Russia and he rediscovered his patriotism at first: the eventual defeats brought home to him that the war would in a few years mark the end of the landowning class as an intellectual élite and the sole source of revolutionary or reformist ideas. *Rudin* is an enlargement of Turgenev's powers: it establishes him as a dispassionate, apolitical novelist who watches political ideas as they filter into individual character. Only at the very end of the book is there an overt political act; and that was added years later.

The first draft of *Rudin* was written in seven weeks. The manuscript was later rewritten after severe criticism by his friends. Before writing it, Turgenev had taken pains to formulate a method which was to sustain him for his finest and mature novels. In his apprenticeship the novelist learns that he must put his limitations to positive use. Turgenev knew he could draw still portraits: he must somehow create the illusion of life rippling through them. He was by nature summary and intense. He now wrote down a list of the types that interested him, putting the real names of the persons, often several similar people compressed into one. Since he had no faculty for dramatic plot, he wrote a minute factual biography of each one, adding to it and noting every trait and gesture. His experience as a playwright led him to choose the closed scene in which people come in and go off, as on the stage; and his practice as a writer of short stories made him build his novels of short episodes complete in themselves, with a pause or interval between them, after which the next movement can begin in a new key. As André Mazon has said, the leisurely narrative of a *conteur* is his strength. A disturbing visitor arrives at a country house, there's a walk in the garden, a debate at lunch, a lady of the house talks with a peasant, there is a lovers' tête-à-tête, a declaration of love in which a man is caught between two loves—then farewells between two people, thoughts of the young man alone. It is the pattern of *A Month in the Country* and in outline it seems slight. But what we are conscious of is the outer watchful timeless silence of Russia. The words of comedy are grave in their undertone and around the people we feel the sparkle or the stare of Nature which is as indifferent to them as it is to the passing of time itself.

In *Rudin* the disturbing visitor who arrives on the stage of the country house was, in real life, Bakunin, the Bakunin of his Berlin years, before '48 in Paris when he had become an exuberant political conspirator. When Turgenev was writing the novel, the real Bakunin was serving the beginning of his four years in prison and his eight years in Siberia. This aspect of Bakunin's life is ignored until the last page: and in consequence there is little resemblance between Rudin and his original. Rudin is not a flamboyant revolutionary. He is no giant. He is not the extremist whom Herzen eventually described as a Columbus without an America or even a ship. The genuine Bakunin-like traits are his eloquence, his spell over the young, his meddling with minds and hearts, his incorrigible sponging, his inborn dishonesty, his foredoomed life as a penniless nomad—a brilliant mind going to seed. He is a chronic romantic philanderer. There is in fact a good deal of the evasive Turgenev in Rudin, and in the portrait Turgenev is punishing himself.

Before Rudin arrives at the country house the main characters are settled. Darya Mihailovna is a rich Muscovite and lion-huntress in her fifties, a fashionable provincial and would-be-*précieuse,* who looks down on her neighbours and likes to fill her house in the summer with clever men if she can find them. "Provincial ladies she could not endure." She is sitting about with the latest French pamphlet in her hand and has to content herself with the local self-educated blusterer and misogynist Pigasov. If any disaster occurs, if a flood has wrecked a mill or a peasant has sliced his hand with an axe, Pigasov always asks "What's her name?": for him women are at the back of every calamity. Darya Mihailovna has a hanger-on called Pandalevsky living at her expense and a young daughter called Natalya with whom a neighbour called Volintzev is stubbornly and shyly in love. There is an eager tutor called Basistov and a tart French governess, Mlle. Boncourt. The summer hangs over the house and the estate, the birds sing. Then Rudin arrives, a tall, broad-chested, stooping man, eyes brilliant, a fine nose and with a thin voice. His reserve goes when he gets into a battle of words with Pigasov about general propositions and convictions. Pigasov believes in facts.

"It follows that there is no such thing as conviction according to you."

"No it doesn't exist."

"Is that your conviction?"

"Yes."

"But here you have one at the very first turn."

Before the day is over the comic Pigasov is routed, Rudin has captivated the young tutor by his eloquence. Natalya sees him as a genius. Pandalevsky sees his position as a privileged hanger-on is in danger and can only bide his time. Rudin stays for a week and is triumphant until a neighboring landowner, Lezhnyov, arrives. It is he who will eventually reveal he has known Rudin only too well in Berlin when they were students. He has been the victim, as Turgenev was in his friendship with Bakunin, of Bakunin's meddling in a love-affair and causing it to wither. Turgenev now puts Rudin to the test of love: it is the test all his characters in stories and novels are put to. And lightly, yet gravely, he proceeds to expose Rudin who has captivated Natalya. Rudin is the classic egoist in his sentiments. He knows the whole keyboard from the evocation of "pure souls" to effective hints of private sorrow: he tells Natalya that she has restored his belief in himself after a wasted life and then, when he finds he has won her, he at once looks for escape by the back door of "submission to Fate." It all sounds uncomfortably like Turgenev's own behaviour in love with young girls. Rudin has no money, no career, nothing. There are none so easily carried away, Turgenev notes, as men without passion: talk of "submission to Fate" is the self-protective device of the drifting and cold-hearted man.

The permanence of Turgenev's love stories owes everything to his sense of love as spiritual test, and test of moral character; but they are also diagnoses of the condition of a generation. In the earlier, *A Correspondence,* the young woman speaks of how intelligent women "who are not satisfied with the worries of domestic life" yearn for the love of a man who will guide their minds.

If he were a hero, he would fire her, would teach her to sacrifice herself and all sacrifices would be easy for her! But there are no heroes in our times . . . And so the parting comes. Happy the girl who realises at once that it is the end of everything . . . But you valorous, just men, for the most part have not the pluck nor even the desire to tell us the truth.

She will be strong only when hard experience makes her find her "true self." The discovery of "the true self" is at the heart of the lovers' dilemma and, by implication, it is Russia's.

Pandalevsky, the hanger-on who fears his security as a *cavalier servant,* turns spy; reports the meetings of the lovers to Darya Mihailovna who gives her daughter a dressing-down in unaristo-cratic language. Natalya's heart is broken but she grows from a simple girl into a decisive, clear-headed young woman: the old theme of Onegin has a long life in the history of Russian love, the theme of hardening off.

It falls to Lezhnyov to explain why they have all fallen under Rudin's spell. Why especially did he put such a spell on the young and inspire them with idealism? The answer lies in his prodigious memory, his eloquence which jumps from image to image, without intervals of exact thought, his power of generalising and coming to conclusions which made "all that seemed disconnected fall into a whole."

Try to tell young people that you cannot give them the whole truth and they will not listen to you.

The young must have conclusions.

Lezhnyov shows Rudin as a cheat, a sponger—soon very evident —also sexless, calculating, flamboyant out of vanity.

So, in the drawing-room of Darya Mihailovna's boudoir, in the trysts in the garden, Rudin appears and it is all set against the background of the comic jealousies of the hangers-on and the tart phrases of the French governess. Rudin is caught out and he leaves. And now—with the skill of a playwright—the truthful Turgenev reverses and widens his judgment. Rudin's visit had been one more fling by a penniless man in search of a patroness. In the final chapters we see him on the road in a remote province, the mountebank down on his luck. Here by chance Lezhnyov meets him, pities him and alters his own opinion. He comes back to the country house and tells them all about the meeting:

I blamed him for coldness. I was right and wrong too when I did so. The coldness is in his blood—that is not his fault and not in his head. He is not an actor, as I called him nor a cheat, nor a scoundrel; he lives at other people's expense not like a swindler but like a child ... Rudin's misfortune is that he does not understand Russia and that is certainly a misfortune. Russia can do without everyone of us but not one of us can do without her. Cosmopolitanism is all twaddle, the cosmopolitan is a nonentity—worse than a nonentity, without nationality there is no art, no truth, nor life, nor anything

What captivates us is the simplicity, the easy grace of this novel, the tact with which he makes short chapters crystallise and contain the talk and the silences in which each character grows more clearly under our eyes. Turgenev is a natural master of conversation and of the silent thoughts it starts in people's minds so that the whole thing is leisurely yet, in detail, is always quickened. There will be a change of tone as the people themselves know one another better; each sentence is an event and we are alert for it and its mood as we are in a play. Comedy rises casually as in small things. For example, Darya Mihailovna is delighted with Rudin. *"C'est un homme comme il faut,"* she thinks but mentally she pronounces those words in Russian.

But *Rudin* is not sure in its construction. Lezhnyov's sudden reversal of his judgment is dramatic and this is too obviously a device, and once it has its effect the story droops into hearsay in the last chapters, although Rudin's shame-faced and seedy confession of his subsequent disasters is diverting. His accounts of how patrons always tire of him, and of how one absurd fellow without a penny joined him in a scheme—practical, one reflects, a hundred years later—of making a river navigable, are funny and even touching. The fact is that Turgenev had difficulties. He changed his mind. He listened to the advice of friends. They, like himself, were puzzled by how to end a story that was ebbing away. Four years after the publication, he tacked on a last page where Rudin is seen, without any warrant from the story, dying on the barricades in the Revolution of '48 in Paris. This does an ironical justice to a character who is too infused with the novelist himself and who has become a figment of debate; but the page is excellent reporting.

The broken revolutionaries were running for their lives from their barricades as the troops came at them, when a tall man in an old overcoat with a red sash and a straw hat on his grey dishevelled hair jumped on top of an overturned omnibus and shouted in a strained shrill voice. In one hand he held a red flag, in the other a blunt curved sabre. He was at once shot dead. *"Tiens!"* said one of the escaping revolutionaries. *"On vient de tuer le Polonais."*

Bakunin did not die in such a way when he escaped from Siberia; he came back to stir up trouble, a conspirator who did not know he was out of date. He was a type of *déclassé* who lives by making reckless gestures in other people's revolutions, very much a prophetic figure who, by a turn of the historical wheel, reappeared as the "Westerner" of our own thirties in the Spanish Civil War. However, perhaps that remark of Herzen himself in Paris when he saw the revolt fail had stuck in Turgenev's mind. As we have seen, he had heard Herzen say he wished he had died sword in hand in the streets, for then at least he would have retained one of his illusions.

In attempting a novel Turgenev was not by nature equipped for the epic length and the large scheme—he shrank fastidiously from Balzac's exuberance which he found coarse—he had been up to now simply a master of the short story. He had yet to find a coherent way of placing several stories, not into a series but into an organic whole, in which narrative and commentary flow together harmoniously. In Pushkin one is always aware of the voice in attendance on the emotion or dashing tale and giving it the drive of meaning and the authority of a judgment. Turgenev looked back to Pushkin's classical lesson: the commentary is to be part of the composition as a continuing aspect of the story, as Freeborn says in some cogent pages on Turgenev's achievement in *Turgenev: The Novelist's Novelist.* Turgenev himself may address us as "gentle reader" once or twice, but he can allow the role of commentator to be taken by Lezhnyov who is involved in the tale. We have the sensation of people living in and out of their changing judgments on one another and all in a single, clear stream. In Freeborn's words:

> The distinction of Turgenev's novels which begin with *Rudin* lies in their historical authenticity. They are portraits not only of particular heroes or heroines but of particular epochs . . . Moreover it is in the unity given to the fiction by the central figure that a balance is

maintained between the ideological matter on the one hand and the human problem on the other.

We are given two views of human destiny; there is a double narrator:

> Man as the rational being who aspires to put his ideas to a service of realizable ideals; and of man as the insignificant creature of a single day, at the mercy of nature and eternity. It is in this duality that the real "realism" of Turgenev's four great novels resides.

Is a non-hero like Rudin strong enough to hold the novel together? That is very doubtful. But we have confidence in Turgenev's truthful feeling for experience. The moments of life are swallowed by the whole. Rudin has left disaster for Natalya behind him; if for others everything had fallen comfortably back into its old order, to Natalya

> Life seemed so cruel, so hateful and so sordid, she was so ashamed of herself, her love and her sorrow that she would have been glad at that moment to die . . . but she was young—life had scarcely begun for her and sooner or later life asserts its claims. Whatever blow has fallen on a man, he must—forgive the coarseness of the expression—eat that day or at least the next, and that is the first step to consolation.

Chapter 7

WHILE Turgenev was writing his epitaph on a lost leader of his youth, the Tsar Nicholas, the dull, military "bald eagle," had led Russia to slaughter and defeat in the Crimea. He died and his heir Alexander II was persuaded by Turgenev's friends at Court to allow him to return to Petersburg though he refused to lift the surveillance by the police. The effect of this was to prevent him from leaving Russia. There was no point in leaving since, despite his letters, Pauline rarely wrote and on her side interest in him had gone dead. He sent her a translation of Pushkin's poem, *Adieu,* in reproach. The last verse goes:

> *Reçois donc, compagne lointaine*
> *L'adieu de mon coeur*
> *Comme une épouse devenue veuve*
> *Comme une amie qui étreint en silence son ami*
> *Avant son éxil.*

His letters suggest that Paulinette was troublesome and had been put into a boarding-school: there is even a suggestion that she be sent back to Russia but Turgenev refused to have her, saying that her position would be impossible for her there. Although he was rich in land he was often short of ready money and often late in sending it for the child's support—a cholera epidemic, the effects of the war, crop failures and bad management of the estate had meant a large if temporary loss. The Tyutchevs had cost him 300,000 francs and a hundred thousand of that had, he said, been thrown out of the window; wages had gone up, no improvements had been made and his income had been cut by a third. Turgenev was turning out to be as improvident as many of the bad landowners. So he got rid of the Tyutchevs—they parted friends—and he got in his kindly old uncle who had married again and who brought in a crowd of his wife's relatives. It was one of Turgenev's lazy decisions and in the long run turned out to be just as bad as the arrangement with Tyutchev. The novelist was a natural victim in these matters and notorious for being at the mercy of his servants. One thing his mother had done to him was to remove the voice and capacity of command. And that must have been an additional reason for his failure with Pauline.

He came back to Petersburg grey-haired but still a dandy, a wit and a gourmet and made effective play with a pose of saying "Farewell to life." He began to end all his phrases with a favourite word "Enough." It grew on him and was a kind of signature tune. His arrival in Petersburg was celebrated by dinners given by his friends on *The Contemporary*, on which he was the leading contributor. *Rudin* was a success, although those who heard that the central character was based on Bakunin said that it was far more a portrait of Turgenev himself.

He allowed himself further dissipations. He said to a friend that he was "going the rounds of the suburban dances with a charming Polish woman, giving her silver plate and spending nights with her until eight in the morning," but that after two months of it he had to give it up out of physical exhaustion. This Polish adventure, his youthful seduction, the touching affair with the miller's wife—who asked him for no more than some scented soap so that her hands would smell as sweetly as the hands of the society ladies he kissed —and some casual incidents he reported to the Goncourts, are the only known episodes of his sexual life besides the two that produced children. There may have been more in Paris and Italy but he was shocked when Tolstoy told him of his debauches. If Rakitin in *A Month in the Country* is in some respects a self-portrait, Turgenev always said he was not a Don Juan. To the Goncourts, the *"doux géant"* said he was timid in love; he approached women with respect, emotion and was surprised, he said, at his happiness. Yet among the pious, aristocratic ladies of Petersburg he had the reputation of "living immorally." They meant that he had rejected the Orthodox Church. When he was staying with the Aksakovs in the country his hostess said that his ideals were sullied and that he was "only capable of physical sensations: all his impressions pour through his nerves, he is not capable of either understanding or of feeling the spiritual side of things." He might be a huge man but —this was wounding—"he lacked even pagan force." On this Yarmolinsky in his *Life* makes a far more sensitive commentary:

> Certainly his response did not stop short of spiritual matters. With him, as with so many artists, the intense perception of the physical world alone was so transcendent an experience as to unlock the gates of the spirit.

One glance at his stories shows the truth of this and it is illustrated by a passage in one of his finest pieces of prose, *A Tour of the Forest*, part of which was being written at this time—he added to it in old age. It has a Shakespearean echo:

> I raised my head and saw at the very end of a delicate twig one of those large flies with emerald head and long body and four transparent wings, which the fanciful French call 'maidens' while our guileless people call them 'bucket yokes'. For a long time, more than an hour I did not take my eyes off her. Soaked through and through with sunshine she did not stir, only from time to time turning her head from side to side and shaking her lifted wings. . . . that was all. Looking at her, it suddenly seemed to me that I understood the life of nature, understood its clear and unmistakable though mysterious significance. There is a subdued, quiet animation, an unhasting restrained use of sensation and powers, an equilibrium of health in each separate creature. Everything that goes beyond this level, above or below, she flings away as worthless. Many insects die as soon as they know the joys of love, which destroys the equilibrium. The sick beast plunges into the thicket and expires alone . . . and the man who from his own fault or from the fault of others is faring ill in the world—ought, at least, to know how to keep silence.

If the pious Vera Aksakov spoke bitterly of Turgenev, there was another no less religious woman living in the highest circles of the Court who thought to rescue him from impiety and the paralysing effects of his love for Pauline Viardot which all his friends deplored and his enemies mocked him for. She was the Countess Lambert. He was cultivating her because she had influence with the Tsar and he was begging her to use it to get him a passport, precisely for the reasons she did not favour. A friendship that lasted began and on his side was one of the *amitiés amoureuses* or confessional philanderings in which his charm made him expert. He ended by troubling her feelings and she was for a time closer to him than Pauline and there is a trace of her in his next novel, *A Nest of Gentlefolk*. The bond between them was that they were both unhappy.

The Countess was of French and German stock and was unhappily married to one of the aides de camp of the Tsar—a plain woman of thirty-five, who had given up the vanities of her high social position and, but for her children, would have become a Sister of Charity. Brought up as a Lutheran, she was a strict convert to the Orthodox Church and her piety and Turgenev's atheism gave a piquancy to their talks when he spent his evenings with her. If she was trying to save his soul, he, of course, was the novelist who was studying her. She listened to the sad story of his frustrated love for Pauline not without jealousy and said she admired Pauline as a singer but added that Pauline had made him waspish and bitter; that he was a pagan who was "corrupted by the cult of Venus" and she appealed to him to replace it by the sterner call of Christian duty. She received him but propriety and a taste for the long-winded in personal relationships led her to prefer knowing him by correspondence which—for her at least—made their occasional meetings more disturbing. She was inclined to tears. If she could have converted him she would have been lost. On his side, Turgenev was careful to play the man of the world and, in time, she had to remind him sharply that she was "a creature of reason," and wished to be treated "as a true friend." When, in one of his letters, he wrote that he "respectfully kissed her charming hands," she replied sharply that "a woman would prefer to have a little more ardour from men without compromising them."

The bond between them was that they were both fanciful enough to declare that "life was over," that they were already on the brink of old age though under forty. Both were hypochondriacs. She did not entirely approve of his work, for politically she was very conservative; and when he came to write *First Love* she told him it was "one of his bad deeds" but that he committed evil or sin in an irresistible manner. The Empress had hated the story, she said, but the Emperor had thought it delightful. Many times they got on to the subject of the "ideal" in literature and there he had to correct her. She was at heart a sentimentalist; she supposed, he told her, that the ideal should be an addition or an embellishment in the portrayal of character and he replied with the faith he had learned from Goethe:

> *Tout être étudié avec une sympathie sincère et ardent, peut dégager pour nous la vérité qui est la base de la vie. C'est en cela précisément que consiste ce qu'on appelle l'idéalisation artistique.*

The part of confidante was consoling to both parties but it affected him less than it affected her. She was more than half in love with him and was unhappy when she saw she could neither make him give up his "paganism" or his destructive love of Pauline. The question of the passport was always there as an humiliation. Against all her arguments, he said he had as much of Don Quixote in himself as Hamlet. She had to get as much consolation as she could from a letter she wrote to him telling him not to see Pauline again—as all his friends did—not "to knock his head against a brick wall," and drift back into his "gypsy life." He agreed wryly that he was about to commit a folly, and made it worse by saying:

> Don Quixote at least believed in the beauty of his Dulcinea but the Don Quixotes of our time realise that Dulcinea is an ugly hag and yet keep running after her . . . we have no ideal, that is the trouble.

The poor woman tried to make him jealous by taking up with Grigorovich, another writer, but although Turgenev had his vanity, jealousy affected him very little. He got his passport and he left for France. For a long time their correspondence went on and then fizzled out. Turgenev's objection to her was not so much that she was a spiritual Siren but that she had the reactionary opinions of Court society; and indeed she was deeply shocked later by the political tendency of his writing and was, as he knew she would be, in the enemy camp. The high-minded lady wished devoutly that he would write "popular" work. The final blow must have come some years later when she found him at Ems, where she had gone for the cure in the company of a Ukrainian woman writer of short stories, Marko Vovtchok, another object of his platonic tenderness.

For an artist to whom the company of women was indispensable, the friendship with the Countess was more than an exchange of woes: it quickened the imagination of the storyteller, who was, as he said, "saturated with femininity." One thing he saw in the Countess was a deep fear and misunderstanding of what was sacred to him: art and its perception of *"la vérité qui est la base de la vie."* With Dostoevsky he believed that "art lives man's life with him." Turgenev's talk with the Countess about Goethe had fertilised him. He sat down to write *Faust,* one of his most accomplished stories. It is the first of his ghost stories, a genre he did not approach again until his last years, and even were we to object—as Herzen did in his brusque rational way—to the suggestion of a ghostly presence, a psychologist would find no objection to it. The story has a double theme: the awakening of the imagination and the maturing and enlarging of our nature through immersion in works of art; and the deadening of the soul that occurs when an interior will imposed by others crushes the free imagination. Vera, the young girl in the story, has been trained by her mother to abjure novels and poetry and to read about useful subjects only. The mother's motive is not ignorant; it is even high-minded; but behind it are primitive influences of family history. Her mother, a delightful person, says:

> "You tell me that reading poetry is *both* useful and pleasant. I consider one must make one's choice early in life; either the useful or the pleasant and abide by it once and for all. I tried at one time to unite the two. That's impossible and leads to ruin and vulgarity."

The subject runs all the risks of being a trite moral story for the schoolroom, written to educate the Countess. With the incomparable delicacy and dramatic tact with which Turgenev can show the growth of love, he can also show the shadow of guilt, the terror of an alien overpowering will running alongside of ourselves like a shadow and a fate; it will blast Vera with the images that break the nerve. He floats the tale out of the schoolroom into the clear air of real life. And, as always, a minor droll character—Vera's husband— brings the playwright's intervals of perspective and rest to a narrative that might otherwise be sententious and too high-flown. The special technical difficulty in this story is that he has to make a formal reading of *Faust* endurable to the reader; yet he manages this cleverly by bringing in the husband who cannot bear poetry-reading, and a comic German who keeps crying out "How wonderful! How sublime!" and even "How profound!" Turgenev was also a master of the tentative and of aside.

> I touched on the old legend of Doctor Faust, the significance of Mephistopheles and Goethe himself and asked them to stop me if anything struck them as obscure. Then I cleared my throat—Priemkov asked me if I wouldn't have some sugar water and one could perceive that he was very well satisfied with himself for having put this question to me. I refused.

From the biographer's point of view the statement at the end of the story indicates that there was a decisive and lasting change in Turgenev's mind at this critical period of his life:

> One conviction I have gained from the experience of the last years —that life is not just an amusement: life is not even enjoyable . . . life is hard labour. Renunciation, continual renunciation—that is its secret meaning; its solution. Not the fulfilment of cherished dreams and aspirations, however lofty they may be—the fulfilment of duty, that is what must be the care of man . . . But in youth we think— the freer the better, the further one will get. Youth may be excused for thinking so . . . Now I would say try to live, it is not so easy as it seems.

The Countess might think she had convinced him but in fact his was not the Christian's renunciation: it was far bleaker—the stoicism of the atheist and pagan and not without its incurable fear of death that gave intensity to the living moment.

Pauline Viardot disliked the story when she eventually read it, perhaps because she had her jealousy of the new Muse. Incidentally, since she knew little Russian, Turgenev's claim that everything he wrote he submitted to her first must be modified: he would read it aloud, translating into French as he went along—not a satisfying method for either party. Another suggestion, not mentioned by Turgenev's biographers, occurs to me. In its circumstances the situation of Vera in *Faust* and Pauline in life are alike: the happy young wife with three children and a doting, dull and anxious husband falls in love with a gifted young man. Vera declares her love and her passion is thwarted—by whom? Not the husband, not another lover; not by a family counsellor—but by the ghost or image of the mother who calls her daughter back to duty. Was it Mme. Garcia, with a family history as exotic as the history of Vera's mother, who imposed her will and made Pauline break? And was Priemkov, too, like Louis Viardot? Or was Turgenev describing the fatal influence of Varvara Petrovna on his own will and heart: ghosts are always the unconscious.

Early in 1856 before he left to knock his head against the brick wall of Courtavenel, Turgenev invited the new young writer Tolstoy to stay with him in his flat in Petersburg: "in Stepanov's house at the Arnicktov Bridge on the Fontanka." Tolstoy was twenty-six, ten years younger than Turgenev and they knew each other only by correspondence in which Turgenev had enthused over Tolstoy's *Childhood* and the Sebastopol sketches which had made him an instant celebrity in Petersburg. The Tsar himself was so enthusiastic that he had ordered them to be translated into French at once. Balls and dinners were given for the fierce artillery officer who had come up to the capital straight from his battery in the Crimea. Self-conscious about the imagined defects in his appearance, Tolstoy had brushed up his stiff hair to give himself a high forehead, given a devilish twist to his frowning brows and had grown curving side-whiskers and a thick moustache to cover his heavy upper lip. He intensified the aggressive stare of his small eyes which appeared to some to be searching for the weakness of an opponent he could crush; he was suspicious of praise, quick to accuse of hypocrisy, ready to pick a quarrel; yet he could also be caressing. The Puritan had been the guest of the beautiful Mme. Panaev at a dinner given by Nekrassov, the editor of *The Contemporary;* Nekrassov and Panaev were known as the co-husbands, for Nekrassov had become her lover. Turgenev and others began to praise George Sand and Tolstoy shouted angrily across the table that a woman of such loose sexual morality ought to be tied to a hangman's cart and dragged through the streets as a public example. An embarrassing dinner party. Yet while he was in Petersburg Tolstoy passed his nights in carousals with gypsies and gambling. Inside a week he had challenged someone to a duel. It is true he confessed his self-disgust in his diaries about his resort to brothels: "Horrible. But absolutely the last time. This is no longer temperament but habitual lechery." And again, after going to some place of amusement: "Disgusting. Girls, stupid music, girls, an artificial nightingale, girls, heat, cigarette smoke, girls, vodka, cheese, wild shrieks, girls, girls, girls."

Turgenev put up Tolstoy in his flat and was nearly driven out of his mind by a guest who was clearly jealous of Turgenev's own fame and his gifts—Tolstoy was at this time an awkward and slovenly writer—and one who declared all Turgenev's opinions were insincere. He found Turgenev's friendly and gentle manner patronising; he was even annoyed by the knowledge that Turgenev's estate was larger than his and accused him of hypocrisy in freeing his serfs and of coldness of heart. Turgenev himself was not Varvara Petrovna's son for nothing: he could scream with rage when provoked, but he was at once ashamed of his rage. A man with little consciousness of his own rank, he could not help thinking Tolstoy's pride in his title of Count, and his contempt for writers who, at that time, were more accomplished than he, were ridiculous. As with so many Puritan diarists, Tolstoy's fits of remorse were the expression of his own inordinate belief in his own virtue alone. He was the only good man because he exclusively knew what goodness was. At the time of his meeting with Turgenev he was no doubt under strain, for he had come straight from the battlefield, but the arrogance and the pride were endemic as we know from the famous Rules he made for himself. His pride was to last all his life until it destroyed him.

In August 1856 Turgenev left for France and he met Tolstoy several times in Paris. "Tolstoy speaks of Paris as Sodom and Gomorrah," Turgenev wrote. "He is a blend of poet, Calvinist, fanatic and landowner's son—somewhat reminiscent of Rousseau—a highly moral and at the same time an uncongenial being." If he saw into the division of Tolstoy's character, he loved the writer. To Botkin, a great friend, he said mildly:

Tolstoy is here and looks at everything with his eyes bulging. But he
is ill at ease with himself and hence not quite comfortable with others.
I rejoice in looking at him, to tell the truth he is the sole hope of our
literature . . . a poet and a complete nature such as Tolstoy's will finish
and clearly and completely what I have merely hinted at.

"I rejoice in looking at him"—their relationship was a curious battle
of the eyes, for if Tolstoy stared aggressively, Turgenev scrutinised
with detachment. Tolstoy could not bear these passive inspections
from a man who was older and more famous, at this time, than
himself.

Turgenev had only to say that Tolstoy "was the sole hope of
literature," for Tolstoy to become the reactionary Count and to say
that he despised art and literary men.

Their comedy continued. There was some affable vanity in Turgenev's habit of self-disparagement when he told Tolstoy that he
himself was "a writer of a transitional period. I am fit only for people
in a transitional state." He reflected on Tolstoy's reckless, extrovert
life of action and remorse and concluded that the fault of his own
generation was that "we have little contact with real life, i.e. with
living people, we read too much and think abstractly." On his part,
Tolstoy found Turgenev's good manners and his quick, cultivated
conversation superficial.

———

Not hearing anything from Pauline he wrote to her mother at
Courtavenel that he was taking the boat at Stettin and travelling via
Berlin, Brussels, Ostend and London and would be in Courtavenel
in August. "I shall be putting on my grey coat, unhappily not the
only greyness in my person."

He was enchanted when he arrived to see the pointed towers and
the drawbridge, the moat he had once drained, the pretty gardens.
The misgivings of the journey vanished at once. The house, as usual,
was crowded with guests; Pauline back from success in London
charmed them and welcomed him as if the crisis in Moscow three
years before had been forgotten. It was incredible: there was no brick
wall at all. Louis Viardot, now sixty, was eager for the shooting and
discussed the sins of French translators in the *Revue des Deux
Mondes* who had mutilated Turgenov's work in translation; they

———

had added rhetorical flourishes and even an extra character or two to some things and cut *Mumu* to pieces. Whatever sadness he—or Pauline—felt about the past disappeared in the fun of that summer and that autumn. He was no longer the unknown writer. He was famous and an addition to the celebrities she was used to entertaining—Liszt, and Saint-Saëns, Ary Scheffer and Lord Leighton, the painters Doré and Renan were on her list. The famous actress, used to applause, imposed her spell. He had only to look about him to see she had made a success of a marriage that had been imposed on her.

He, too, forgot his morbidity. "The last flowers of autumn," he wrote, "are sweeter than the first blooms of spring." If youth was over he was "as happy as a trout in a stream when sun shines on its limpid waters." His upbringing at Spasskoye had split his nature, so that an artificial or adoptive family seemed to him the only desirable one; by a trick of the heart Louis and Pauline had taken the place of his father and mother.

The enchantment of that late summer and autumn at Courtavenel held. Turgenev loved children and played with Pauline's daughters—after Louise two had been born—and they played practical jokes on him. One morning he was woken up by a chicken they had put into the cupboard in his bedroom. The guests rowed round the moat of the grey mossy château: Pauline played the guitar on the lawns in the evenings. There were concerts. Pauline and her daughter played their way through Beethoven; in the little private theatre they acted Racine—Paulinette now fourteen, did well as Iphigenia. Turgenev clowned as he loved to do and told stories that amazed and made everyone laugh, and solid Louis Viardot read Victor Hugo aloud. Turgenev, who had a talent for drawing, did a rather disturbing comic drawing of a sportsman coming home, not with birds but with a bag of infants—a drawing that must have appealed to the children's taste for comic horrors. The talent for drawing was turned into an amusement of the adults. He invented what was to become a permanent game in the family: the Portrait Game. He drew portraits of grotesque people and it was the duty of the guests to analyse the characters suggested. A number of these have survived—see Marion Mainwaring's *The Portrait Game.* To take one example—Turgenev writes of one long-nosed, heavy-chinned, furry-browed man:

Old French-language-and-grammar teacher in a school. Stodgy, paro-
chial, inveterate snuff-taker, tedious, kindly enough at bottom, fond
of joking in a donnish way. He is tall, stooped, sunken-chested; he is
a bachelor, likes to go strolling along the quais: he's inquisitive, he'll
stand and stare. He never goes out without an umbrella and wears big
green gloves.

The novelist's impartiality is at work, but Pauline is sharper on the
same man:

Head clerk in a banking house, disingenuous, spiteful, commonplace,
greedy, his fingernails have never been clean—he breathes very heavily, and you hear all kinds of noises issue from his nose and throat—
his eyes are dirty too, as for his teeth!

The comments were read aloud and were given either the *grande
médaille d'honneur* or *la bêtise la plus complète*—awards which had
to be accepted with grateful thanks.

One of the guest-players in this witty game was the local doctor,
a Radical, who though he shared Louis Viardot's detestation of
Napoleon III, privately regarded the company at Courtavenel as a
collection of typical bourgeois liberal intellectuals who would do
nothing for the working class. His name was Dr. Frisson and his
comments on the portraits were solemn. Seven years on, when the
Viardots left for Baden-Baden, Courtavenel was pulled down and
sold piecemeal and it is not quite surprising that Dr. Frisson super-
vised the operation.

One comic disturbance did occur at Courtavenel. The soldier poet
Fet arrived, having characteristically made a mistake in the day of
his invitation. He was a neighbor of Turgenev's at Spasskoye, a great
friend of Tolstoy's who, like him at this time, was opposed to the
emancipation of the serfs and was a roaring reactionary. Turgenev
loved him and quarrelled with him and said "Fet lies so sweetly that
one wants to kiss him." He was a poet and for Turgenev that was
enough. Fet was a rough lonely fellow who hated Paris and spoke
French badly and was turned out like "an officer endimanché with
rings on his fingers and the ribbon of St. Anna in his buttonhole:"
he told stupid stories in broken French so that the humour disappeared—"His eyes," Turgenev wrote to Tolstoy, "were wide open,
his mouth rounded with astonishment, yet open-hearted astonish-

ment was on his face." He was blundering, bored everyone and he did not conceal that he wanted to get away up to Turgenev's room and have a real Russian shouting match. He did so and everyone was alarmed by the row going on upstairs. He was simply attacking Turgenev's democratic ideas as usual; also his folly in leaving Russia and for hanging on to the skirts of Pauline Viardot. Turgenev lost his temper too and said that for him *her* decisions on everything were absolute. Fet had come to get Turgenev out of the mess he was in.

"I am really only happy," Turgenev said, "when a woman puts her heel on my neck and grinds me into the dust. What luck it is for a woman to be hideous."

That is how Fet reported their row afterwards when he wrote his memoirs in old age. No one ever really believed what "the sweetest of liars" said. Still, Turgenev himself had spoken to the Countess Lambert about "ugly Dulcineas." He had his malice. When someone in the party went up to see who was killing whom, the quarrel stopped and they came down quietly like children. The row had started because Turgenev had said how delighted he was to see his daughter had forgotten her Russian and had become entirely French.

In October, with the shooting done, the Viardots returned to their house in Paris and Turgenev took a flat there. His daughter was at school in Paris. She had been thrilled to see her father, for the lonely child needed an ally and was glad to get him away from his fascination with the Viardot girls. It is said that she was put out when Pauline Viardot came to see him at the flat, for the watchful adolescent thought, jealously, that Pauline treated Turgenev as if he were a husband and was indignant. It may be that in her managing way Pauline started complaining about the disorder in which Turgenev lived and his daughter did not understand the actress's business-like gush. Once in Paris, Pauline had become the singer again and now the warmth of the country holiday had gone: indeed she became firm and cold. And not from caprice. She told Turgenev she was pregnant again.

It has been suggested by Magarshack and others that the child was Turgenev's or that Pauline did not know whether it was his or her husband's. The child was a boy called Paul who was said by some to resemble Turgenev. Against this is the fact that Turgenev took little interest in the boy; his deep affections in after years were for Pauline's daughters. Those who have gone thoroughly into the gossip concerning Turgenev's relations with Pauline and the parentage of her children—especially the possibility of Didie and Paul being his children—have found no evidence that he was the father of either of them. It is true he established a dowry for Didie, but she was conceived and born in a period when there were no known meetings between Turgenev and her mother. His special affection sprang from the fact that he saw the mother reborn in her, especially when she grew up. Turgenev confided in his brother Nikolai, and his brother absolutely denied that there was anything in the gossip which became general, especially among Russians who hated Pauline for getting him away from his country. There is nothing in the fact that Turgenev sent Pauline an enthusiastic telegram when Paul was born. He congratulated Pauline on everything and even invented a biographical entry for Grove's biographical dictionary for "the son of Louis and Pauline Viardot." He foresaw the boy would grow up to be a musician and the flattery of the prophecy is entirely in keeping with Turgenev's gifts of fantasy. He made one request of the Viardots: that the children should regard him as their godfather. His imaginary, unreal, poetic family was complete.

One thing seems certain: the news of the pregnancy was a violent shock to him. He became ill at once, as he always did in these crises. And for many years after, indeed until Pauline retired from the stage, they were once more on very distant terms, even if they occasionally met. It is possible that Turgenev made advances to her that summer which angered her. It may be that this and not the earlier occasion in his youth was what she referred to when she wrote in a letter to the conductor Jules Rietz, quoted in April Fitzlyon's *Life:*

> without Ary Scheffer I would have committed a great sin—for I had lost my will-power—I recovered in time to *break my heart* and do my duty—I had my reward later—ah! I too had my gypsy instincts to combat—to kill passion . . . Scheffer watched over me like a father.

The sporting and literary friendship between Louis Viardot and Turgenev continued in a dignified way. Turgenev talked of translating Viardot's French version of *Don Quixote* into Russian. He did not do so, but he arranged for it to be published.

So Turgenev had, after all, "broken his head against the brick wall." His illness was "the bladder complaint" he said, which had killed his father. The illness brought on neuralgia and long periods of depression; and as always with him a dramatic rush of fantastic images into his head. He said he had become an ant heap poked about by children, a shed falling to pieces, as brittle as glass; that he was rotting like frozen fish when the thaw comes on, that he was as foul as a squashed mushroom, a heap of rubbish not worth sweeping up and that a snake was gnawing at his vitals. If Turgenev was still malicious about others, he was savage with self-ridicule. He would never write another line and, remembering not to follow the mad Gogol's example, he had not *burned* his manuscripts, but had torn them up and thrown them in the water closet. Tolstoy saw him in Paris and felt a mixture of contempt and pity for this victim of love. The illness wore off but Turgenev's depression lasted. He was seen about in Russian society in Paris but he loathed the city and called Lamartine a whiner, George Sand garrulous and hated Hugo's tremolo. He had met Mérimée many times but his cold obscenities disgusted him, though he was glad to use an introduction to Monckton Milnes and Palmerston when soon after he went off to London.

He went there to visit Herzen and to attend a public dinner for the Royal Literary Fund where he saw Disraeli and talked with Carlyle, and in an account of English solemnities he gave his famous analysis of the diction of Lord Palmerston. He noted that at seventy-five Palmerston had an old man's voice, but clear and strong and that he spoke slowly punctuating his phrases with "er-er," but always finished his sentences beautifully. These stutterings were a studied habit with English public speakers and, in fact, the manner was pleasant because it added a touch of naturalness to speech, a touch of good humour and surprise. And it amused him that Mérimée, who had tried all his life to achieve the English coldness and reserve, could only stumble in English and was lost without the formal aids of French rhetoric. Afterwards Carlyle tried to convince him that the best government was autocratic, like the Russian!

After London he went to Sinzig, the spa on the Rhine, where he was tortured by a pain like toothache which went on all day until midnight. Nevertheless the little town brought back memories of his youth. From the deck of a Rhine steamer he had seen an old woman and a young girl placidly looking out of different windows of an old house and, for some reason of memory working upon his present life, he wrote an excellent long story called *Acia* which Tolstoy disliked. Delicately, in a few lines, Turgenev catches the charm of the town as he had seen it himself as a young man drinking the delicious wine, breathing the smell of the lime trees that embalmed the place, listening to the voices of the pretty German girls who "even when the moon appeared and made each cobble of the streets distinct" did not go home. For all his affectations of premature old age and his misery, the sensations of youth were an inexhaustible spring to which the poet in him could always return. The story is an odd one: it portrays a wilful, naïve young Russian girl—a Russian "orphan," and her first awkward awakening to love. The original upon whom he worked is said to be a child of his uncle's, but perhaps it was his own "orphan" Paulinette who came to his mind as he looked into her future.

Tolstoy wrote to him from Baden-Baden to say he had ruined himself at roulette, and to borrow money. Turgenev sent it and wrote: "If you knew how difficult I find things and how sad I am. Take a lesson from me: do not let life slip through your fingers." Soon after Tolstoy came to Sinzig to borrow more—he had lost at the tables again. Turgenev himself had to borrow in order to rescue him and Tolstoy wrote in his diary "Vanicha . . . was very severe with me." Turgenev told him he was living in a cesspool. He told him to roll up his sleeves and get to the workers' bench. Their comedy was still held at a harmless stage by Turgenev's tolerance.

But he was not cured of love by the short reunion at Courtavenel. He was a man of recollections, never to be cured of the past which shadowed him. Whether it was because he was indulging the strange pleasure of tormenting himself and could not resist the brick wall, he made one more brief visit to Courtavenel. Pauline was away in Budapest and he passed the time with Louis Viardot shooting. At last Turgenev's friends took action. Botkin, the tea merchant and epicurean, a man of large appetites—"a man," Turgenev said, "with a number of extra mouths, aesthetic, philosophical and fleshly, who munched noisily with all of them"—persuaded him to go to Italy and above all Rome, and Turgenev did begin writing a draft of his next novel, *A Nest of Gentlefolk,* there. He was stirred to exasperation by the Russian colony in Rome; the nobility were alarmed by the news that the problem of emancipating the serfs was at last being seriously approached in Petersburg. He stood his ground, albeit nervously: his opponents in Rome were alarmed because emancipation would affect their incomes—it would affect his own. He wrote to Countess Lambert: "I shall be a landowner and a gentleman, not a serf-owner." The novelist was creating, in his mind, a hero—a practical projection of his own unpractical self: Lavretsky.

Botkin and Turgenev spent some time among the painters in Rome. One short essay, a portrait of the Russian painter Ivanov, shows Turgenev, the critic-artist-traveller, in good form. Ivanov had been working for years on his huge picture, *Christ Appearing to the People,* a work which the strange mystic and ascetic had started and re-started over and over again, something Balzacian, a *chef d'oeuvre inconnu,* an obsession. Ivanov lived in a state of involuntary semi-starvation and had reached a point of mania. He refused to eat in restaurants, because he said the waiters were plotting to poison him.

> It is said [Turgenev writes] that Ivanov copied the head of Apollo Belvedere and the head of the Byzantine Christ he had discovered in Palermo over 30 times and gradually bringing them together at last succeeded in painting his John the Baptist . . . But true artists do not create in that way.

Ivanov was not a good painter but he belonged to "the transitory period"—as Turgenev more and more thought he himself did. Ivanov, he said, was imperfect and obscure, attempting something beyond his powers; but his great merit, as an idealist and thinker, consists chiefly in the fact that he pointed out the models to use, "leads us to them, awakens us, stirs us. He himself may not satisfy but he does not offer cheap satisfactions to others." Once Turgenev showed Ivanov an album of good caricatures. Ivanov examined them and then raising his head said "Christ never laughed." The naïveté of Ivanov delighted Turgenev, who was drawn to the beautiful observation of his small simple sketches. Where he succeeded was in commonplace things, not in the huge clumsy grandiose "master-piece" which he had laboured at for twenty years. These small things contained the tranquillity of the artist—the quality which Turgenev himself carried in his own nature.

The travellers went on to Florence and Venice and returned to Paris. His friends were relieved to see Turgenev returned to health. But like the hero of Italo Svevo's *Confessions of Zeno,* Turgenev replied with one of his ready fantasies that cherish illness as a religion:

> Ah, but don't you see, the organisms of people who have a chronic disease like mine, seem to be stronger than ordinary people. The disease is taking a rest, letting nature do its best for the patient so as to be able to break out with greater force later on. I should not be surprised if I dropped dead suddenly to the astonishment of all my friends.

The actor was sticking to his part and returned to Russia to a round of dinners and to the drawing-room of the Countess Lambert to whom he had written from Paris reproaching her for "the tone" of her letters about Pauline Viardot and saying:

> What has died in me is not my emotions, no, but the opportunity to satisfy them . . . The only thing left for a person like myself is to let himself be carried on the waves of life for the time being and think about port after he has found a sweet dear Comrade such as you, a Comrade in emotion, ideas and, the main thing, in attitude. (You and I expect very little for ourselves)—to hold his hand firmly and float along.

Not surprisingly she accused him of being a coquettish author. Pauline Viardot was writing in much the same terms as Turgenev to her confidant Jules Rietz.

Turgenev as a child. From a portrait, c. 1824. *Turgenev Museum, Orel*

ABOVE: Turgenev's mansion at Spasskoye. *Radio Times Hulton Picture Library*
BELOW: The church and school at Spasskoye, built by Turgenev.
Radio Times Hulton Picture Library

Turgenev's estate: the memorial chapel to the Emperor Alexander II;
the drawing-room and divan; the study; the Turgenev family crypt; peasants
on the estate. *Radio Times Hulton Picture Library*

"Exile's Avenue," Turgenev's estate. *Radio Times Hulton Picture Library*

ABOVE: Turgenev: a drawing by L. Pietsch, 1866. *Stadtgeschichtliche
Sammlungen, Baden-Baden*
BELOW: Pauline Viardot on her first visit to St. Petersburg.
Radio Times Hulton Picture Library

ABOVE: Turgenev's funeral, 1883: the cortege en route to the Volkov cemetery.
Radio Times Hulton Picture Library
BELOW: Ivan Turgenev, 1882. *Radio Times Hulton Picture Library*

Baden-Baden. *Radio Times Hulton Picture Library*

Authors who wrote for the *Sovremennik* magazine. Sitting (left to right):
I. Goncharov, I. Turgenev, A. Druzhinin, A. Ostrovsky.
Standing: L. Tolstoy, D. Grigorovich. *Society for Cultural
Relations with the USSR Library*

Chapter 8

TURGENEV became declamatory: one seems to see him on a stage saying "I have now said Farewell to dreams of happiness for good." He went back to Spasskoye but he was often in Petersburg, killing his boredom. If Pauline rarely wrote to him, he wrote often to her; there was a slight edge to his news:

> I am in good health. I go out a lot, but only to one house, Countess Lambert's. She is charming, no longer young—

(She was thirty-eight, very little older than Pauline)

> her hair is greyer than mine—but no one could have more heart or wit—but there's no one word one can describe wit and heart together —hers are very fine. She has become a great friend—I spend all my evenings with her.

And he went on to say he had started a novel and incidentally tells Pauline what she is missing:

> I have already mentioned that I am writing a novel. How happy I would have been to show you my plan and the characters, the theme I have in my mind, etc., and how precious I would have found your

judgements on them. I have brooded a long time on my subject and I hope to avoid the crude mistakes and faults of impatience which you quite rightly once pointed out to me in the past. I am in vain, if the ardour of youth is now far away, but I write with a coolness and composure which astonishes me: I trust the book won't suffer from that. *Qui dit froid dit médiocre.*

In the next six years during which the friendship with Pauline Viardot scarcely existed, Turgenev reached his highest powers as a novelist and worked hardest. He liked to pass himself off as a man without will and he had many of the distractions of a rich man who did not have to toil to earn his daily bread as Dostoevsky, Schedrin or Goncharov did; but the inner will of the artist was strong. The impatience caused by lack of self-confidence we detect in *Rudin* vanished in his next book, *A House of Gentlefolk*—or a "Nest" as it is sometimes called more appropriately, for the lack of a real "nest" of his own was the repeated complaint throughout his life. The novel is not the finest thing he did, but it was a favourite with his readers and the critics and established his reputation as the leading Russian writer. With *The Sportsman's Sketches* it is the only book for which he was not afterwards abused even in the most virulent Russian quarters. The Countess admired it and was flattered in seeing something of herself and her religious influence in the character of Lisa, the heroine. In the words of one critic, the novel brought "a truce of God" because it pleased the two factions: Westerners like himself and their opponents, the Slavophils. The burden of being Russian as it was felt by the educated Russian upper class of his generation —the class for whom he expressly wrote, for no other readers had yet appeared—was shared equally by his characters and he saw it with his usual detachment in individual lives. Despite his own strong commitments, equilibrium or balance is the essence of his work— that equilibrium which he saw at the heart of Nature.

Once more he set his novel in the country house in which the people had been established for generations. This was, as we have seen, the closed—or rather not quite closed scene—suited to the classical, play-like structure natural to him: each chapter is short and shapely—there is a pause and a light spring to the next scene, carrying the people and the theme forward with assurance and simplicity. The animation of the prose gives one the illusion of actuality, and even something contemporary with ourselves to the tone, so that even old history seems as near as the morning in which we are reading it. All is movement as we pass in and out of a drawing-room into a garden, from a garden to a coach, from a coach to another house and another, from morning to afternoon, from day to evening. People reveal themselves and their conflicts—it seems to us—less by the author's direction than by the course of nature. Even in the debates about ideas or in his "biographical" passages Turgenev is not giving us the static, explanatory essays or summaries we find in older novelists like Scott or Balzac—in him past and present ripple along intermingled, action rises from the stream of conversation and flashes to the surface. Turgenev looks forward as he looks back. And although he is a portraitist who gives the surface of people, we feel also that they are organic creatures that Russia has been forming in its long restless sleep.

The important thing is that in his chief character, Lavretsky, Turgenev has at last found someone who approaches the positive hero. He is not master of his fate, but he has reserves of strength which enable him to outgrow a bad and confused education, to endure and to work; unlike Rudin he is not negative nor is he a vagrant. He is not brilliant but he does not give in. But let us first look at a lesser character, Lavretsky's rival, to see Turgenev's analytical manner at work. We see Panshin first as the latest type of young, up-to-the minute political and social climber from Petersburg. He has all the graces, is musical, can even paint and write a bit. What has formed this waterfly? We hear his father—whom we never see but are at once convinced we have seen him somewhere—we hear his father was

> a retired cavalry officer and a notorious gambler, a man with insinuating eyes, a battered countenance and a nervous twitch about the mouth

who has shrewdly pushed his climbing son into Society:

> He never lost an opportunity while shuffling cards between two rubbers or playing a successful trump, of dropping a hint about his Volodka to any personage of importance. . . .

It is that simple act of "shuffling cards" and thinking of something else while he does it that makes him present for a moment—and then disposes of him. Turgenev makes his thumbnail sketches work for the novel: they are not there only to divert us.

So, in the first chapter, it will be a comic smirking gossip, one of the inevitable toadies of the country house, who will come slavering over a titbit of scandal, into Maria Dmitrievna's drawing-room, to show us where the centre of the drama will lie. The news is that Lavretsky, a neighbouring landowner, has had the nerve to come back from Paris without his wife and to be indifferent to pity and ridicule. How can he face public opinion when it is notorious that he has been cuckolded by his wife who has deserted him in Paris? A man who can't control his own wife is not only a fool: he is reproachable. He has let decent society down. With a playwright's skill, Turgenev delays Lavretsky's arrival in Marya Dmitrievna's drawing room for seven chapters. Turgenev's timing and touch are always perfect: Lavretsky drops in casually at Marya Dmitrievna's, on some farming business, and the first person he meets in the doorway is her daughter Lisa who is nineteen and who was no more than a child when he last saw her.

"You don't recognise me?" he said taking off his hat. "I'm Lavretsky. Is your mother at home?"

So the meeting of hero and future heroine is lightly accomplished.

And, in the classical manner—"we must ask the reader's permission to break off the thread of our story for a time"—the most important "biography," the history of the Lavretsky family, is insinuated and suddenly the novel is deepened: it is no longer, as Turgenev called it, "our story." It is a living slice of the passions, the accidents and the ideas that have created Lavretsky's forbears and himself. He is a man who will carry his generation on his shoulders. In many respects Fedya Lavretsky has the violent history of Turgenev's mother's family, the Lutovinovs in him—there is gypsy blood—and of Turgenev's father. Lavretsky's own father had in his youth been abroad and had come back a supercilious Frenchified dandy, disgusted by Russian life. *His* father, our Lavretsky's grandfather, roars into the present:

The puppy won't eat, he can't bear the heat and close smell of the room; the sight of folks drunk upsets him; one daren't flog anyone in front of him; he doesn't want to go into the government service, he's weakly as you see in health . . . And all because he's read Voltaire.

Not only Voltaire and Diderot but Rousseau too! All the "new" nonsense of the eighteenth century had been in his head; but Turgenev says:

It was there in him, but without mixing in his blood, not penetrating to his soul, nor shaping itself in any firm convictions. But indeed what could one expect from a young man of 50 years ago when, even at the present day we have not succeeded in attaining them.

One notices that like Stendhal, Turgenev is caustic in dating the minds of his people. It is a way of making time stereoscopic. This high-minded Voltairean soon seduced a serf girl: that was acceptable. What was unacceptable was that on enlightened principles he married her. And his father, in his dressing-gown trimmed with squirrel fur, literally chased him out of the house.

And slippers on his bare feet, flew at Ivan Petrovitch with his fists . . . all over the house, the kitchen garden, the pleasure grounds, across the road . . .

shouting "Stop you scoundrel! Stop or I'll curse you."

The young man got to Petersburg, deserted his serf-wife, got a place in the Embassy in London. Years later when the father died he returned to Russia, a sour anglomaniac, with a wooden laugh— Turgenev could not bear the English laugh—speaking curtly through his teeth and his head stuffed with political economy. At home he found his wife has died and left him a son, Fedya—our Lavretsky—and he put him through a spartan Richard-Feverel-like moral training system which makes the boy grow up tough, self-conscious and halting with women. A natural development has been arrested. This Meredithian touch is interesting. Probably Turgenev never read him but he had read Thackeray and widely in the English novel and was very aware of the stern Victorian theories regarding the education of young gentlemen. There are many scenes that come straight from Turgenev's own childhood in these pages; and

the fanatic aunt Glafira is one more of Turgenev's portraits of his
own terrifying mother, though Glafira lacks her moments of naïve
charm.

Fedya becomes just the young man who will easily be trapped by
a sly and fortune-hunting girl, the daughter of a peculating and
shabby General in whom

> the good nature innate in all Russians was intensified by that special
> geniality which is peculiar to people who have done something dis-
> graceful.

Fedya Lavretsky, the victim of a patched-up parody of Western
ideas, exploited and deserted by a shrewd girl, is in his turn back
from Paris. If he has strength it will be the submissive but lasting
strength of the peasant mother he does not remember. He has to
learn to be a Russian—but what is that?

Turgenev's mind—as we know—was apolitical. A Westerner by
conviction, he had many friends among the leading Slavophils—the
Aksakovs were close to him—and he watched the effect of their
convictions upon them. Conviction is always a questioning word in
his novels; like Stendhal, as I have said, he knows how to "place"
the changes of conviction historically. In a remarkable scene with an
old university friend called Mikhalevich, Lavretsky has a serious yet
farcical friendly row all through one night. Mikhalevich is a man
whose high hopes at the university have failed him—he has sunk to
being clerk to a spirit-tax contractor—but he is out to wake up
Lavretsky:

> "I want above all to know what you are like, what are your views and
> convictions, what you have become, what life has taught you."

Mikhalevich (Turgenev notes) still preserved the phraseology of
1830, and he is soon shouting that Lavretsky is a loafing Voltairean:

> You know which leg the German limps on, you know what's amiss
> with the English and the French and your pitiful culture goes to make
> it worse, your shameful idleness, your abominable inactivity is justified
> by it.

That is an attack on the signs of the sleepy Slavophil he sees in Lavretsky, who, whether he has "convictions" or not, at any rate believes that if one is a landowner there is one thing one ought to know: how to farm one's land.

But if Lavretsky is a disillusioned Westerner he is not a fashionable and opportunist Westerner like Panshin. Lavretsky listens to Panshin speaking in Marya Dmitrievna's drawing-room where Panshin is trying to court her daughter Lisa. Panshin says:

> We are sick from having only half become Europeans, we must take a hair of the dog that bit us . . . The best heads, *les meilleures têtes*, among us have long been convinced of it. All people are essentially alike; only introduce among them good institutions, the job is done. Of course there may be adaptations to the existing national life: that is our affair—the affair of the official (he almost said "governing" class) . . . Marya Dmitrievna most feelingly assented to all Panshin said. "What a clever man," she thought, "is talking in my drawing room." Lisa sat in silence leaning back against the window; Lavretsky too was silent. Marfa Timofyevna playing cards with her old friend in the corner, muttered something to herself.

Lavretsky argues back in semi-Slavophil fashion for

> "a recognition of the true spirit of the people and submission to it without which a courageous combat against error is impossible.

Turgenev is leaning a little towards Slavophils and for the purpose of irony has set the novel in a remote part of Russia where the old traditions are unchanged. One would expect Marya Dmitrievna's daughter to be either a worldly or rebellious girl; but she is simple and in fact she has been deeply influenced by her personal maid who is religious to a state of exaltation. Lisa holds to the old Orthodox beliefs and although she is drawn to Lavretsky she is shocked when he says he refuses to be reconciled to his wife and will not forgive her in his own mind. Marriage, she says, is forever, whatever wrongs are done. She sees—as Countess Lambert saw in Turgenev—a soul to be saved, an atheist to be redeemed, but the more she says this the more her heart is drawn to him.

Lavretsky is helped towards his love for Lisa by his sympathy for her lonely and homesick old German music master, a petulant old man, who is maddened because his talents have been almost extinguished by having to earn a miserable living among the gentry and outside his own country. Lavretsky listens to the old German and in his own loneliness visits him in his little house in the nearby town. The old man is sure that he had genius once and longs for one brief outburst in which what has been forgotten will reappear. One night when Lavretsky is there, the German suddenly plays superbly: what has inspired him is his discernment of the love Lavretsky tries to conceal: his genius has been awakened and, as he listens, Lavretsky understands his own love. This scene is unquestionably one of the sublest revelationary things Turgenev wrote about love and music. He is always excellent in his portraits of musicians, in their struggles with their art (again) but this scene also goes to the heart of Turgenev's feeling for art as the supreme resource of the human spirit: art lives our life with us. Lavretsky the dogged farmer is transformed.

A newspaper reports that Lavretsky's wife has died in Paris. Lavretsky is free to declare himself to Lisa, who now begs him to go to church and pray for his dead wife's soul, and indeed herself prays for her and for Lavretsky. Even so, Lisa's religious conscience is troubled. She loves passionately but while she is in a trance of hesitation she hears the news of the wife's death is false. Indeed the wife turns up dramatically at Lavretsky's house with a child she says is his. That is the tragic end of the love affair which, as in so many of Turgenev's stories, is on the brink of a happiness that is swept away.

The reappearance of Lavretsky's wife is a violent shock to the reader. Lavretsky detects an unpleasant smell of patchouli at once as he comes back into his little manor farm. The wife is standing with her luggage and her child; the bad romantic plays of the period have led her to see herself as *La Dame aux Camélias*—now having a popular run in Paris—but without the tuberculosis of the heroine. She falls on her knees before her husband and vulgarly acts out the part of contrition. Lavretsky's dream of happiness is wrecked: she is his wife, clearly after a large allowance, the big house he has closed, and for rehabilitation in Russian society, and she uses her child—which may or may not be his—as an emotional blackmail. It is part of the cruel irony that Lisa herself persuades Lavretsky, on religious grounds, to give in to her: innocently Lisa and he have done wrong and must accept God's punishment, a God Lavretsky does not believe in. Lavretsky puts his wife into the big house; she soon takes up with Panshin, then leaves him and goes off again to Paris, the corrupt West, and to resume her love affairs there.

This part of the novel breaks with the spirit of the whole and there is an uncomfortable element of "strong" plot which, for Turgenev, is unnatural. There is a particularly artificial scene in which Marya Dmitrievna tries to persuade Lavretsky to acknowledge the child while the wife hides behind a screen and comes out at the critical moment: sentimental melodrama. In the end, Lisa goes into a convent and Lavretsky has to live out his life without happiness, but it is made plain that Lisa and Lavretsky are not destroyed by submitting to suffering and fate: they survive as best they can by acts of will.

Eight years later, when he has become a sound middle-aged farmer, Lavretsky makes one more visit to the house. The older generation have died off. As on his first visit, a young girl runs into him as he comes into the drawing-room; once more he says "I am Lavretsky." All the laughing young people who are playing a game are almost strangers to him: he simply knows that time has gone on. He looks at the bench in the garden where he and Lisa sat, and at the piano:

> He touched one of the keys; it gave out a faint clear sound; on that note had begun the inspired melody with which long ago on that same happy night the dead Lemm had thrown him into such transports.

This last chapter recalls those scenes in Chekhov's plays where passing cries of happiness are unbearable and make us weep.

"Welcome lonely old age, burn out useless life," Lavretsky thinks as he goes off, and the joyous cries sound more loudly in the garden.

We dab our eyes and then it strikes us again that Turgenev himself is moved by the rise and fall of love and not by the fullness of love realised. Hail and farewell. Spring and autumn. No high summer of fulfilment. Therefore no tragedy, only sadness. The pessimism of Turgenev is absolute.

What is most lasting in our minds when we put the book down is the natural ease with which Turgenev evokes the essential solitariness of Lavretsky's mind and his life as he travels across the steppe:

and as he watched the furrowed fields open like a fan before him, the willow bushes as they slowly came into sight and the dull ravens and rooks who looked sidelong with stupid suspicion at the approaching carriage . . . as he watched the fresh fertile wilderness and solitude of this steppe country, the greenness, the long slopes, and valleys with stunted oaks, the grey villages and the birch trees—the whole Russian landscape, so long unseen by him, stirred emotion at once pleasant, sweet and almost painful in his heart and he felt weighed down by a kind of pleasant oppression.

He nods off to sleep and when he opens his eyes again:

. . . the same fields, the stame steppe scenery; the polished shoes of the trace horse flashed alternately through the driving dust, the coachman's shirt, yellow with red gussets, puffed out by the wind

until the arrival at the house:

"So here I am at home, here I am back again," thought Lavretsky as he walked the diminutive passages while one after another the shutters were being opened with much creaking and knocking and the light of day poured into the deserted rooms.

And when at last he went to bed that night

It seemed to him that the darkness surrounding him on all sides could not be accustomed to the new inhabitant, the very walls of the house seemed amazed.

It was about this novel that Countess Lambert said it was written by a pagan who had "not yet renounced the cult of Venus, but already understands the sterner call of duty towards which his sick soul is drawn, rather against his will."

He went up to Petersburg that winter to enjoy the fame and social success his novel had given him. The railway from Moscow to Petersburg was not yet finished and the journey was as bad as ever. He gave a few readings in the capital, caught laryngitis in that damp cold climate, heard through the papers that Pauline was giving something like fifty concerts in England. He went off to Vichy for

one of his cures and thought the place ugly compared with the pretty
German spas; it was half-empty. The Germans would never have
allowed a horrible barrel-organ to play under his window. The rain
fell. The river was sickly yellow. So he turned to reading Pascal and
wrote to Pauline—for he kept up his side of the correspondence—
that Pascal treads down all that is most dear to man, pushes you
down in the mud and offers for consolation a religion that is bitter
and violent *"qui vous abêtit, c'est son mot"*—which even repels
Pascal himself but which he says it is one's duty to accept in order
to crush the cravings of the heart. Turgenev goes on:

> I venture to say the humane view of character is the opposite of the
> Christian, if one reduces it to the cowardly and narrow doctrine of
> personal salvation and egoism. But no one has ever written with the
> force of Pascal; his anguish, his imprecations are terrible. Byron is a
> pure stream compared with him. And how lucid and profound Pascal
> is. What grandeur he has. "Nous sommes incapables de savoir cer-
> tainement et d'ignorer absolument. Nous voguons sur un milieu vaste,
> toujours incertains et flottants, poussés d'un bout vers l'autre. Quelque
> terme où nous pensions nous attacher et nous affermir—il branle et
> nous quitte; et si nous le suivons, il échappe à nos prises, nous glisse
> et fuit d'une *fuite éternelle.*

And what crushing blows Pascal gives us. The heart of man is full
of filth. And

> Le dernier acte est sanglant, quelque belle qui soit la comédie en tout
> le reste. On jette enfin de la terre *sur la tête* et en voilà pour jamais.

The waters of Vichy and Pascal between them had made Turgenev
bitter. He added a note for Louis Viardot as he often did to his
letters, and said he hoped to find him at Courtavenel.

From Pascal he turned to the humanity of Cervantes and Shakespeare who were closer to him. The novelist who read too much had
been working on a brilliant pair of character studies of Hamlet
and Don Quixote and he had given a public reading of this in Petersburg; and it was, by transference, a study of his own character.
Louis Viardot had translated *Don Quixote* as we have seen and
it strikes one that another bond of the long family friendship
with the Viardots was language: the sounds of French, En-

glish, German and Russian, melting into the language of music.

The influence of Don Quixote on Russian literature had been powerful in Gogol and was to be so in Dostoevsky's *The Idiot*, but Turgenev believed that in his time there had been more Hamlets than Quixotes in Russia. They are, he says, two ways of conceiving the ideal: one is inside human nature, the other is outside. In one the individual will predominates; in the other something outside the "I" which the individual prefers to the "I." In his person Don Quixote expresses above all the faith in something eternal and unchangeable, faith in truth, the truth that is outside. He is saturated with the love of the ideal. Life gives the opportunity to pursue the ideal, to establish the triumph of truth and the reign of justice on earth. He is without egoism, his thought never dwells on himself, he is all devotion and self-sacrifice. But, it must be observed, he is slow to feel compassion and finds it difficult to move his mind from one thing to another. He is free to change his opinions. Indeed he is something of a casuist: in love, when he notices his mistress is squalid, he blames this on the magicians. His dreams are chaste; at heart he knows there is no hope of possessing the loved person, indeed he rather dreads that. He is hurt by the world.

"But who hurts Hamlet but Hamlet himself?" Turgenev quotes the Russian proverb: "Those who mock me today will do me a good turn tomorrow." Hamlet is all egotism, analysis, he is scepticism in person. As an egoist he can have no faith in himself but he clings to the "I" in which he has no faith. He is absorbed in his own personality: he thinks of himself strategically, not of his duties. He has no pity for himself, for his spirit is too elaborately critical to allow him to be content with what he finds inside himself. He delights in self-flagellation, is fascinated by his faults, studies himself night and day. His self-awareness is itself a force. One cannot love him, for he loves no one, but one can't help admiring him because his outer man, his melancholy, his pallor are attractive. One also rather likes him because he has a tendency to be plump. He never makes Don Quixote's wild mistakes: windmills will never be giants for him and he won't take up arms and fight.

The Hamlets of this world are of no use to the masses—they offer nothing, are going nowhere, for they have no end in view. Love they can only simulate; yet his scepticism is not the scepticism of indifference: hence its significance and power and he will indeed fight against injustice . . . The most important service of Hamlet is that he will develop such men as Horatio.

In Vichy he had begun writing his next novel, *On the Eve*—the title meant "on the eve of the emancipation of the serfs." He knew that the Crimean War had changed the climate of intellectual opinion, especially among men younger than himself who had already politely suggested that up till now his novels, long or short, had been simply sensitive love stories: "the wanderings of Odysseus always ends in Calypso's isle." They were demanding direct political commitment to social reform and in an incoherent way to revolution: the emancipation of the serfs, if it ever came, would merely be a beginning and itself would not go far in solving Russia's problem. They were, in effect, asking Turgenev to reverse his method: to proceed from idea—the radical idea—to character and not (as he did) to build on character first and to watch ideas at work in it. More than this, they required a Radical hero.

The story opens on an idyllic summer day in the country with a philosophical discussion between two young men, a feckless painter and a minor academic. Shabin is the painter, Bersenyev the scholar:

"Is there nothing higher than happiness?" Bersenyev says.
"And what, for instance?" asked Shabin.
"Why, for instance, you and I are, as you say young; we are good men, let us suppose, each of us desires happiness for himself . . . But is that word, happiness, one that could unite us, set us both on fire and make us clasp each other's hands? Isn't that an egoistic one; I mean, isn't it a source of disunion?"
"Do you know words, then, that unite men?"
"Yes, and they are not few in number; and you know them too."
"What words?"
"Well, even Art—since you are an artist—Country, Science, Freedom, Justice."
"And what of love?" asked Shabin.
"Love too is a word that unites but not the love you are eager for now; the love which is not enjoyment, the love which is self-sacrifice."

Presently, when we are introduced to the family with whom the young men are staying, we meet Insarov, the man who is in the minds of these philosophers.

Insarov is a poor Bulgarian student who is slowly revealed to us as a man deeply involved in a conspiracy to free Bulgaria from Turkish domination, a man determined on self-sacrifice. He is a consumptive. A young girl, Yelena, falls in love with him and his cause. She goes off with him when the call comes. They get as far as Venice and while they are waiting to be smuggled across the Adriatic, Insarov dies and the girl goes on and vanishes into a war where she is nursing the wounded. No more is heard of her.

Despite Turgenev's delicacy and his power to move us from joy to tears, despite his "irresistible" qualities, the reader at once realises there is something wrong with *On The Eve*. The fundamental reason is the astonishing one that in his search for a hero he worked from another writer's manuscript. A few years before, one of his young neighbours, a certain Vassily Karatayev had given him the story of a girl he had once known who had fallen in love with a Bulgarian patriot and had gone to Bulgaria with him and died. Karatayev had tried to write the story but found he lacked the talent and gave the manuscript to Turgenev and told him to do what he liked with it. Turgenev wrote:

> The figure of the heroine Yelena, in those days still a new type in Russian life, was outlined clearly in my mind; but I lacked the hero, a person Yelena could give herself to in her still vague, though powerful, craving for freedom.

He retained only one of Karatayev's chapters about a jaunt to a country town near Moscow, though he amended it. It is crudely out of tone with the rest of Turgenev's narrative; but the weakness of the rest of the novel is that it labours. Turgenev himself wrote to Countess Lambert:

> Planning a novel is very fatiguing work, particularly as it leaves no visible traces behind it; you lie on the sofa turning some character and situation over in your mind, then you suddenly realise that three or four hours have passed and you don't seem to have anything to show for it . . . to tell you the truth there are very few pleasures in our trade.

And quite right too; everybody, even artists, even scholars must live by their sweat of their faces.

The bother is that Turgenev could not succeed with an unfelt and unknown character. He knew nothing about conspiracy—that required a novelist with a gift for the novel of plot and exciting action. Insarov is a dour, dull, cardboard figure: the only sign of action in him appears when, in the chapter Turgenev retained, Insarov violently pitches a drunken German into a pond. The conspiracy exists only by hearsay. The only originality is one of approach: the book examines Yelena from the point of view of each character and one of these, the painter Shabin, is a silly caricature of the conventional Bohemian artist and an embarrassment to the reader, who skips past him as fast as he can.

The other characters are a collection of drolls, whose opinions of Yelena are not worth hearing. No doubt Turgenev had not rid himself of the "type" figure—the superfluous man—and was arguing that there was no Russian male with convictions and vigour who would be worthy of Yelena and her force of character—an argument that made the young critics indignant. *On the Eve* marks the beginning of a crack in his reputation which later became a gulf. Yet when he lets Yelena live for herself before our eyes she is a real, troubled girl whose doubts and courage are clear to us. If Turgenev fails to create a hero he does create a heroine simply because of his gift for showing a girl grow into independent determined womanhood through loss, disillusion or, as in this case, fatality. Once more the son of Varvara Petrovna can draw Russian women who are becoming strong; indeed in all his best work the fully drawn women, whether evil or good, are stronger than the men. The critics who denounced him for his lack of social commitment were wrong in dismissing his love stories as fairy tales: they were tests.

Of course there are fine things and some of the criticism was puerile—the critics were annoyed that the conspirator was a Bulgarian: surely the condition of Russia was more important than the overthrow of a government in Bulgaria? What annoyed the official classes—of whom the Countess Lambert was a typical member—was that a revolutionary or patriotic conspiracy should be approved in the portrait of Insarov and that a Russian girl should deny morality, her family and society and go off with him. Ruling society had become prudish by the mid-century: the days of Pushkin had gone.

And there was more trouble. The young critics who attacked him had been taken on by *The Contemporary*, in which Turgenev was the star. In one of his fits of temper he broke with the periodical and from then on they began personal attacks on him. He was mocked as a fashionable novelist who is "trailing in the wake of a singer and arranging ovations for her at provincial theatres abroad."

Once his temper had calmed, Turgenev bore no malice to his critics and indeed often expressed his admiration for them. This can, of course, be taken as masochism, a false humility, a desire to keep in with "the movement" and the young, and a form of Olympian patronage. But he had his unchanging views of the values of art which they denied; for the utilitarians it must be socially "useful." Before he died, he was telling Tolstoy to stop preaching and to return to his art; and in the next generation Chekov was to attack the utilitarian doctrine.

Turgenev's spirits were low when he wrote *On the Eve*. He told the Countess that his heart had turned to stone. And the novel brought with it another painful quarrel which had its roots in something more than ordinary literary jealousy. For many years Ivan Goncharov, the author of *Oblomov*, had been, to all appearances, a close and admiring friend. They had been in the habit of meeting and reading works in progress to each other in the peculiar Russian custom which suggests not so much a lack of self-confidence or dramatic vanity as a curious desire for consensus. Turgenev himself more than once accepted the advice of his friends, deleted passages they disapproved of, adding what they suggested. But in these exchanges Goncharov scarcely concealed a jealousy that was turning into paranoia. His novel, *Oblomov*, had appeared at the time of *The House of Gentlefolk* and had far less success. Even in the course of their private readings, Goncharov had accused Turgenev of stealing a scene from his own novel and Turgenev, always willing to bow to others, removed the scene. But Goncharov had also read part of the manuscript of a novel called *The Ravine*—it was not finished until thirteen years later—and Goncharov now told friends that Turgenev had stolen *On the Eve* from him. The matter became a scandal. A committee of friends sat in arbitration on it and said that any resemblances were due to the fact that "the events were common to the times and to the Russian soil." Turgenev was angered that the committee was not more explicit and broke with Goncharov though, in his usual dignified manner, soon forgot the matter. But Goncharov's fantasy became something like insanity. He said Turgenev not only copied him but that when he went to Paris he passed his ideas to his European friends so that Alphonse Daudet, the Goncourts and George Sand, and even Flaubert, were using them at his expense. The ease with which some Russian temperaments take to suspicious envy and paranoia—it is striking in Dostoevsky—seems to indicate a real difference of character between the Russians and Western Europeans.

The quarrel itself is unimportant but Goncharov's personal history does throw an oblique light on Turgenev's position in Russian letters, and also on Tolstoy's, at this time. Goncharov was not an aristocrat: his family came from the laborious merchant class—they had been in the grain and candle-making trades and certainly produced men of intelligence and, as his first novel, *A Simple Story*, shows, he came under Romantic influences close to those that affected all his generation. The family came from Simbirsk, a town which was a byword for sleepiness. They rose by diligence, but a diligence so applied that it left Goncharov with a deep melancholia and reserve beneath the hard, ironical surface of his character. The hard-working Goncharov had a core of lethargy in his nature which indeed enabled him to create the beatifically idle Oblomov of his great novel and above all the blessed somnolence of the most deeply Russian part of it: "Oblomov's Dream." Goncharov admired the aristocratic ease of Turgenev, the grace of manners, the taste, the critical excellence and tact of his writings: he himself wrote slowly, awkwardly, lost himself in inward divagations: it took him years to write a single novel and this was not entirely due to having to earn his living as a civil servant. The tedious necessity of the desk was a source of pride and he told Turgenev: "you slide through life superficially . . . I plough a deep furrow," and envied him his education, his talent, his income of ten thousand roubles, and freedom and "earthly paradise beside a beloved woman"—the paradise above all; he envied Turgenev's freedom to travel if he liked to the sun of Europe, whereas he had to sit at a desk in the gloom, fog and cold winds of Petersburg, like one of Gogol's poor clerks and indeed felt obliged to accept the ungrateful task of Chief Censor when the liberal reforms came in during the sixties.

Goncharov's view of Turgenev as an effete and fashionable figure and his resentment of Turgenev's life abroad was shared by some circles in Petersburg; but it is characteristic of Goncharov's deep personal malady that, after the quarrel, he craved to do small services for Turgenev. One sees a similar split in Dostoevsky's attitude to Turgenev. The tragic irony is that, in *Oblomov*, he had created a comic character on a scale far greater than anything within Turgenev's powers, a figure at once Russian and universal. *Oblomov* is one of the finest, most generous, broken monuments in Russian fiction. The strange thing is that where Goncharov failed in *Oblomov* was in its long and tedious love story in which (one is inclined to say), *he* was trying, and failing, to copy Turgenev. There is further irony in the fact that *Oblomov* satisfied the committed critics who saw the novel as an attack on Russian landlordism, when its greatness arises from the active Goncharov's buried craving for inertia as a quality almost saintly.

If Turgenev quarrelled in Petersburg, at Spasskoye he worked. After the failure of *On the Eve*, he turned to his past and produced a masterpiece in the art most natural to him, the story that runs to a hundred pages. The story is *First Love*, the tale, which he said was autobiographical, of a father and his sixteen-year-old son who are in love with the same young girl. It was the story that shocked Countess Lambert. It also shocked Louis Viardot when he read it in translation in the *Revue des Deux Mondes*. Viardot, the older man and husband, wrote sternly as friend to friend, that it was nothing but a glorification of adultery à la *Dame Aux Camélias* and that Turgenev was drifting into the sewer of the modern novel. The characters of the dirty, snuff-taking Princess and her daughter were odious. How could the father in the story be charming and adorable when he had cynically married a rich woman in order to spend her fortune on his mistresses? Why not, at the very least, make him a widower —the censor had made a similar complaint years before when he rejected *A Month in the Country*. Worst of all, Viardot said, the narrator is a man of forty who ought to have known better than to expose the vices of his father. This letter gives us one of those rare sights of the remote Louis Viardot who struck people as being an outsider in his own family and who indeed is known to have complained to his wife that the manner in which she left him out of the conversation with her famous friends at Courtavenel was causing gossip. He begged her to restrain herself. The respectable atheist and Republican enjoyed an extremely indecent piece of *gauloiserie* so long as it had the blessing of history and concerned the vices of Kings and Courts, but he held sternly to the morality of the middle class.

The story and its intention are, of course, quite unlike Louis Viardot's caricature of it which can only have sprung from the anger of a good man who had had to endure the insinuations conventionally made about an elderly husband married to a famous young wife. The story is a study of the devastating loss of innocence and the revelation of the nature of adult passion and, as usual in Turgenev's stories, it turns on the growth of knowledge of the heart. Love is not the simple yet tormenting rapture of a touching adolescent; it is a violent, awe-inspiring passion which leaves its trail of jealousies and guilt. There was some truth in the criticism that Turgenev's love stories have something of the emblem or fairy tale in them, but *First Love*, like the later *Torrents of Spring* and the love story in *Smoke*, contains one of his rare statements about the nature of physical passion—rare because of his own romantic idealism or the conventions of the time. There is no pressing on the pedal in the powerful scenes: they are quiet. Truthtelling—quite different from the highly coloured naturalism which Louis Viardot had read into the story—rules every turn of feeling. The boy sees his father at night talking to a woman at the open window of a house. She is Zinaida with whom the boy is in love. She is refusing the father something:

My father gave a shrug of his shoulders, and set his hat straight on his head, which with him was always a sign of impatience . . . then I could hear the words "Vous devez vous séparer de cette . . ." Zinaida straightened herself and held out her hand. Then something unbelievable took place before my eyes. My father suddenly lifted his riding-crop, with which he had been flicking the dust off the folds of his coat, and I heard the sound of a sharp blow struck across her arm which was bared to the elbow. It was all I could do to prevent myself from crying out. Zinaida quivered—looked silently at my father—and rais-

ing her arm slowly to her lips, kissed the scar which glowed crimson
upon it.

And the boy goes home thinking "That is love, that's passion
. . . But how could one bear to be struck by any hand, however dear
- and yet it seems one can if one is in love."

My father flung away the crop and bounding quickly up the steps to
the porch, broke into the house. Zinaida turned round, stretched out
her arms, tossed her head back—and also moved away from the
window.

That is the climax of a story which has passed through the
comic antics of Zinaida's admirers. We have seen various kinds of
love. We have seen feelings change into their opposite. The boy's
startled jealousy of his father is violent, then absurd, then turns to
admiration amounting to worship, and then is quietly dissolved in
the events of ordinary life. What is sometimes called leisurely in
Turgenev is not so much a sense of timelessness as one of space in
which everything will eventually be accounted for or vanish. Life is
affirmed not only in its intense moments but in its continuing: the
fact that the boy cannot know all, that indeed no one knows all,
gives Turgenev's realism its essential truth-telling quality. In this
his realism is finer than Tolstoy's assertion of all knowledge. The
story goes on:

Two months later I entered the University, and six months after that
my father died (as the result of a stroke) in St. Petersburg, where he
had only just moved with my mother and me. Several days before his
death he had received a letter from Moscow which upset him greatly.
He went to beg some sort of favour of my mother and, so they told
me, actually broke down and wept—he, my father! On the morning
of the very day on which he had the stroke he had begun a letter to
me, written in French. "My son," he wrote, "beware the love of
women; beware of that ecstasy, that slow poison." My mother, after
his death, sent a considerable sum of money to Moscow.

But, for Turgenev, explanation is not an end. Life is not enclosed
reminiscence:

During the past month I had suddenly grown much older, and my love, with all its violent excitements and its torments now seemed even to me so very puny and childish and pitiful beside that other unknown something which I could hardly begin to guess at, but which struck terror into me like an unfamiliar, beautiful, but awe-inspiring face whose features one strains in vain to discern in the gathering darkness.

And now the story becomes still more spacious than its observed drama. Years ripple on, "everything melts away like wax in the sun . . . like snow" and the writer hears of Zinaida's death in childbirth. "So that was the final goal to which this young life, all glitter and ardour and excitement went hurrying along." What had he left now, in old age, fresher and dearer than his memory of "that brief storm that came and went so swiftly one morning in the spring?" Far more than this personal memory of love and death. He recalls that some days after he heard of Zinaida's death, obeying an irresistible impulse he was present at the death of a poor old woman who had known nothing but bitter struggle with daily want and had had no joy or happiness—wouldn't she be glad to die? No, she feared death and fought it and kept whispering "Lord forgive my sins." We are brought back to Zinaida's, his father's and his own desire for life:

by the death-bed of that poor old woman, I grew afraid, afraid for Zinaida, and I wanted to say a prayer for her, my father—and for myself.

This is Louis Viardot's vulgar story of adultery! A story that begins as a comedy of intrigue and becomes a tragedy that disperses us into the common lot! We recall Turgenev's quotation from Pascal:

Le dernier acte est sanglant, quelque soit la comédie en tout le reste. On jette enfin de la terre sur la tête.

The quarrel with Goncharov opened a period of quarrels in Turgenev's life which became a storm when his next and finest novel, *Fathers and Sons,* was published. Before that, in 1860 and 1861, Turgenev was travelling in Europe. He was in Soden near Coblenz with Tolstoy's brother Nikolai, a delightful companion. Turgenev remarked:

> The humility Leo Tolstoy developed theoretically, his brother actually practised in real life. He always lived in the most impossible lodgings, almost hovels . . . and shared all he had with the poorest outcasts.

In Soden Nikolai was slowly dying of tuberculosis and wrote to Leo that Turgenev was with him

> so well that he confesses that he is "quite well." He has found some German girl and goes into ecstasies about her. We (this relates to our dearest Turgenev) play chess together but somehow it does not go as it should: he is thinking of his German girl and I of my cure.

The poor man died at Hyères in the autumn of 1860. The relations between Tolstoy and Turgenev continued to be in flux. Tolstoy admired *Faust*, thought *Acia* rubbish and, contrary to most critics, thought *On the Eve* was much better than *The House of Gentlefolk*. Tolstoy's judgment is erratic—he thought the awful painter Shabin "an excellent negative character."

> The rest are not types, even their conception, their position is not typical . . . The girl is hopelessly bad. "Ah how I love thee . . . her eyelashes were long" . . . It always surprises me that Turgenev with his mental powers and poetic sensibility should even in his methods not be able to refrain from banality. There is no humanity or sympathy for the characters, but the author exhibits monsters whom he scolds but does not pity. This jars painfully with the tone and intention of liberalism in everything else.

Turgenev wrote in a droll verse letter to their common friend Fet:

> Indeed I know he bears me little love
> And I love him as little. Too differently
> Are mixed those elements of which we're formed.

After his brother's death, Tolstoy was in more sympathetic mood. He and Turgenev were fairly near neighbours in Russia, as Russian distances go, and Tolstoy came to Spasskoye on a visit with their friend Fet in 1862. The meeting was amiable. Turgenev had just finished *Fathers and Sons* and gave it to Tolstoy to look at. He lay on Spasskoye's famous divan in the drawing-room, began to read and fell asleep over it. Ominous. Tolstoy woke up to see Turgenev's back impatiently disappearing through the doorway.

The two set off, nevertheless, to stay with Fet. Turgenev loved good food. Champagne flowed. After the meal, Tolstoy, Fet and Turgenev went for a walk and lay down in the grass talking with abandon. The next morning they came down to breakfast, with Mme. Fet seated before the samovar. Disaster. Kind Mme. Fet asked Turgenev whether he was satisfied with the English governess he had found for Paulinette. It seemed a comfortable question, even though it may have raised in Turgenev's mind the trouble the girl had been in the Viardot family, and the bother he had had in finding a flat for her and a governess in Paris. Turgenev took the question easily and said the governess was excellent, though she had of course the English mania for liking things to be clear and exact. She had asked Turgenev what precise sum the now eighteen-year-old girl ought to give to charity. Turgenev went on:

And now she requires my daughter to take in hand and mend the tattered clothes of the poor.

Tolstoy bristled at once: he saw an opportunity of attacking Turgenev's belief in a foreign education.

"And you consider that good?"
"Certainly it places the doer of charity in touch with every day needs."
"And I consider," Tolstoy exclaimed, "that a well-dressed girl with dirty rags on her lap is acting an insincere and theatrical farce."
"I beg you not to say that," said Turgenev. "Why should I not say what I am convinced is true," replied Tolstoy.

Once more the idea of "conviction" haunts every Russian quarrel of the period; no one has opinions. They have absolute convictions.

"Then you consider I educate my daughter badly?" Tolstoy said he did. Turgenev jumped up from the table, white with rage, and exclaimed, "If you speak in that way I will punch your head," and rushed into the next room. A second later he rushed back and said to Mme. Fet: "Please excuse my improper conduct which I deeply regret," and once more left the room.

Turgenev had the habit of pacing in and out of rooms when he was agitated. The gentle man's passions flared up though he would repent very quickly. The uncharacteristic thing was the threat of any physical violence: the champagne of the previous evening must have been too lavish, but of course Tolstoy—who had himself fathered an illegitimate child—had aimed precisely at Turgenev's guilt and his difficulties with the girl and also at his dignity and his virtue. Turgenev had been determined to turn Paulinette into a nice French girl, for he knew that in Russia she would be open to slights and unhappiness, even though his long absences from her showed him to be a negligent father.

The two men left the house in a temper and the quarrel became a farce. It was simple for Turgenev to stalk out because he had a carriage. Tolstoy had no carriage and Fet could not lend him the only carriage he had because he only had horses that had not yet been broken in. Tolstoy had to hire a conveyance at the nearest post station. At the first country house he reached, Tolstoy wrote to demand an apology from Turgenev and told him to send it to the post house at Boguslav where it would be picked up. The dust of the country roads blew up around the quarrel. Turgenev replied in the formal tones of an elder statesman raising a minor point in a Treaty. He said that manners had required him to apologise first to Mme. Fet but not to her guest. The point being made, he now proceeded to a majestic apology: he confessed to the insult—though in fact Tolstoy had insulted *him*—and even asked pardon.

> What happened this morning proved clearly that attempts at intimacy between opposite natures as yours and mine can lead to no good results,

and had the honour to remain, Gracious Sir, your most humble servant. Alas, with typical incompetence, he forgot to send the document to Boguslav, but had it delivered by messenger to Fet's house so that the message arrived very late. Tolstoy was not satisfied. He went to Boguslav for pistols and issued a challenge, adding the sneer that he meant "a real fight and not the sort of formality with champagne to follow, usual in military circles."

Turgenev answered that he did not see what more he could add and that he would willingly stand his fire in order to efface "My truly insane words." Tolstoy, he said, had a perfect right to call him out. The comings and goings of carriages, messengers and horses enlivened the country roads. Fortunately the weather was good. The unhappy Fet tried to bring the two men together but Tolstoy now turned on Fet and said he would return any further letters from him unopened.

Then, of course, after four months Tolstoy made one of his familiar somersaults into repentance. He wrote to Turgenev saying:

> I have insulted you: forgive. I find it unendurably hard to think I have an enemy.

But once more the natural inertia of Russian life spoiled the effect. More letters seemed to have miscarried than to have arrived. Turgenev went off to France and, not knowing his address, Tolstoy sent his own letter to a bookseller in Petersburg asking him to forward it and it took more than three months to get into Turgenev's hands.

This led to a new twist to a quarrel which was turning into a short novel, with Dostoevskian overtones. Passing through Petersburg, Turgenev wrote to Fet:

> I learned from certain "reliable people"—oh those reliable people!— that copies of Tolstoy's last letter (the letter in which he says he despises me), are circulating in Moscow and are said to have been distributed by Tolstoy himself. That enraged me and I sent him a challenge to fight when I return to Russia. Tolstoy has answered that the circulation of the copies is pure invention and he enclosed another letter in which, recapitulating that and how I insulted him, he asks my forgiveness and declines my challenge.

When he at last received Tolstoy's letter through the bookseller, Turgenev wrote again to Fet that obviously the stars of Turgenev and Tolstoy were not in conjunction:

> But you may write and tell him that I (without phrase or joke), love him very much from afar, respect him and watch his fate with sympathetic interest . . . we must live as though we inhabited different planets or different countries.

When he heard about it, Turgenev's genial friend Botkin's opinion was that Tolstoy, the younger man, wanted to love Turgenev ardently and unfortunately his impulsive feeling encountered merely mild good-natured indifference. His mind was in a chaos. Turgenev's was not.

Chapter 9

THE attacks on Turgenev by Goncharov and Tolstoy were personal attacks on his honour and dignity as a man; he was by nature excitable but his irony and judgment soon restored his balance. In the next few years he found himself in the middle of a quarrel with Russia itself, both with the educated élite of Right and Left and with young men of humbler class who had become vocal after the Crimean War. Confusion and extremism appeared on the scene and he was at once in the difficult position of the man of strong, committed liberal principles who has to meet the usual charges of being a waverer.

He was in Paris in 1861, because he was concerned about his daughter who wanted to get married but could not make up her mind about her suitors, when the Emancipation of the serfs was proclaimed and he went to the Thanksgiving Service at the Russian Church and, like many others, wept with joy. Herzen, the exile who could not return, told him that the author of *The Sportsman's Sketches* ought to be in Russia. Turgenev had, however, settled matters with his own peasants before the proclamation. He had given them a fifth of his land for nothing and at Spasskoye itself—the most intimate part of his estate and his home—he had given them the land on which their houses stood, and was soon building a small hospital, a home for the aged and had started a school.

All over Russia the peasants were bewildered by their freedom and often suspicious of the new dispensation. Many preferred the old ways to which they were accustomed. At Spasskoye they continued their traditional sport of stealing wood and, knowing Turgenev was an easy man, they grazed their horses on his flower beds. Elsewhere there were rows about the size of individual holdings and the redemption money. There were family rows between husbands and wives, and between brothers. The peasants were illiterate and often refused to put their mark on legal papers. They found they had to pay taxes and many regarded Emancipation as a landlord's trick—and among the bad landlords so it became. Many peasants sold their strips and left the land and there were not enough hands left to get in the harvest. Presently in Petersburg there were outbreaks of fire which were thought to be the work of terrorists belonging to the Land and Liberty League who, without any clear idea of policy, were calling for Revolution. The new Tsar had begun as a liberal but was now in panic; Radicals were arrested and sent into exile.

These events are in the background of the new novel Turgenev had written, *Fathers and Sons*, the tragedy of the conflict between two generations. The book set off a storm that was to last the rest of his life. It is his masterpiece. To foreign readers the savagery of the quarrel has seemed incomprehensible until recent times. In his brilliant Romanes Lectures given in Oxford in 1970—by far the most illuminating exposition we have of Turgenev's growth and achievement as a novelist—Sir Isaiah Berlin adds an important corrective to our judgement. A book like *Fathers and Sons*, he points out, no longer seems happily remote to us in the violent conditions of our own times. His characters are not delightful Russian incurables but are now present and recognisable, now revolutionary change occurs everywhere in our own world. Turgenev was not withdrawn from disturbing realities; he was apolitical in the party sense, but he had his own commitment and could not resist his fascination with what frightened him or the duty he felt the artist had to observe and understand the types he saw dramatically opposed in his country.

The storm caused by his novel arose out of his portrait of "its tragic hero": Bazarov. The Radicals thought it a libel on the younger generation who called for revolution or reform; the Conservatives accused him of siding with the enemies of order. In his *Reminis-*

cences, Turgenev is enlightening on the origins of the character and especially on his methods. Once more he says:

> I have heard it said . . . not once but many times that in my works I always "started with an idea or developed an idea" . . . I never attempted "to create a character" unless I had as my starting point not an idea but a living person to whom the appropriate elements were later on gradually attached and added. Not possessing a great amount of free inventive power, I always felt the need of some firm ground on which I could plant my feet.

He goes on to say that the basis of Bazarov was a young provincial doctor he had met in a train. The man had since died. The impression was still vague but in that man

> I could watch the embodiment of the principle which had scarcely come to life but was just beginning to stir at the time which later received the name of "nihilism."

It is an oddity of social history that well-off Russians were in the habit of going to Ventnor in the Isle of Wight for the sea-bathing. Turgenev went there and there was talk of a "new Russian type"— someone said he would be Rudin reborn. Walking alone on the beach, the novelist told them that he had had a sudden vision of a dead man: Bazarov must be tragic. But the sources of a novelist's characters are not only parts of new persons suddenly met, but go back also to literature and literary experience. Some said that in Bazarov, Turgenev had put something of the young Radical critic Dobrolyubov who had been outrageously rude to him. Turgenev denied this, but Bazarov is famous for his rudeness—and Sir Isaiah Berlin points to the possibility of Belinsky as a source of Bazarov's brusqueness, directness, his explosions of sarcasm at hypocrisy and that there may be a link with Dobrolyubov's "ferocious militant, anti-aestheticism." Belinsky died tragically and the gifted Dobrolyubov died tragically young also in 1861 while the novel was being written. The random finality of death was always Turgenev's haunting preoccupation; but the hostile critics took Bazarov's untimely death at the end of the novel as a final attempt by Turgenev to make his "hero" trivial and to punish him for his nihilism.

The moment we open the novel we understand that Turgenev is

not writing the didactic work which both the Left and the Right imagined and called for in the hysteria of the time. His art rests on his ability to unself himself and to become the people he writes about. He observes and listens so that they appear to us clearly, untrammelled and living, as human beings do, in their own effortless justification. This, we say, is what they felt themselves naturally to be in the times they were living in, moving into the days that follow.

As usual the novel was carefully planned in play-like fashion in four long acts, though the scenes run with more intimacy than in his earlier work. They are less story-like and more flowing than in the manner of a European novel. In the first act we see Arkady Kirsanov, a student who has just graduated, arriving at his father's small property in the country. He brings with him his idol and friend, young Bazarov, who is coming to the end of his medical training and who is on the way to visit his own much poorer parents, fifty miles or more further on. The elder Kirsanov's property has 100 serfs—or as Nikolai Kirsanov prefers to say, for he is an enlightened man—5,000 acres. The year is 1859. He has anticipated the Emancipation by putting his peasants on the quit-rent system and is having endless trouble with them. They are suspicious. They steal, they break his machines through incompetence. Nikolai is a warm, tender, unpractical man, a reader of the classics and a liberal of good family, but short of money and easily swindled. He is also a widower and is embarrassed to admit to his son that while the boy was away at the University he has taken an innkeeper's daughter called Fenichka to live with him and that she has lately given birth to their child. Arkady tells his father that he and his friend Bazarov are above out-of-date prejudices about marriage, so father and son are on shy good terms at once. Nikolai shares the house with his brother Pavel, once a Guards officer, very much the Petersburg aristocrat and dandy who wears high, marble-white collars, a man of culture who affects stiff English manners. He had been famous for a long love affair with a Princess who had "enigmatic" eyes. She had died and Pavel had given up his life in society, travelled to all the fashionable resorts and had come at last to live in correct and austere melancholy with his brother. At sight, Pavel takes against Bazarov, Arkady's lower-class "long-haired" friend. And this first act is mostly about their growing enmity. "This Bazarov. What is he?" Pavel asks Arkady about his friend.

He is a nihilist, Arkady says. A nihilist is a man who doesn't take any principle for granted.

> "Indeed," [says Pavel]. "Well I can see this is not our cup of tea. We of the older generation think that without principles" (Pavel Petrovich pronounced the word as if it were French, whereas Arkady put the stress on the first syllable)—"without principles taken as you say on trust one cannot move an inch or draw a single breath. *Vous avez changé tout cela,* may God grant you health and a general's rank, but we shall be content to look on and admire Messieurs les . . . what was it?"
> "Nihilists," said Arkady, speaking very distinctly.
> "Yes. It used to be Hegelians, and now there are nihilists. We shall see how you manage to exist in a void, in an airless vacuum; and now please ring the bell, brother Nikolai, it is time for me to drink my cocoa."

When Pavel forces Bazarov into the argument, Bazarov is off-hand and says he has no interest in anything outside of physics and the natural sciences. A decent chemist is twenty times more useful than a poet like Schiller or Goethe, the gods of Pavel's generation. Pavel says:

> "I take it you do not acknowledge art then?"
> "The art of making money or of advertising pills for piles!" exclaimed Bazarov with a contemptuous laugh.
> ". . . So you reject all that? Very well. So you only believe in science?"
> "I have already explained to you I don't believe in anything: and what is science—science in the abstract? There are sciences, as there are trades and professions, but Abstract science just doesn't exist."

For Pavel, Bazarov is an impudent barbarian; for Bazarov, Pavel is a ridiculous aristocrat. His fame as the unhappy pursuer of the Princess, who has anyway been long dead, is pathetic.

> ". . . a fellow who has staked his whole life on the one card of a woman's love, and when that card fails, turns sour and lets himself go till he's fit for nothing, is not a man, is not a male creature . . . And what are these mysterious relations between a man and a woman? We physiologists know what they are."

147

Pavel had been taken by the "enigmatic" eyes of the Princess.

> "You study the anatomy of the eye; and where does that enigmatic look you talk about come in? That's all romantic rot, mouldy aesthetics."

As for kindly old Nikolai Kirsanov's love of nature. Bazarov says:

> "Nature is not a temple, it is a workshop and man is the workman in it."

These sarcasms lead at last to a grand quarrel in which Arkady and Bazarov are on one side and Pavel on the other. Bazarov says that it is useless to go on talking about Russia and social disease. Reformers never do anything. All they talk about is art and parliaments when the important question is getting enough to eat. Russia is stifled by superstition, industry is a mess because the people at the top aren't honest. Nothing is likely to come out of this talk about emancipating the serf; the peasants will simply rob one another and drink themselves silly. And so, says Pavel:

> "[You] decided not to do anything serious yourselves."
> "And decided not to do anything serious," Bazarov repeated grimly. He suddenly felt vexed with himself for having spoken so freely in front of this member of the upper class.
> "But to confine yourself to abuse."
> "To confine ourselves to abuse."
> "And that is called nihilism?"
> "And that is called nihilism," Bazarov repeated again, this time with marked insolence.
> . . . .
> "We destroy because we are a force," remarked Arkady . . . . "Yes, a force, and therefore not accountable to anyone."

To which Pavel Kirsanov replies frostily that he might as well say that the wild Kalmuk or the Mongols are a force. He and the aristocracy believe in principles and civilisation and all its fruits. The proper home for Arkady and Bazarov is a Kalmuk tent.

In the second act Bazarov and Arkady leave the idyllic estate on which they have annoyed everybody and Turgenev now turns first to farce. The young men go to the provincial capital and call on a ridiculous "advanced" young woman, Yevdoxia Kukshin, and an absurd, brash young climber, Sitnikov, who is the son of a spirit merchant and ashamed of it. Yevdoxia seems to live on champagne and cigarettes. Her room is littered with books and papers and her talk is an inconsequent litter of headlong ideas.

> "Are you interested in chemistry? That is my passion. I have even invented a new sort of mastic myself." . . . To make dolls' heads so they can't break . . . I have still got to read Liebig. Have you seen Kislyakov's article on female labour in the *Moscow News?* Do read it. You are interested in women's emancipation, I suppose. And in the schools' problem too?"

How out of date George Sand is; not to be compared to Emerson, knows nothing of physiology and hasn't even heard of embryology and in these days how can one get on without that?

Farce turns to the comedy of provincial manners when the two young men escape to the Ball the visiting panjandrum is giving. We see the grand man's struttings and snubbings. But the note changes when a beautiful and rich widow invites the young men to stay at her mansion. Bazarov, who has mocked Pavel Kirsanov for his fatal love of his "enigmatic" Princess, finds himself snared into what he despises: romantic love for a cold, intelligent, rich woman who talks well and who is drawn to Bazarov's rebellious ideas.

> Bazarov was a pursuer of women but had no time for ideal or romantic love which he regarded as an aberration: If a woman takes your fancy, he would say, "try to gain your end and if you don't succeed—well don't bother; there are plenty more good fish in the sea." Mme. Odintsov appealed to him; the rumours about her, the freedom and independence of her ideas, her unmistakable liking for him—all seemed to be in his favour; but he soon discovered that he would not "gain his end," and as for turning his back on her, he found, to his own bewilderment, that it was more than he could do. His blood took fire the moment he thought of her; he could easily have mastered his blood but something else was taking possession of him . . . when he was alone he recognized with indignation a romantic strain in himself.

To rid himself of it he decides to leave and when she hears this she tries to stop him. In one last dangerous tack Bazarov cannot control himself. She is apparently tempting him too far and he angrily blurts out that he loves her and tries to embrace her. Madame Odintsov is astonished and physically frightened. She is not a conscious flirt: she is used to power and ease—her house runs like clockwork—and for her the relationship has been one of intellectual curiosity with a pleasant element of mild emotional flutter in it. She "believes" in his gifts and that he may become a "great man" but she would certainly not love him, a poor young man outside her own class. Bazarov sees he has made a fool of himself only too clearly and leaves. He returns to Arkady's house to pick up his luggage and his medical books and goes on to stay, as he originally intended, with his own parents. Arkady goes with him.

In the next act the two young men are seen there. The parents' place is a small farm of a hundred acres and one serf. His father, an old army doctor, and his adoring mother greet the young men with touching, overwhelming love; indeed it suffocates Bazarov and although they try to leave him alone to work they cannot bear it. They tiptoe from room to room longing to be with him. These are the most touching portraits in a book in which the conflict between the generations is most felt. The young men decide to leave but promise to come back. The parents cannot understand what they have done to offend their son as he prepares to go.

> From early morning the house was filled with depression: the plate fell out of Anfisushka's hands; even Fedka [the servant] did not know what he was doing and ended by taking off his boots.

He had worn boots especially in honour of the two young men.

> . . . when Bazarov, after repeated promises to come back within a month at the latest, at last tore himself from [his parents'] clinging embraces and took his seat in the tarantass; when the horses moved off, the bells tinkled, and the wheels spun round—when there was nothing left to gaze after, the dust had settled and Timofeich, all bent and tottering, had crept back to his tiny room; when the two old people found themselves alone in the house, which suddenly seemed as shrunken and decrepit as they—then Vassily Ivanych, who a few moments before had been vigorously waving his handkerchief on the

steps, slumped into a chair and let his head drop on his chest.
"He has gone, left us!" he faltered. "Gone, because he found it dull
here with us. I'm a lonely man now, lonely as this finger," he repeated
again and again, and each time he thrust out his hand with his
forefinger pointing away from the rest.

Bazarov and Arkady return to the Kirsanovs. There is a watchful
truce between Bazarov and Pavel Petrovich. Pavel even shows polite
curiosity about Bazarov's microscope. But Bazarov is morose and he
eventually tries to rid himself of Madame Odintsov's image by
recovering his audacity with women. He sets out to see if the simple
Fenichka is vulnerable. Once more the test of love appears in the
story. Fenichka is an ingenuous young mother; Bazarov puts her at
her ease. The only person she fears is Pavel Petrovich who keeps an
eye on her. In fact, the old aristocrat sees something of his own lost
Madame Odintsov, the Princess, in the blooming face of the young
mother and his gazes are almost but not quite innocent; he longs for
the impossible return of youth, the wild youth which Bazarov has
and he guesses what Bazarov is up to. One day he sees and hears
Bazarov making up to Fenichka, who is confused and does not know
what to do when Bazarov suddenly kisses her. The opportunity for
revenge has arrived for Pavel.

In a splendid, icy, formal scene he challenges Bazarov to a duel.
Bazarov of course regards this as farcical, but the very pointlessness,
the destructive aspect, makes him accept at once. He'll certainly
stand up to a gentleman. (Turgenev the sportsman is excellent in
duel scenes: he has one very good short story on the subject and
knows that duels conceal an underlying attraction between the parties.) This one satirises the formalities and is comical. Bazarov
wounds Pavel, who falls and behaves with polite sang-froid and is
obliged to let Bazarov attend to his wound. Pavel eventually recovers
and realises he has acted a good deal out of snobbery. The fact is
that Turgenev is preparing, once more, a test of love for his characters: Pavel tells his brother and Fenichka that if they love each other
they must marry. They overcome their nervous shyness—they were
afraid of Pavel's authority.

In the final act, Bazarov packs up once more and while he does
so he tells Arkady that their friendship is over. Not because of the
trouble he has caused but because Arkady, he says, has changed.

Arkady, who had also been sentimentally in love with Madame Odintsov, has been drawn to her younger sister whom she has dominated in her regal way. In this Turgenev shows his subtlety in showing the two sisters in another light. Madame Odintsov's idle, exalté mind veils a managing, possessive nature. Bazarov sees that Arkady has been clear-headed in love when he himself is still suffering from the romantic disease and has failed. He is not rancorous but he tells Arkady that in accepting the conventions of marriage he has lost the Nihilist spirit.

> "There's no audacity in you; no venom . . . Your sort, the gentry, can never go farther than well-bred resignation and that's futile . . . you won't stand up and fight . . . you enjoy finding fault with yourself; but we've had enough of all that—give us fresh victims! We must smash people!

Bazarov returns to his parents. This is the moving finale of the novel. The old people realise that their son has changed and dare not ask him what is on his mind. They are relieved when they see him taking an interest in helping his father in doctoring the peasants from time to time. The father listens with admiration to his son's talk of new knowledge in medicine. The doting mother restrains her effusive love and is in awe of him. But an accident occurs. Bazarov goes off to perform an autopsy on a peasant who has died of typhus and in doing so makes a small cut in his finger. He comes back asking for silver nitrate. There is none in this backward part of the country and Bazarov understands—and so does his father—that he is a dead man if he has caught the infection.

The scene of Bazarov's death is famous. It is one of the most moving and beautifully observed things that the great observer ever wrote—Chekhov admired it as a doctor and as an artist who himself was a master of recording human sorrow. The power of this narrative owes something to the hypochondria and sense of the presence of death which Turgenev felt so continuously in his own life; and in this the writing is one of those cleansings which a great artist achieves in his maturity. If the death, by such a small misadventure, may strike one as trivial and therefore not tragic—the point made by hostile critics—it has its own ironic logic: for Bazarov the Nihilist cannot object to accident or the random hostility of nature. When the death occurs, Turgenev writes, the experience of life on earth is not altogether in our hands. The last lines that describe the visit of the parents to Bazarov's grave are devastating:

> Vassily Ivanych was seized by a sudden frenzy. "I said I would rebel," he shouted hoarsely, his face inflamed and distorted, waving his clenched fist in the air as though threatening someone—"And I will rebel, I will!" But Arina Vlassyevna, suffused in tears, hung her arms round his neck and both fell prone together. "And so," as Anfisushka related afterwards in the servants' rooms, "side by side they bowed their poor heads like lambs in the heat of noonday . . . "

In the years that follow, the two frail old people support each other as they walk, year after year, to the cemetery, kneel at their son's grave, yearning over the silent stone.

The storm caused by *Fathers and Sons* was violent and went on rumbling for years. The Right did not enjoy the ironical portrait of Pavel Kirsanov and Turgenev's tolerance of Bazarov. The word "nihilist" had caught on—very much as the idea of "the superfluous man" had done years before—and the Radicals thought the portrait of Bazarov a libel on the young generation and their views. Bazarov is indeed silent on what he and his friends would do once the task of destruction was done; whereas those among the Nihilists who did think about this had a belief in some kind of Populist democracy which was too vague to become an effective Cause. Turgenev was in the impossible situation of being an apolitical man, a detached diagnostician in a period when the politically minded called for polemic and propaganda. Turgenev made matters worse by his comments. To the Conservative Countess Lambert he wrote:

> The convictions of my youth have not changed. But I never have been and never will be occupied with politics. It is alien and uninteresting to me. I pay attention to politics only in so far as a writer who is called upon to depict contemporary life must. You do wrong to demand from me in literature what I cannot give—fruits that do not grow on my tree. I have never *written for the people* . . . I have written for that class of the public to which I belong.

To others he wrote that he found himself agreeing with most of the views of Bazarov, excepts his views on art and literature. That sounds harmless enough but it was damaging, for under Russian despotism, with political discussion subject to censorship, art and literature had a peculiar covert political prestige. All literature was judged—as it continues to be in Russia today—by its social "tendency." But for Turgenev, as Sir Isaiah Berlin says, "acts, ideas, art, literature were expressions of individuals, not of objective forces of which the actors or thinkers were merely the embodiments. The reduction of men to the function of being primarily carriers or agents were as deeply repellent to Turgenev as it had been to Herzen or, in his later phase, to his revered friend Belinsky."

Politically Bazarov was not a revolutionary but a pre-Revolutionary; a type thrown up by a period which seemed "on the eve" of perhaps violent change: the peasantry were 80 percent of the population of the country. Bazarov thought them stupid. Two objections to him have some point: first, he was not, in the Nihilist sense, a true type, for he was not really an urban figure—as the active politicals inevitably were. Secondly, his ruling interest was not in politics but in natural science. Had he been a writer he could have been prophetic of Chekhov who, as a doctor, also stood outside the philosophical and literary influences which had formed the main stream of Russian novelists—including Turgenev himself.

The only weakness of the novel—it seems to me—is in the chapter on the visit to Madame Odintsov. It has some of that over-scented claustrophobic sentimentality into which Turgenev sometimes falls. She is the standard dissatisfied rich woman, but there is an embarrassing lushness in his writing when he tries to probe her mind:

> Sometimes, emerging all warm and languorous from a fragrant bath, she would fall to musing on the futility of life, its sorrow and toil and cruelty . . . Like all women who have not succeeded in falling in love she hankered after something without knowing what it was. In reality there was nothing she wanted, though it seemed to her that she wanted everything.

It is not hard to believe that Bazarov would feel the angry sensations of lust in her presence, but that he could have endured all those long, educative walks in the woods and the solemn conversations in her drawing-room is hard to believe, although we take the ironic point. We suspect Turgenev of one of his bouts of self-castigation for the long drawn out "ideal" love for Pauline Viardot and his chats with Countess Lambert, and that here the book suffers from the blur of autobiography unassimilated.

Of course there were critics who defended Turgenev, even among the political young; but the attacks wounded him deeply. He had been looked upon as a leader by the young of his generation, now the new generation of young people despised him. They were indeed supplanted in their turn but for one who drew so much from the springs of youth as he did and who regretted the loss of his youth so bitterly—as the early pose of precocious old age shows—the blow was terrible. The effects lasted into his real old age.

As he had said in *Rudin*, the young require simple answers even if they are illusory. The irony is that Tolstoy and Dostoevsky, who were hostile to radical politics, were treated with respect. The reason —apart from the fact that their range and strength as novelists was far greater—was that they were obsessed men. They had their missions which, in their different ways, were aspects of the feeling that Russia had an untainted Messianic role to play in the world; both had their religion and indeed in Dostoevsky's journalism the idea of mission was politically imperial: the Russian right to Constantinople. Turgenev had no mission: he thought Dostoevsky's large talk of humanity mere rhetoric. Like Pavel Kirsanov, though not in his arthritic way, he stood for "civilisation," spelled out letter by letter, for what had been a long, patient, intricate growth.

———

The philandering friendship with Countess Lambert limped on, despite her disapproval of *Fathers and Sons.* He still annoyed her by playing the man of the world and she annoyed him with her sentimental philistinism.

There was a good deal of talk on his part of how his heart had died and that there was no hope for him but to prepare himself to face the lugubrious facts of mortality. The only thing he or she could do, he said, was to allow themselves to float together hand in hand on the waves of life. She with a firm grip on his hand, one notices, not hers firmly gripped by his. No master steersman he, nor was he very complimentary. "You and I expect so little for ourselves," he said. The Countess, who disapproved of his politics, his books and his lack of religion, was piqued to hear that she would get very little as they floated along.

Floating was very much in his mind. About this time, sick of Russia, he turned to fantasy. For some reason or other the dream he had told Pauline about when he was a young man at Courtavenel came into his mind and he wrote a strange story, *Phantoms.* It can be read as an erotic dream or even as a tour of the futile history of political power in the world; or as a literary experiment by a poetic realist who has felt an impulse towards surrealism, or as a non-mystical venture into the occult. The reader looks for allegory or for images from the unconscious—does it tell one something of the life the rationalist has buried?—but Turgenev said that *Phantoms* was simply a stream of disconnected pictures without allegorical meaning. A woman in white who appears to be spun out of mist seizes the writer, in the familiar way of such erotic dreams, declares she loves him. By unlucky chance Turgenev gave her the English name of Ellis; he may have intended Alice. He feels the touch of her lips—"Leeches might prick so in mild or drowsy mood"—and she bears him away night after night into the sky and they fly over the world into the civilisations of the past. He sees Caesar's Rome, Pompeii, the Russian steppe, Paris, Germany, St. Petersburg in a series of nightmare and splenetic pictures in a grotesque travelogue of terror. The woman cannot reveal who she is except that she is a spirit in limbo craving not to be utterly extinguished until she sees

> a thing bulky, dark, yellow-black, spotted like a lizard's belly, not a storm cloud, not smoke was crawling with a snake-like motion over the earth. A wide rhythmic undulating movement from above downwards and from below upwards, an undulation revealing the malignant sweep of the vulture as it sweeps over its prey; at times an indescribably revolting, grovelling in the earth, as of a spider stooping over its captured fly . . . It was a power moving; that power which there is no resisting, to which all is subject, sightless, shapeless, senseless, sees all, knows all . . . Ellis," I cried. "It is death itself."

If there is the bizarre attraction of meaningless horror, the suggestion of a sexual struggle against extinction in *Phantoms,* it was
followed by *Enough* which might be called a rationalist's Commina-
tion service, a Psalm of despair. Turgenev was noted for saying
"Enough," as if in angered longing for an End of some kind: it
suggests the desire to be done with all that accompanies the bril-
liance of a mind, the force of a desire intellectually before it can be
lived through, the malady of the sentimentalist. It is more obviously
an utterance about the evanescence and futility of life. Nature is
inexorable.

> She knows not art as she knows not freedom as she knows not good.
> . . . Man is her child; but man's work—art—is hostile to her just
> because it strives to be unchanging and immortal . . . [Nature] creates
> in destroying and she cares not whether she creates or she destroys.

Russian critics fell upon *Enough* and though it has a fine sustained and dominant rhythm in which each sentence and phrase
strikes hard as an energetic statement of pessimism, it is altogether
too personal to be effective. Tolstoy made a sensible remark about
it. He said: "The personal and subjective is only good when it is full
of life and passion, while here we have subjectivity full of lifeless
suffering." Turgenev, the spectator, had little gift for bringing his
inner life to the surface. But one understands that he has reached
total despair.

Chapter 10

IN these the gloomiest days of his life surprising news came to him. Pauline Viardot had decided to give her last performances in the great opera houses of London and Paris: she had her last triumphs in Dublin and Paris, but she knew her voice had lost its highest quality. The voice that had ruled as if it were a separate being inside her began to lose its range. Drastic with others, the perfectionist had enslaved and over-strained her voice and coming of a long-headed family with an austere tradition of musical discipline, she was not going to expose herself to fiasco.

Compared with hers, Turgenev's life had not been driven. Her journeys from city to city in Europe in the first decades of the railway age were long and exhausting. She arrived at each place and had to begin daily rehearsals at once. In one year, she gave fifty performances in England. She had lately created the part of Lady Macbeth in Verdi's opera. Her role in *Macbeth* was considered one of her greatest acting parts and not without a meaning irony Turgenev wrote to her saying that if they could play it together in her little theatre at Courtavenel, he would be glad to play the part of Banquo. In 1861 she had given Gluck's *Orpheus* a hundred and twenty-one times. In a letter to the conductor Rietz—quoted by April Fitzlyon —she wrote about learning her parts:

I have the impression I have a little theatre in my head where my little
actors move. Even at night in my sleep my private theatre pursues me
—it becomes unbearable at times.

The Viardots decided to give up Courtavenel, and let the house in
the rue de Douai. Louis Viardot had often been alone there, playing
"mother" to the children. He fumed with hatred of Napoleon III,
his politics and his morals and wanted to get out of Paris. The couple
settled on Baden-Baden as the ideal place for a semi-retirement in
which she could give occasional performances when she wished and
turn to composition and rich pupils.

In choosing Baden-Baden the Viardots showed their acumen.
Pauline had commanded a kingdom of huge applauding audiences;
now she needed a small Court in a place where the élite and fashionable settled and money abounded—in short a Principality. The
Germans had been adept at preserving princelings, grand dukes and
margraves who combined the overfed bourgeois flush with the elegance of royal satiety and ease. The Rhineland was the country of
the *Schloss* with its stagey medieval appeal to the middle-class
century; a spa ministered to the most exclusive of diseases: gout,
rheumatism, paralysis and the stone. A few miles across the Rhine
from Strasbourg and twenty-three miles up the Rhine from Karlsruhe on the main line from Ostend and Brussels, Baden-Baden had
become Europe's and especially the Parisian's summer resort, a
Monte Carlo without need of a Mediterranean. It had its *Schloss*,
indeed it had two. Famous statesmen, great artists in music, the
theatre and painting found the season at Baden-Baden indispensable
to their health and amusement. It was a pretty town, adroitly placed
where nature was a seductive mixture of mountain, forest, decorous
waterfalls and streams. Beyond the little valley that climbed gently
from the orchards of the Rhineland and the hills where the vineyards
stood in peaceable regiments were the tall pines of the Black Forest;
in the sheltered avenues of the town itself were a profusion of
beeches, acacias, chestnuts, willows and firs, all neatly labelled as in
a botanist's paradise. The scene was graceful, instructive and sooth-
ing to the indulgent sentiments of middle age. The cakes were rich
and creamy, the wines light and tender. The little river Oos running
through the gardens from the hills was packed with trout; the mountain lakes (to German fancy), with water sprites. The fountains

---

played, the statues offered their antique suggestions. In the summer and early autumn evenings a lilac haze gave the scene the sweet wilfulness and contentment of a Victorian painting. At appropriate hours one lay in the baths of ionised minerals, drank the water at a Kurhaus, or sat in long rows listening to the orchestra, paraded to see who had arrived and filed into the gambling tables. Whiskered officers pranced on their horses. Ladies and grooms galloped down the Allées. The age of uniforms, clinking spurs and the crinoline had come. The rich built themselves villas in the grey, steep-roofed château style of Louis XIII. When Viardot sold Courtavenel he brought his distinguished collection of pictures as a compliment to the town, and Pauline soon established her Court.

If Turgenev had almost lost touch with Pauline, he was often in correspondence with Louis Viardot, who received moneys for the education and pension of Paulinette, and also about translations. He was helping Viardot to translate *Onegin* into French when he heard of the move to Baden and made this the excuse for a visit. It was very short and difficult. But in 1863 the embarrassment had receded sufficiently for him to be allowed—there can be no other word—to take a flat in the Schillerstrasse not far from the Viardots' house.

Some biographers, including David Magarshack, think that Pauline's softening towards Turgenev was unscrupulous and one does detect here and there in his work that he knew he was being used. She was proposing to publish several albums of Russian songs and she needed the support of his famous name. His figure would be indispensable to her salon. April Fitzlyon more sympathetically suggests that now Pauline had given up the great opera houses she had time for family life and the emotions she had been obliged to subdue as an artist. In the confessional letters, strange in their erotic overtones, Pauline had written to Rietz, the testy father figure to whom she had turned at the time when Turgenev had attached himself to the Countess Lambert, and said outright that she had crushed her heart ruthlessly. She certainly knew at once when she saw Turgenev in Baden and needed him that she could dominate him absolutely whenever she wished. She wanted a small theatre. Turgenev was soon building one of those steep-roofed Louis XIII–style houses for himself, planting its large gardens and building a theatre for her in the grounds.

Why, after all his sufferings, did he return to the Viardots and accept, finally as it turned out, the life of an expatriate? The "empty nest" at Spasskoye knew him now only as an occasional visitor. Was it only because, as he sometimes said, and others said quite seriously too, that Pauline's extraordinary eyes had hypnotised him? Did he inevitably submit to the will of others? She had obviously imposed her will on her husband. Of course, Turgenev loved family life by proxy. Her children were growing up and he loved children although his own child bored him. One does not imagine that she was a woman to forget a wrong or that she would accept any criticism of her own behaviour. She had a tongue and in the Spanish way cherished a jealousy. There is one scene, of which almost nothing is known, which may have been important. He brought his daughter Paulinette for a visit to Baden and Paulinette made a violent attack on Pauline: Turgenev was the witness. If we knew the words that passed we would probably know everything about Pauline and Turgenev's relationship in the past; it would tell us what Pauline must have understood when she heard him silence his daughter and saw her only victory: that such victories are dangerous, even though they are victories at the expense of another woman's child and the child's father. Still it does seem that a warmer reconciliation with Turgenev dates from soon after this time. And that what kept Turgenev out of Russia was a renewal, of what he called an autumnal love on his side and, just possibly, on hers.

That happiness can, of course, be regarded as a danger for him as a writer, for he wrote less when he was with her.

Although his life-long complaint was that he had been obliged to live "on the edge of another man's nest," he had in his early years held the opinion that it was not a good thing for an artist to marry. The artist must serve the Muse, serve her and no one else. "An unhappy marriage may do something for a talent, but a happy one is no good at all." It was a mistake to be absorbed in a feeling for one person alone. And he said that he himself found he could work best in the glow of a casual affair "especially with a married woman who could manage both herself and her passions." He may have taken this attitude because of his mother's domination: it is common for men who have been dominated in that way to shy away especially from women of their own class. It is true that in the long separations from Pauline his talent reached his greatest powers; yet what may have been his spiritual love of her was certainly a marriage at its most exacting. He was very aware of the impoverishing effect of expatriation and his own friends did not stop reminding him of it. But Russia, we must remember, had turned on him, indeed on his greatest book and not only that, threatened him. He had had one unforgettable taste of arrest and exile which had put an end to his happiness when he was a young man.

There was a powerful reason, almost as powerful as love, for keeping out of Russia now. The extreme radical manifestos, the acts of terrorism that followed the emancipation of the serfs and the fact that the conservatives saw Turgenev as sympathetic to the Nihilists, aroused real fears that they might incriminate him. Turgenev knew, as every Russian did, that his freedom of movement was in the hands of the Tsar who could easily find the pretext for sending him into exile once more, even for confiscating his estate. In 1862 Turgenev's Radical opponent, Chernyshevsky, a member of what Herzen called "the bilious set" whose attacks had led to Turgenev's quarrel with *The Contemporary*, was arrested on charges connected with revolutionary socialism and was deported to Siberia, where he remained until 1883. Turgenev was not in the same danger—he had been careful to keep his well-placed aristocratic friends—but he knew how remote from the minds of his countrymen the liberal spirit was: they had been formed for despotism, its paternal thrashings and its Byzantine chicaneries.

A reminder of his own danger had come to Turgenev in 1863. He had gone to London and had visited Herzen, whose brilliant periodical *Kolokol*, or *The Bell*, was still powerful as the voice of dissident Russians abroad. With him was Bakunin, the now dilapidated friend of Turgenev's youth. In 1861, Bakunin, the perpetual revolutionary, had achieved his most romantic coup—he had been in prison then in Siberia when the Austrians handed him over to the Russians in '48. Now, with impertinent ease, he had escaped through Japan and arrived in London via New York, eager for news of revolution. Herzen wrote in *My Past and Thoughts:*

> He had piously preserved all the habits and customs of his fatherland, that is of student-life in Moscow: heaps of tobacco lay on his table like stores of forage, cigar-ash covered his papers, together with half-finished glasses of tea . . . He argued, lectured, made arrangements, shouted, decided, directed, organised and encouraged all day long, all

night long . . . and set to work to write five, ten, fifteen letters to Semipalatinsk and Arad, to Belgrade and Tsargrad, to Bessarabia, Moldavia and Belokrinitsa . . . His activity, his laziness, his appetite, and everything else, like his gigantic statue and the everlasting sweat he was in, everything, in fact, was on a superhuman scale, as he was himself; and he was himself a giant with his leonine head and tousled mane.

At fifty he was still the wandering student, living from day to day, borrowing indiscriminately, throwing other people's money away, giving away his last penny except what he needed for cigarettes and tea. In London he soon got money from Turgenev, who was sorry for the old agitator who had grown up coarse but incurable in his hopes of finding a revolution somewhere. He nevertheless derided Turgenev's views and egged Herzen on to support the Polish insurrection in *The Bell*—a folly as Herzen later admitted. Bakunin was flamboyant as a conspirator and wildly reckless in his correspondence and described the meeting with Turgenev in a letter which was easily picked up by the Russian secret police in Paris and the upshot was that Turgenev was commanded to return to St. Petersburg to be questioned in secret by the Senate. This was alarming and Turgenev wrote a letter to the Tsar protesting that he was a writer with no involvement with politics; but he had to go. He knew one or two of his judges who received him politely: in fact before the first hearing he had gone to a grand soirée given by a Marquis Pepoli who had married a singer. He wrote to Pauline:

And Prince Dolgorouki (listen to this!)the head of all the police in the Empire, one of the most influential people in the government chatted with me for a while; Prince Souvorov (of the Council of State and military government of Petersburg) was charming to me which shows that they don't regard me as a conspirator.

Indeed the fat judge, Venevitinov, once a friend of Pushkin and Gogol, told him the whole affair was a miserable waste of time.

So it turned out. The judges studied the Dossier, asked him one or two questions where his name was mentioned in it and told him he was free to leave Russia whenever he liked, and sympathised with him. He was having one of his first attacks of gout. He went off to arrange for the publication of the first album of Pauline's Russian songs and spent an evening with "kind old Countess Lambert" whose health was improving.

The exasperating aspect of the case was that it took place after an exchange of published letters with Herzen in 1862 in which Turgenev had explained his profound differences with Herzen's ostensibly Left-ward move in politics which seemed to Turgenev reactionary. One more sad and important quarrel with a friend of many years was the outcome.

The purpose of *The Bell* was described in the four volumes of Herzen's collected writings:

> You can work on men [he wrote] only by dreaming their dreams more clearly than they can dream them themselves, not by demonstrating their ideas to them as geometrical theories are demonstrated.

In the fifties he had settled in London, living at first in a grotesque room in Primrose Hill which contained, to his sardonic amusement, a bust of Queen Victoria and of Lola Montez. He was freer in London than he had ever been in his harassed wanderings in Europe but:

> My heart was not lighter for this freedom but yet I looked out of the window with a greeting to the sombre trees in the park which were hardly visible through the smoky fog and thanked them for their peacefulness. There is no town in the world which is more adapted for training one away from people and training one into solitude than London.

Until the sixties, Herzen, like Turgenev, had been a convinced Westerner but now he changed his mind. The rich Russian aristocrat and revolutionary, noted for his fine bearing and his excellent clothes, could not bear to see the rise of the lower middle class in industrialised Europe.

> Their vulgarity is cramping to art, above all their decorum, moderation and punctuality.

Their life was

> full of small defects and small virtues; it is self-restrained, often nig-
> gardly and shuns what is extreme and superfluous. The petit bourgeois
> ideal is the little house with little windows looking on to the street,
> a school for the son, a dress for the daughter, a servant for the hard
> work.

To Herzen the success of the new ideal was a degradation; he was
aging and yearned to be back in peasant Russia and dreamed that
a society less mean and calculating, something closer to the old
Slavophil teaching, would somehow appear. It is an extraordinary
reversal of belief and when Turgenev read the six long letters addressed to himself in *The Bell,* he replied hotly to the accusation
that his own belief in Western Europe and its traditions was due to
laziness and epicureanism. The hope of a new society lay with the
educated class who transmit civilisation. Herzen, he said, was worshipping the peasant's sheepskin coat; left to themselves the peasants would soon become as bourgeois as Europe and would be averse
to all civic responsibility and independent action.

> You diagnose contemporary mankind with unusual subtlety and sensi-
> tivity [Turgenev wrote], but why must this [i.e., the petit bourgeois]
> be Western Man and not *bipedes* in general.

Herzen, he said, was like a doctor who after examining the symptoms
of a chronic illness says that the whole trouble comes from the
patient's being a Frenchman. If Herzen has lost his faith in civilisation and finally revolution, let him admit it "without evident or
implied exceptions in favour of a Russian Messiah who is expected
at any moment and in whom you really believe as little as you do
in the Hebrew one."

This dispute lost its amiable note after his "trial" in Petersburg,
and, Turgenev read in *The Bell* a nasty paragraph, thought to have
been written by Bakunin, which accused Turgenev of betraying the
conspirators to the judges and in which he was called "a grey haired
Magdalene of masculine gender" who had written to the Emperor
because she feared he was unaware of her repentance with the result
that she had lost strength, appetite and her hair and teeth are falling

out. The language of Russian controversy has always been gaudy in personal insult. It was too much that Bakunin who had borrowed money from him should now spread slanders.

> But [he wrote to Herzen] I did not expect you in just the same way to fling mud at a man you have known for almost twenty years—solely because his convictions are different from yours.

Herzen never apologised: he had been infected by Bakunin with the mistrust that Bakunin always sowed between his friends—the characteristic that Turgenev had noted years before in the portrait of Rudin. There was a long breach. It is characteristic of Turgenev that he tried to comfort Herzen when *The Bell* finally lost its readers and came to an end.

Fashionable society in Baden, frivolous though it was, paid its peculiar tribute to the fame of the artists who came there. Pauline's fame in opera, Turgenev's fame as a novelist, drew people to them. Louis Viardot's mild distinction as a scholar himself benefited from the glow of his wife's and Turgenev's achievements. Other musical people had caused royal frostiness and a drawing in of skirts, but this respectable liaison offered no revelations to the outside world and was so clearly domestic, middle-aged and high-minded that it ruffled no one except the Russians and the French who, in their airy way, could not believe that two of Pauline's children, Claudine and Paul, were not Turgenev's, but had no secrets of the alcove to report. Pauline had the advantage of being the model for *Consuelo* who had never strayed, despite her alarming experiences. And then the Viardot group were well-off and intellectually formidable. The most the ironical could notice was that Turgenev, who had so often spoken of his old age and approaching death even in his thirties, now at forty-five had the tact to be as white-haired as the husband who was more than twenty years older than himself. In this town where the Russian visitors shouted and the courtesans from Paris were overdressed, there was social reassurance in the sight of the two staid and white-haired men going off shooting together or escorting the vigorous and commanding young singer who struck one, in her severe plainness, as being the male of the three. Her salon was soon the most exclusive in Baden and was visited by the ruling Prince himself.

The climate of Baden improved Turgenev's health: he was free of the laryngitis, colds and bronchitis of Petersburg. He no longer wore a respirator or spat blood. He stuck, however, to mufflers, comforters and rugs in the winter and longed for Russian stoves.

Turgenev's letters to Pauline when she is occasionally away singing in Germany recover the liveliness of his youthful adoration; the flowery worshipping phrases in German which had almost vanished now reappear in the mid-sixties, and although we have none of her letters we can tell from his that she now wrote often and more warmly. The next few years were the happiest in their lives. Turgenev was in high spirits. He loved dancing and play-acting. He became a child among her children. He appointed himself an additional father or a godfather who, as he said, adored them all, played with them, taught them. The young pupils of Pauline Viardot were in awe of her, but it was Turgenev who put them at their ease with his chatter. Louis Viardot was silent, uttered the word that brought them to order, was strict, but could make a pun. He was the just man with strict moral views: he was very French in being the man whose ideas were arranged in an orderly manner. But he did find himself effaced at times by a famous wife and the famous novelist. In Alexander Zviguilsky's introduction to new letters of Turgenev (Librairie des Cinq Continents, 1871), there is a reference to Gustave Dulay's *Pauline Viardot, Tragédienne Lyrique*, which comments on a letter Louis Viardot wrote to his wife in 1865. He says he has never for a moment thought his wife indulged in sentiments or conduct unworthy of her. But one has to be careful not to give rise to gossip. He complains, without mentioning Turgenev, that there have often been occasions in conversations, in musical matters or relations with their children "that his place has been taken by another." What would Pauline think if she found some other woman, George Sand, for example, taking *her* place the whole time in the affections and duties of those nearest to her, so that she was made to feel irrelevant? Pauline appears to have replied that he was having an attack of the blue devils, but he replied that he wished it were just that, but:

> my heart is sound, it is filled with you, loves and reveres you. Let us work together and give me back my peace, cheerfulness and let me

enjoy to the full my happiness and pride in having you for my wife
and friend.

The passion of Louis Viardot for the wife who respected but did not
love him, is resigned but deep. She was a woman indeed with two
lovers: the husband almost silent who, when she was away once,
wrote to Turgenev that he was now sadly left "to be the mother of
the family," fussing for her return; and the other, vivacious, brilliant,
talkative and longing for her too, when he had to go to Paris or
Russia. There is an important difference between the two men:
Louis is proud of his marriage to her and feels that she belongs to
him: for Turgenev the feeling is different. He tells her constantly he
belongs to *her* and the little girls whom he adores: She is a tree, he
says, she is his root and his crown. "I fall down at your feet and kiss
them a thousand times, am yours forever and ever." Once more this
is written in German, the love language of his youth, the language
of music; and one can be certain it is the influence of her voice
singing which has passed into these words. It strikes one again that
language was his instrument.

The wounding quarrel about *Fathers and Sons* went on. Journal-
ists, Turgenev noted, had called him a Vidocq, a Judas, bought for
gold, poison toad and spittoon. But he was not only helping Pauline
with her Albums and even composing an *operétte* with her—he was
writing a new novel, *Smoke,* in which he had one more fling at the
Russian question. The Russian visitors in Baden talked incessantly
through the nights about it.

In *Smoke,* all Turgenev's sense of outrage at the reception of
Fathers and Sons, breaks out in his fierce caricature of Russian
society. Since the novel is set in Baden, among an international set,
it naturally strikes one as being adventitiously a European novel in
which the Russian characters have a stupefied, often an absurd
anachronistic role. We are no longer dragging our way across the
steppe or sitting in happy out-of-date lethargy in out-of-date country
houses and among people who, for all their surface sophistication,
belong to an order which has not been known in Europe for at least
two hundred years. The very lightness of manner, the treatment of
the theme, seems "modern" in its restlessness, its quickness, its wit

and a new kind of psychological penetration. The upper-class Russians may cling together, but they are seen bemused by an active clash of cultures and are, as far as Europe is concerned, "on the spot." Baden is a town in an advanced, industrialised country: people come and go not by diligence but by train. The smoke of the title is railway smoke, as well as having other symbolical duties. (The title was not Turgenev's: the publisher took it, very fittingly, from one of the last pages of the book.)

There is no raggedness in the carefully constructed story. Baden suits it perfectly in being the closed scene which is a substitute for the country house and in which the skills of the secret playwright can be displayed and where the characters, being transients, can bring their past to a head and to the test before, once more, they depart. The flowery August season is at its height. We see the yawning and glum Russian colony bickering and boasting under the *"arbre russe"* in the gardens, "the *fine fleur* of our society," among them people like Baron Z, writer, orator, administrator and card-sharper; Prince Y, friend of the people and the church, who made a fortune out of selling doped vodka; the Countess S, a "Medusa in a bonnet"; a Princess Babette who boasted, as a thousand others did, that Chopin had died in her arms. The French are there in swarms, especially the *demi-monde* to whose buffooneries the Russians listen with awe, having no wit themselves. The opening chapter of *Smoke* is ferocious caricature of the Russian gentry abroad. Here, on his way back to Russia after four years studying economics and agricultural methods abroad, a young man called Litvinov pauses for a few days. He is waiting for his fiancée and her Aunt to arrive from Karlsruhe before he goes back to Russia to put modern ideas into practice on his land. Litvinov is a new kind of hero. He is the son of a modest, industrious clerk of serious mind who late in life had married a woman of noble extraction with large estates: this lady had run her houses in the orderly European fashion and seen to her son's education. Litvinov takes his future as a landowner seriously and studiously and is an earnest, simple young plebeian. He knows that now the Emancipation has occurred, his task will require practical and intelligent handling. He is well-equipped to do this and has no time for the fashionable young Russian officers on leave, the reactionary Generals or what he regards as the blather of the Russian Radicals. As a hero he is nice but dull: Turgenev advances him in the cause of common sense. While he is waiting, he is dragged into the two main Russian parties: the dispiriting Radicals who gather round the famous Gubaryov—maliciously drawn from Herzen's friend, the poet Ogarev, and the new kind of Slavophil Radical who believes that all hopes lie in the hidden genius of the Russian peasant. Litvinov is bored and next finds himself with the old Generals and young aristocrats who are still determined to resist the changes brought about by the Emancipation. He goes off for a long walk up the mountain to the old *Schloss* and there runs into a party of aristocratic young officers. They spot the plebeian in Litvinov at once and snub him with majestic affability and contempt:

> All were born with the same cachet of correctness, each one of them appearing to be profoundly convinced of his own importance, of his future place in the State. Meanwhile they had that touch of petulance and carelessness into which one plunges quite naturally when one is abroad, which agreeably disguises the fact that the feeling of superiority is absolute.

One hearty old General makes a speech:

> I am not an enemy of what is called progress, but all these universities and colleges, schools for the people, students, priests' sons and restaurant keepers, these scrapings from the bottom of the sack who are worse than the proletariat—*they* are what frighten me . . . No, I've nothing against progress, but don't swamp us with lawyers and juries and leave military discipline alone.

For Litvinov this is bad enough but when he looks at the ladies to whom the officers are showing off, he has a shock. Among them he sees a young woman with whom he had been deeply in love ten years before when he was a green student and who had thrown him over for a rich man. Litvinov gets away as fast as he can: he is horrified by what Society has made of her.

Down in Baden when he is walking in the gardens, an interesting, shy, intelligent man called Potugin, rather older than himself, attaches himself to him and Potugin becomes the chief voice of the debating part of the novel. Potugin is a haunted melancholy fellow, but he shares Turgenev's own views on the Russian situation: his dislike of the Slavophil faith in the Russian mission and the "untutored instinct of the Russian people."

Potugin's speeches to Litvinov are long and the essence of them has already been given in the letters Turgenev had written to Herzen. Turgenev knows how to make them come out with explosive passion from a human being who is modest and even tentative by nature. We hear the argument about the nature of civilisation:

> We owe everything we know about the sciences, industry, justice to civilisation and more—even our sense of the beautiful and of poetry cannot grow without its influence—what one calls spontaneous national talent is nonsense. Even in Homer one can trace the germs of a rich and sophisticated culture . . . I repeat, without civilisation there is no poetry. Have you ever asked yourself what the poetic ideal of the primitive Russian is? Look at our legends. If love appears in them, it is the result of chance or a magic charm. Our epic literature, alone in the literature of Europe and Asia, offers not a single example of two people who love: the hero of holy Russia begins his courtship by treating her without mercy.

The Russian is a natural slave, who calls for a master whom he calls his leader. He is a natural liar out of indifference and love of mischief.

In the course of the novel these conversations go on. They are well-done, but we begin to see that Turgenev has blurred the novel by giving it in effect *two* central characters who are convenient aspects of himself. What redeems the novel is the love story which puts Litvinov to the test, a test which in some degree is the larger moral and political theme of the novel. It is true that Potugin's private rôle in the love story is, at one point, incredible. There is a tangle of hearsay about dealings with an illegitimate child which is hard to follow. It is confusing because Turgenev is secretive here— he is telling what might be a private story of his own through the victimised Potugin, when the real victim in the novel is going to be Litvinov. The duplication is a strange mistake; nevertheless the story recovers.

It now turns out that the young woman who had jilted him had sent Potugin to get Litvinov to come and see her. She wishes to explain why she jilted him. Irina Ramirov—as she now is—is one of

Turgenev's destructive heroines, torn in half by her desires, bewitching, sensual, calculating but incalculable and tenacious. But what is remarkable about the portrait of Irina is Turgenev's sympathy and delicacy in showing the the confusion of self-will, greed, real feeling and lust in her nature. She will turn out to be a mixture of the sly adventuress and the guilty neurotic who must have her victory if only for a moment. The story is an account of her gradual seduction of Litvinov. We fear for Litvinov and we fear for her as she tells him that she only wants to confess her shame in jilting him in favour of a "protector"; that her marriage to Ramirov has shown her the shallowness of society and the mistaken vanity that made her crave for it. She has to fight Litvinov's cold revulsion. She at once knows and does not know what she is doing as she advances inch by inch to her difficult victory. She is completely a woman. She is one of the very few women in Turgenev's novels who are openly moved by sexual desire. Her feelings proceed from guilt about the past to bitter jealousy of Litvinov's love for his fiancée (who will soon arrive). This desire is made intense by her indignation at his eventual remorse at his loss of honour in breaking with an innocent girl. (To Turgenev, in his novels as in his life, questions of honour are crucial.) In other stories of young love, the insight that jealousy is an actual *source* of love does not arise. Love is simply born; a discovered faculty. But in these later loves, like Irina's, jealousy is the prime mover: the greed for power and possession is there without innocence. This is more than love; it is passion and passion knows good and evil.

The scenes in which this is shown are done exactly and delicately; the duologue is astonishingly true, alarming and fresh. There is no melodrama which so commonly occurs in Victorian novels where sensuality and love are the theme and, except in *First Love,* the deviousness and drive of passion have not yet appeared in Turgenev's writing—and indeed the lack of them sometimes suggests something tepid in his view of love and a desire to evade its reality. But in *Smoke* we have a real sense of passion taking possession of Litvinov against his will. Why is Turgenev now willing to show the other half of love? If there is a personal reason we can only surmise. But, as far as the novel is concerned, we are given a strange hint in a throw-away line about the Osinins, Irina's family. They were, he briefly says, an ancient family of Princes who having been maliciously accused of witchcraft, fell into disgrace; they were ruined without mercy, their titles were abolished, they were sent into exile and never recovered their power.

Romantic nonsense? It was Turgenev's habit to account for every detail of a character's background when he planned his books and the word "witchcraft" was meant to stick, for a vein of atavistic superstition ran through his rational mind though, as in his "uneasy" stories, it put a question into which the psychologist must go. For him "bewitchment" meant what it meant to Litvinov when he is shaken by finding he loves Irina for the second time in his life against his will. He says:

> Another life has infiltrated you; you cannot free yourself of it; you will never be cured of this poison.

He is "possessed" and against every honourable wish.

The account of Litvinov's incapacity to think when he is under Irina's spell shows a far greater moral penetration into the inner life than Turgenev has shown us in his passages of romantic tenderness and melancholy. After a first parting with Irina—which for him is final, yet not final, Litvinov

> felt no pain and did not weep; a glum *engourdissement* carried him away. He had never before felt like this: there was an intolerable sense of emptiness, an emptiness in himself and around himself, everywhere. He was not thinking of Irina or Tatiana. He felt one thing: that the knife had fallen, the rope that held him to the quay had broken and he was seized by something icy and unknown. Sometimes it seemed that a whirlwind was passing over him and he felt that rapid swirl, the uneven beating of black wings in the air. But he was resolved. He was going to leave Baden. In his mind he had already left; he was in a clattering and smoky train carrying him forward, on and on to a far-off, lost and desolate country.

That emptiness describes the loss of his moral existence. He goes back to Irina, nevertheless. The time has come for Irina to advance to the next stage of her victory and she *murmurs* that she loves him and will follow him to the ends of the earth. That finishes him, for her willingness to go off with him presents itself as a wild revenge as well as a recovery of the love she once gave and took away. He goes off to prepare for the meeting with Tatiana, who is arriving the next day at the railway station:

> Confidence, peace, self-respect had vanished in him; he stood in the debris of his moral collapse; what had just happened had put a mask upon his past. His sensations were new, intense, vivid, but hateful; a mysterious parasite had entered the sanctuary and sat there in silence and mastered him as one takes possession of a new dwelling. Litvinov was ashamed of himself no longer, but he was afraid: he burned with an intense and desperate fear: prisoners experience these opposite feelings and thieves after their first theft.

The disturbing moments before the seduction, itself halting, half-sulking, inevitable, are carefully given that air of accident so necessary to incitement and yet covering the act. There is a tiny incident in which some dresses Irina has bought for a Ball that night slip off a table to the floor. They are expensive dresses such as she always craves, but now petulantly she stamps on them and bursts into tears; exactly the igniting detail required. What strikes one in this scene is something we had not noticed in this designing woman: she, too, at the last moment, has to find courage. Turgenev understands the strangeness of that.

Of course, once the seduction is accomplished, she fails to live up to her promise that they will go off together, taking their "freedom." She is, after all, a coward in doing evil and tries to wheedle him into coming to Petersburg where he can be her lover from time to time at a discreet address, while she goes on enjoying the wealth of her husband and, since he is already suspicious and jealous, enjoy the excitement of using her skills in deceiving him. Litvinov refuses. In victory Irina has lost her power.

This is an interesting and subtle conclusion: when untried young girls win or lose in first love, in Turgenev's stories, they are shown moving into womanhood, but Irina—the experienced—is diminished by her success. In years to come she will be written off by old and young in Petersburg as a *fantasque*—the fashionable cliché of the time. They fear her and keep away. She makes life a meaningless byword.

As for Litvinov, he goes home to recover his self-respect and to be forgiven by Tatiana. That sounds trite but unhappiness has turned *her* into a woman; her childish insipidity has gone.

The story of Irina is said to be taken in part from the life of a Petersburg girl well-known to be the Tsar's mistress, and the publisher was nervous and wanted to make alterations which Turgenev refused to do. What has surprised biographers is that Pauline Viardot approved of *Smoke*, for so plainly does the story contain one strong aspect of her character. The stress on Irina's "witchcraft," her hypnotic power and her possession of him, is surely taken from Pauline's nature, as he saw it, and indeed as his friends saw it. This is not to say she is like Irina in any other way, any more than Litvinov resembles Turgenev. But Turgenev is an infallible observer of *how* certain events happen; he can be ecstatic about feeling but—such was his dual nature, he never missed a physical gesture or a fact in a scene and one can be pretty certain that the scene in which Irina seduces Litvinov is taken from life: that fluster of the senses, that stamping foot, those tears which are not tears! If at any time Pauline and Turgenev became lovers it would have been briefly and wildly like this: certainly Pauline would have refused to go off with him. Still, this is, of course, speculation. But it is strange that what has been called his second love for her was so clearly acceptable to her in Baden. The novel could have been done in malice, of course— for he did not lack it—and we cannot but note it has a great deal of angered caricature and fierce irony. He was in his drily masochistic way aware that his strange love had exposed him to being used. He and Pauline were, by all accounts, on cool terms in the early sixties and there must have been times of rancour and recrimination. Biography has the fundamental weakness that it can rarely tell us what was said or unsaid between the parties: it is a novel without dialogue. Pauline may have simply approved of *Smoke* in a very general way because it came to her as Turgenev translated from the Russian orally; the finer points would vanish and how could she not approve, conventional as she was, when a wicked woman who confuses love with lust comes to a futile end. She would be able to think of many a woman like that. And one thing which, as a very intelligent woman, she may have understood: that Turgenev had penetrated into the inner life of his two lovers, especially in his clear account of Litvinov's torments and remorse, and that this was a development of his talent as a psychologist.

In *Smoke* one sees that Baden is beginning to insulate Turgenev and that although he was deeply aware of its dangers, expatriation had begun to tell. Although his ideas are strongly held he seems to have been trapped by his self-irony and a Narcissim which prevents him from using his dilemma. It was impossible for him to make of his expatriation what Henry James made of his, for James's "international situation" had arisen from two attitudes to a common culture. There was nothing in common between Russia and Europe. Also, as a *rentier*, Turgenev was not aware of the corruption of money although he does see that the love of wealth and ease, as in Irina's and in Madame Odintsov's lives, nullifies them.

Russian critics were enraged by the book. Some were prudish about the "immorality" of the love-story. But the chief objection was to the utterances of Potugin who had said he both "hated and loved" his country—taking the love-hate from Catullus—and had even added that, as far as civilisation was concerned, Russia's disappearance from the face of the earth would be unnoticeable. The defeat of the Crimean War still scalded the patriots. Herzen was annoyed by Potugin and said his speeches ought to have been cut by half (which is true), but Turgenev replied that Potugin did not talk enough and he added that if Herzen were to sniff the vegetable oil the Slavophils smell of, he would restrain his feelings. But Turgenev's vanity was again hurt although he affected to be indifferent to the general rage.

Chapter II

THE public quarrel about *Smoke* was crowned by a farcical row between Turgenev and Dostoevsky when they enacted a scene which might have come straight out of Turgenev's own novel. In August 1867, Dostoevsky and his new wife, Anna, arrived from Dresden. She was the young stenographer to whom he had dictated *The Gambler* and *Crime and Punishment* (which had not long been published), and who had rescued him from his dead brother's predatory family and from the son of his first wife who had encumbered him with debts to the tune of 20,000 roubles. With the money of her own dowry and with the help of his publisher, she had got him out of Russia and into Europe, where they were to travel for four years while he entered on his long struggle to write *The Idiot*. After the misery of his imprisonment in Siberia, the death of his first wife and his destructive affair with Polina Suslova, Dostoevsky was entering on the finest creative period of his life. He had been in Europe before and, like so many Russians, had taken to roulette at the German gambling tables. He was at the height of the gambling fever when he reached Baden-Baden, where he had come solely to play. He had lost every penny: Anna had been obliged to pawn her wedding ring and her earrings, her furs and a lot of her clothes. The couple had once or twice been obliged to live only on tea. After a short euphoric stay at an expensive hotel, they were driven to living in two cheap rooms over a blacksmith's on the outskirts of the town, where the noise of the anvil and the screams of the children were wrecking Dostoevsky's easily damaged nerves. He was soon out on the streets looking for a fellow Russian to borrow from.

He ran into Goncharov, the dour hermetic chief censor, himself afflicted with the paranoia which had caused him to accuse Turgenev of plagiarism a few years before. Goncharov lent him "a piece of gold" and, perhaps not without malice, told Dostoevsky that Turgenev had seen him at the tables the day before but had not spoken to him because there was a convention that one must not talk to a man while he was playing. Of Dostoevsky this was certainly true: ill-luck, he always said, came to him for personal reasons. He had only to catch sight of some cool Englishman or German at play, to see the man as an evil omen, a devil personified, who would make him forget his system. The novelist drew everyone he met into a conspirator in his own drama. That, in itself, marked the ominous difference between himself and Turgenev, as artist and man. Honest Anna persuaded her husband to call on Turgenev because, on an earlier visit to Baden, he had borrowed fifty thalers from him and Turgenev would think he was ashamed of not paying back his debt. A meeting was arranged, but Dostoevsky's pride was already fermenting: he mistook the time and arrived at Turgenev's flat in the Schillerstrasse while he was eating his lunch. What happened is known from Dostoevsky's brilliant novelistic account of it in a letter to his friend, an eminent literary figure called Maikov. He wrote:

> I went to him in the morning at 12 o'clock and found him at lunch. I tell you frankly: even before this I didn't like the man personally. Most unpleasant of all, I owe him money from 1857 [in fact it was from 1863] from Wiesbaden—and have not returned it yet. Also I don't like his aristocratic, pharasaic embrace when he advances to kiss you, but presents his cheek. Terrible; as though he were a General.

Turgenev had the French manner of kissing. There sat Turgenev, the rich writer whom Dostoevsky had, as he said, "adored" when he was young as the model aristocratic and man of genius, now waited on by a butler in a frock coat, eating a cutlet and drinking a glass of wine. Dostoevsky had read *Smoke* and disliked it and began to nettle Turgenev at once, telling him that it wasn't worth while to be as wounded by the critics as Turgenev was.

It is not easy to tell truth from fiction in what happened in the next hour. One can only say that Turgenev was apt to lose his head. It seems likely that he *did* say he was going to write an article denouncing Russophils and Slavophils. In a moment the two were at loggerheads about their convictions. Dostoevsky's hysteria was, as Solzhenitsyn has written in another connection, an evasion of his conflicts. He may not have quoted Potugin's own words from *Smoke* that the only contributions Russia had made to civilisation were "the best shoe, the shaft yoke and the knout—and hadn't even invented them," but at the height of the wrangle, with Turgenev's temper rising—Dostoevsky said he kept calm and ironical—he hit upon one of those small phrases that turn dispute into farce. If Turgenev was trying to write about Russia, he said, he had better get a telescope.

> "A telescope," said the startled Turgenev. "What for?"
> "Because Russia is a great distance from here. Train your telescope upon Russia and it will not be difficult to see us distinctly."

On his decision to settle in Baden-Baden with the Viardots, Turgenev was sensitive. He understood Russian malice. He praised the Germans to Dostoevsky and spoke of the debt his generation owed to German philosophy. At which Dostoevsky said he had found the ordinary Germans a collection of cheats and swindlers. Turgenev denied this and said with rage:

> You insult me personally. You must know I have settled here and that I consider myself a German.

Dostoevsky said he did not know that, but if it was the case, he apologised and left, exalted by indignation. A German!

Such naked combats about convictions, as Mochulsky says in his book on Dostoevsky, rose from the endemic "self-consciousness" in the Russian nature which, more accurately put, is a spontaneous consciousness of the self as an absolute, extended to the universal. (It resembles that capacity of the Spaniard to leap suddenly from his ego into a universal expansion of it.) Dostoevsky believed, as he often said, in going to extremes, in pushing beyond the limit in search of revelation, in going to the brink of the precipice. He was at the beginning of his vision of the Russian Christ, the mission of the Russian people to rule the whole Slav world and under the leadership of the Tsar to save mankind from the corruption of the West—even "with rifles." But, as Mochulsky suggests, the difference between Turgenev and Dostoevsky as artists was fundamental and irreconcilable.

> Turgenev was a fatalist lacking in will and saw history as an impersonal, predetermined process. Dostoevsky affirmed freedom of will and the power of personality. Turgenev wrote "Is there a God? I don't know. But I do know the law of causality. Twice two is four." Dostoevsky, with the frenzy of despair, fought against the law of necessity and by a volitional act "acquired" faith in God.

Dostoevsky was the spiritual gambler: his greatness as a novelist lies in dramatising to the limit the swaying conflict between "knowing" and "not knowing."

The quarrel was part of Dostoevsky's development. He needed an imagined enemy at the roulette table to reanimate his genius. On Turgenev it had no effect but of disgust and the feeling that Dostoevsky was a sick soul. But it had a disagreeable aftermath. After his trajectory from self-abasement to exaltation, Dostoevsky often fell into cunning and double-dealing. He had his report of the quarrel copied and sent to be preserved for posterity "in the archives"; obviously it would be publicised. Turgenev wrote to his friend Polonski in 1871:

> I have been told that Dostoevsky has "unmasked" me. Well, what of it, let him enjoy himself. He came to see me in Baden five years ago, not to pay back the money he had borrowed from me, but to curse me because of *Smoke* which, according to his ideas, ought to be burned by the executioner. I listened to his philippic in silence—and what am I finding out now? That I seem to have expressed every kind of offensive opinion which he hasted to communicate to Bartenev. (Bartenev has written to me about it.) It would be out and out slander if Dostoevsky were not mad which I do not doubt in the slightest. Perhaps it came to him in a dream. But my God, what a petty dirty gossip.

Worse followed. If Turgenev had caricatured the Radicals in his portrait of Herzen's friend Ogarev in *Smoke*, Dostoevsky caricatured Turgenev in *The Devils*: he became the shrill, lisping figure of Karmazinov and a "Red." The portrait is spiteful. Karmazinov is an effeminate, vain, aging celebrity who is mocked from the floor at a public reading; the Baden lunch is more fully guyed, but we learn that Turgenev did at any rate offer him a cutlet and sat with his knees under a plaid rug because, although it was August, he found Baden cold.

Turgenev is made to say "I still cling to honour but only from habit. . . Granted it's from timidity; you see, one must live somehow what's left of one's life." The malice, indeed the hatred, reach their height when he parodies Karmazinov giving a reading of *Phantoms*. Karmazinov says that he has helped the town council to lay a new water pipe.

> I felt in my heart that this question of water pipes in Karlsruhe was dearer and closer to my heart than all the questions of my precious Fatherland.

And then goes on to parody *Enough*, which he called *Merci*, in which Karmazinov says he is laying down his pen for good—as indeed Turgenev often did say—and if angels from heaven or the best society were to implore him, he would not change his mind. Dostoevsky's humour is broad. He underlines his jokes with a heavy hand. But when he parodies *Phantoms* as an account of Turgenev's first kiss, he is very funny indeed about the political tour of the earth. The lovers are sitting near a gorse tree—look up your nature notes —there is a touch of purple in the sky:

> Suddenly they see Pompey or Cassius on the eve of battle and both are penetrated by the chill of ecstasy. Some wood nymph squeaks in the bushes. Gluck plays the violin among the reeds. . . .Meanwhile a fog comes down, everything disappears and the great genius is crossing the Volga in a thaw, such a fog—it was more like a million pillows than a fog. Two and a half pages are filled with the crossing and yet he falls through the ice. The genius is drowning—you imagine he was drowned? Not a bit of it: this was simply in order that when he was drowning and at his last gasp he might catch sight of a bit of ice, the size of a pea, but pure as crystal "as a frozen tear." And in

that tear was reflected Germany, or more accurately the sky of Germany and its iridescent sparkle recalled to his mind the very tear which "Dost thou remember fell from thine eyes when we were sitting under the emerald tree and thou didst cry out joyfully 'There is no crime!' " "No," I said through my tears, "but if that is so there are no righteous. either." We sobbed and parted for ever.

She goes off to visit some caves down the coast and he flies off to dwell for three years under the Suharev Tower in Moscow and hears a hermit sigh. This reminds him of her first sigh thirty-seven years before, when she said:

"Why love? See ochra will cease to grow and I shall cease to love."
Down comes the fog again, the wood nymph whistles a tune from Chopin, Aneus Marcus appears over the roofs of Rome.
A chill of ecstasy ran down our backs and we parted for ever.

This parody has its seamy side. Dostoevsky had published *Phantoms* in his own paper, *Epoca,* because he had thought Turgenev's name would draw readers: the truth is that noble as Dostoevsky seemed to his wife Anna, who passed the quarrel over lightly in the revised version of her account of him at the end of her life, he was undoubtedly a pathologically jealous man, as she knew from her own frightening experiences with him.

Turgenev wrote to a correspondent that Dostoevsky's conduct had not surprised him: "he hated me even when we were both young" and added, "Groundless passions are the strongest and most prolonged." He and "the most spiteful of Christians" did not meet again until they orated from the same platform when they were old men.

During the eight years Turgenev lived in Baden he put on weight and mockingly called himself the "Badenbourgeois" and acted the part: there was always a tension between himself as a personality and himself as an artist. Very aware of the dangers of expatriation he went five times to Russia for visits of a month or two. There were journeys to Paris also where he went to see his daughter, Paulinette, who had been married in 1855 and in one of his letters he complains that spring in Europe lacks the sudden explosiveness of the Russian spring. On one of his Russian visits in 1867—his climacteric year, he said, because he was forty-nine, the multiple of 7×7, one of his mother's superstitions—Pauline was singing in Karlsruhe, Breslau and Berlin and he met her in Berlin when he was on his way to Petersburg. They spent five days together. April Fitzlyon quotes in full the German passage which had been suppressed from an earlier published version of one of his letters to Pauline:

> I cannot tell you how endlessly depressed I was. Those days in Berlin, that unexpected, wonderful meeting, all that—and then a cruel separation—it was really and truly too much for me . . . I was positively broken under the burden of those unforgettable impressions—broken as I have never been before. Oh, my feeling for you is too great, too powerful. I cannot live away from you any more, it's beyond me. I must feel your nearness which is so dear to me, revel in it: the day on which your eyes do not shine on me is a lost day. But enough, enough! Or I shall lose my self-control . . .

He was happy, he said, that everything in him, to his very depths, was linked with her being.

The uncle who had long before succeeded the Tyutchevs had naturally come to feel that he owned Spasskoye. He had become not only lazy and incompetent but angrily obstructive. When Turgenev compared his own income to his brother's who had shared the inheritance and had improved it in a business-like way, he realised the uncle was hopeless as a manager. There was nothing for it but to turn him out. Since his mother's time Turgenev had shied away from confrontations but after the ecstatic days with Pauline he had to face the old fellow who was revelling in a sense of injury and moved on to insults and dangerous threats in his letters. He called his nephew an Assassin. When Turgenev told him he would have to go the old man turned vindictive and presented the two promissory notes Turgenev had left with him as an insurance, but on the understanding they would never be called in. The uncle took steps to distrain on all his nephew's property, in Russia and abroad including the new house at Baden, so that Turgenev had quickly to make it over to the Viardots. He was obliged to explain his financial difficulties to his daughter. Her husband, a glass maker, seems, like her earlier suitors, to have had his eye on Turgenev's money. He had already spared no expense on Paulinette and had given her a substantial dowry. Now he was obliged to write:

> If my uncle had not acted so infamously towards me I would have been in a position to give you 50,000 francs. However, I have just spent 75,000 to buy back the bills of exchange I gave him 11 years ago (without actually receiving a sou), to be presented on my death. And not only did he present them *now* with me alive but he is also demanding to be paid himself with compound interest: that is to say more than twice the principal. That has come as a blow to me and with the present state of my affairs my fortune is pretty well shaken.

He set off for Moscow and Spasskoye to face his uncle. It was in March. The train left at five-thirty in the morning and took him as far as a little place called Serpoukhov; after that he went by sleigh with a new bailiff and a valet. He was ill and at once started coughing. There was a bad journey over the unmade roads which had been torn into holes and gullies as the snow softened in the thaw. By now Turgenev had bronchitis, a high temperature and was forced to stay in a miserable inn. And his gout had started again. Bad health always came to his aid when he wished to dodge a personal crisis, so he sent his bailiff on to deal with his uncle and he himself returned to Moscow, where he quickly recovered.

It is obvious from his correspondence about money, with Louis Viardot, that he was one of those unworldly gentlemen who—like so many of the Russian gentry—had amateur notions about the management of money. To him it was a sort of fluid, capricious in its flow. When short of money owing to his extravagance or to some failure of crops—and he was often short enough to have to borrow his fare from a friend—he simply sold another farm or took to the landowner's common device of selling off more timber from his forests—and put the transfer of the funds to France into the hands of friends who were as amateur and forgetful as himself. He and they mistrusted banks. At home he was easily robbed by his agents. Perhaps he assuaged his guilt as a landowner by agreeing that it was right that he should be robbed and that he was, in any case, the victim of having a position he had not chosen. In his heart he did not and could not think of money as real. To Viardot, of course, it was very real.

Turgenev put off the meeting with his uncle until the June of '68. It was a terrible year of desolation in Russia. To his brother he wrote:

> I spent two weeks in Spasskoye and, like Marius, can say that I have sat upon the ruins of Carthage. In the present year alone the "fetid elder"—that plunderer of money, cattle, carriages, furniture and other possessions—has fleeced me of 3,500 silver roubles. (I had to pay a 5,000 rouble debt of his.) I will not mention that he left the estate in a loathsome disorder and chaos, that he paid no one, tricked every one etc.... During my entire stay at Spasskoye I was like a hare on the run; I could not stick my head in the garden without serfs, muzchiks, small merchants, retired soldiers, sluts, peasant women, the blind, the lame, the neighbouring landowners of both sexes, priests and sextons—my own and other people's—rushing forward from behind trees, from behind bushes and almost out of the ground to assault me—all of them emaciated by hunger with their mouths agape like jackdaws, throwing themselves and shouting hoarsely "Dear master! Ivan Sergeivich, save us! Save us, we are dying." I finally had to save myself by fleeing lest I be stripped of everything. Moreover a terrible year is on the way: the spring crops have perished; the rye is enormous on the stalk, but the ears contain not a kernel. What a picture Russia presents now—this land everyone contends is so rich. The roofs are all uncovered, the fences are down and not a single new building is to be seen except for the taverns. The horses and the cows are dead; the people are thin—three coachmen could hardly lift my trunk between them. Dust is everywhere, like a bank of clouds; around Petersburg everything is burning up—the forests, the houses, the very *land*... The picture is not a happy one, but it is very accurate.

Back in Petersburg he was depressed. The white nights got on his nerves. There was a nasty, sweetish, humid smell in the air. He stayed with his friend Annenknov and his wife and baby, in a dacha which shook at the slightest wind. They sat freezing before the fire, with rugs over their shoulders—it was June. He longed for Baden. He gazed sentimentally at the house on the Nevsky Prospect, opposite the theatre, where he had met Pauline on her first visit to Petersburg twenty-five years before.

One thing he did achieve: he sold a large amount of timber and the money was to go to a fund for Didie's dowry: "I adore that child." Her birth in 1852 had killed all his hopes of a life with Pauline, but he worshipped this daughter. She was very much a dark

Spanish type like her mother and grew up to be a talented painter. When she was ten he said the little girl had an extraordinary power over him—"and she knows it." And adds the words he always used to women he loved: "I kiss her hands." He sent her a caricature of himself as Don Quixote and asked if she would want a Don Quixote like that for a husband when she grew up? There is—he told her mother—"only one Didie in the world. . . and she knows, without my telling her, that I belong to her utterly and she could put a collar round my neck like she does with Flambeau [one of the Viardot dogs], and the worst of it is I wouldn't be cross." The desire to belong, to be a possession, was at the core of his affections.

In Baden, the little theatre he had built for Pauline in the garden of his house was opened and Pauline and her pupils gave performances of three little operas for which Turgenev had written the libretti: he also played minor parts himself; the Queen of Prussia and the Duke and Duchess of Weimar who were present raised their eyebrows at the sight of the great novelist and aristocrat lying on the floor in the part of a ridiculous pasha. The operas were not a success. At Pauline's musical matinées when she played the organ, at which she was remarkable, the Russians were not impressed by the sight of their great writer pumping away at the instrument. They saw him frittering his talents away as a clown.

Turgenev was restless. He went again to Paris to correct the French proofs of a collection of stories and he went to see his daughter and her in-laws. The girl was pregnant, the mother-in-law detested her, the marriage was having its troubles. He went on to see Flaubert who sat red in the face, dressed in red, in a red room. He called on Sainte-Beuve who was ill. The critic took a piece of paper and made a drawing of the cancer of the bowel of which he was dying: he offered drawings of the cancer to all his callers. In June of 1870, Turgenev was off again to Berlin on his way to Petersburg and sat opposite the ominous Moltke at a dinner and studied him. With his fair wig, his calm clean-shaven face and penetrating blue eyes, Moltke seemed the tranquil personification of power, intelligence and will, an enemy Napoleon III had underrated. In Petersburg Turgenev had one of his violent attacks of gout which had now become chronic, worked on the draft of one of his four finest stories,

A Lear of the Steppes and bought 6,000 Russian railway shares for Didie's dowry, which brought the capital value up to 50,000 francs. The beautiful girl was now eighteen.

Unknown to them all, the "autumnal happiness" of Baden was coming to an end. While he was away the Franco-German war had broken out and Moltke's armies were on the move. Herzen had died too soon to see the justification of his belief that bourgeois Europe was a rotten organism.

Turgenev had said once or twice when the builders were slow in building his villa that the first tenant of the house would be a French General. It was soon clear that no French General would enter Baden with his troops. The Viardots were alarmed. They were French citizens. They fled from the town like the rest of the foreign residents. Turgenev returned from Russia in time to take Pauline Viardot and her daughters to Ostend and put them on the boat for England, then returned to Louis Viardot who stayed on for a short time. Turgenev remained. He still believed the French would arrive and knew they could do nothing to him. He, in fact, stayed on until the winter.

In 1848 he had been a spectator of revolution in Paris; now he was a spectator of war and wrote a number of commentaries for a Petersburg newspaper. The articles came to an end because the Russian editors were pro-French and he, from the double influence of the love of the romantic Germany of his youth and his hatred of Louis Napoleon, took the German side.

The German population were astonished by the early German victories. It had always been said that the Rhinelanders would not side with Prussia: now they were amazed to find themselves "befuddled by patriotic joy" in German unity. Turgenev heard the first sound of the German artillery from Yverg Castle, the highest point of the Black Forest from which one could see the whole valley of Alsace with its peaceful regiments of vines, its orchards and wide, hedgeless fields of maize stretching as far as Strasbourg. He saw the first black and red smoke of the explosions—forty to a minute. "It is impossible not to curse the war." He took the German side, he said, because the salvation of civilisation and the free institutions in Europe depended on the donwfall of the monstrous Napoleonic system. He sincerely loved and respected the French people, he said, "but it was time to crush the immoral system that has ruled for 20 years." It was their turn to learn the lesson that Prussians received at Jena, the Austrians at Sadowa and the Russians at Sebastopol. There is one characteristic literary aside in these letters: he had been reading Tolstoy's *War and Peace* as it slowly came out, sometimes admiring it, often sharply critical of its "petty" realism, most of all of its philosophisings and its military comments.

> I can well understand why Tolstoy supports the French side. He finds French phrasemongering repulsive, but he hates sober-mindedness, system and science (in a word the Germans), even more. His novel is based on enmity towards intellect, knowledge and cognition.

Tolstoy thought (he said) that battles are lost and won in the rumblings of adjutants and generals, whereas they are won by plans carried out, as Moltke does, with mathematical precision.

As he wrote, his house shook with the sounds of the bombardment of Strasbourg which had already been half burned down. And by day the French prisoners streamed in. But he was no reporter. He stands apart, absorbed in historical and social meditations . . . "We are still barbarians! And we shall probably remain so until the end of our days."

The war, the surrender and the Commune were ruinous for the Viardots. Their property in Baden was safe enough, but in the collapse of the Funds, their income was vanishing and although she gave concerts in England that year and took on pupils in London, Pauline Viardot could not command the fees she had earned from the rich and even royal pupils she had had in Baden. She and Louis took a house in Seymour Street, and soon after, in Devonshire Place. When Turgenev joined them he took a separate flat in Beaumont Street to avoid gossip, but was at Devonshire Place most of the day. He stayed in England for seven months, except for a month when he was off to Petersburg in the spring of 1871 to raise money to help his daughter whose husband had been ruined by the war and to find a publisher for another of Pauline Viardot's album of songs—they had had only a small success and, this time, secretly, he paid for the publication himself. His new agent at Spasskoye was turning out to be as incompetent and idle as his Uncle Nikolai had been. He had also the duty of seeing Pauline's eldest daughter, Louise, who had left her husband and child in France. She was teaching singing in

the Conservatoire in St. Petersburg. She hated her mother, her
father, her husband and all society. She had cropped her hair short
and seems to have inherited her mother's male, domineering traits,
without having her mother's charm, and had always a submissive
female "slave" in attendance. She repels, Turgenev wrote to the
Viardots, but she aroused his pity. He went to Moscow which he
loathed for its smell of "lamp oil and slavic blubber" and read the
news of the Commune in the paper. Now he was pro-French:

> It's a case of the insurrection of '48 but now triumphant. What will
> happen to France? Will France, the nation to which we owe so much,
> fall into the anarchic state of Poland and Mexico?

What would become of the Viardots' property, their investments,
the farm at Courtavenel?

He had gone to Moscow because the cholera he dreaded had
broken out in Petersburg, the plague he called "Him" or "the green
devil." The very word started bizarre imaginary pains in his body.
In Moscow he received from Pauline one of the few letters we know
of that display anxiety and even passion for him. She was frightened
by the collapse of her career and her home.

> Ah Dear friend, hurry back. Don't stop an hour longer than is abso-
> lutely necessary. I beg you if you have the slightest love for us. Don't
> go back to Petersburg. Promise me not to go back to that fatal city
> —please. Are you going on to Spasskoye? I hope you won't. Send us
> a picture of yourself as a young man. Oh, write every day and come
> back, dear friend, come back to be near those who cannot be happy
> unless you are here.

The cold was intense, the snow crackled under his feet and, he said,
he would give anything for the fogs of London because she was
there, and he came back.

Although they disliked London, the Viardots had excellent
friends there, people who remembered her performances. They
stayed in country houses. She gave her Saturday parties. Eventually
when the situation in France calmed down, Louis Viardot returned
to Baden, to sell the house and pack up their furniture—especially
the valuable organ—and his considerable collection of pictures, all
unharmed by the war.

The happy frontier people of that part of Germany had thrived on French visitors and Baden's small distinction, and no French man or woman, as Turgenev pointed out, had been molested. But the war had awoken French patriotism in Louis Viardot and although Pauline had been the victim of French insularity and intrigue in the operatic world in her youth, she loved the cosmopolitan life of Paris. The only member of the ménage who did not was Turgenev but, as he said, he would follow the Viordots even to Australia if she ordered it.

They got back their house in the rue de Douai and Turgenev discreetly asked if they would let him three rooms at the top of it. It was agreed.

Chapter 12

In 1870 when he was fifty-two, Turgenev wrote to a correspondent that a "Russian writer who has settled in Baden by that very fact condemns his writing to an early end. I have no illusions on that score, but since everything else is impossible, there is no point in talking about it. . . But are you really so submerged in what is 'contemporary' that you will not tolerate any non-contemporary characters?" Such people, he says, have lived and have a right to be portrayed. "I admit no other immortality: and this immortality of human life (in the eyes of art and history), is the basis of my whole world."

What is one to think of his writing in the Baden period? The critics hated *Smoke* for political and patriotic reasons, but it is a very able novel. His visits to Russia were not lost: he had another long book in mind—*Virgin Soil*—but he was not ready for it and turned to the long short stories in which he rarely failed. He was simply, he said, "too full of subjects." In his early fifties he wrote two reminiscent stories—the horrifying tale, *The Brigadier*, based on the incident we already know of in the life of his Lutovinov grandmother who had committed murder. An old and senile brigadier "of the age of Catherine" is seen fishing, accompanied by a bullying servant who ridicules him. The brigadier has become a ruined and childish simpleton, reduced to poverty and ostracism because in middle years he had loved and lived with a terrifying young widow who, in a rage, had killed her page. Out of love and in a fit of honour the brigadier had assumed guilt for her crime and was tried for it but his sentence had been short. The widow and (after her death) her sister, bleed him of all his money until he is destitute. Yet once a week he visits the widow's grave with adoration. At last he knows he is going to die. He knows because of a dream.

> I, as maybe you know, often see Agrippina Ivanov (as he now calls her) in my dreams—heaven's peace be with her—and never can I catch her: I am always running after her but cannot catch her. But last night I dreamed she was standing, as it were, before me, half turned away and laughing. . . I ran up to her at once and caught her. . . and she seemed to turn round quite and said to me "Well, Vassinka, now you have caught me. . . It has come to me that we shall be together again."

The tale is told in the old-fashioned way of picking up the story by hearsay in the manner of a folk tale, but in the servant's mockery there is something of the mockery of Shakespeare's cynical comics, and Turgenev has made it powerful. The hearsay, the careful reader will notice, is not flat but is subtly varied as changes of scene and voice are made to carry it. The theme is, of course, familiar in his writings: a man dominated and enduring abasement and suffering in love. He will give everything to the monster but he lives by his honour which is a kind of exultation. The dream of death as a woman is also a common theme and so—we note once more—is the myth of bewitchment as a psychological fact.

The theme of honour as the real test in love and indeed in all crucial circumstances is of great importance in Turgenev's writing and it must not be read as a romanticisation of an old-fashioned or picturesque idea common enough in the historical novels of the nineteenth century. If the brigadier's honour is not to be questioned this is for reasons of Russian history. Turgenev believed that Russia was uncivilised in the Western sense because there was no experience of an age of chivalry in its culture. And if we look beyond this story to his own life, it would seem that his own Quixote-like concept of love in his feelings for Pauline is a chivalrous vow which once uttered must never be betrayed; in that sense his love of Pauline was not a weakness nor an obsession. It was an anachronism. It was a life-long vigil. It was not even romantic, but a spiritual law, an article of the aristocratic faith. *The Brigadier* is not only an important story, but a very revealing one in another connection. In his own life, Turgenev felt he owed it to himself as a duty of chivalrous principle to give money secretly to revolutionaries like Bakunin and others—the Populist leader, for example—even though he hated violence and terrorism and feared the loss of his property.

The idea of honour abused is at the heart of *An Unhappy Girl*, a story drawn from his student days. The girl is half-Jewish, one of the maltreated "orphans" handed on: the Jewish aspect of her beauty is ancient, ennobled by race, and aristocratic instinct. She is helplessly trapped in a coarse German family. Her tale is remarkable for its scenes of vulgar lower-middle-class life, its gambling episodes and a drunken funeral meal which follows the funeral of the tormented girl who has been driven to suicide. Unfortunately there is an element of plot: it is suggested that the girl may have been poisoned so that her small inheritance would then pass to the awful Germans if she died unmarried. Plot-making was outside Turgenev's competence. The girl's wretched state is well-done but Dostoevsky with his dynamic power of dramatising the inner life of the "insulted and the injured" would have made more of her, for Dostoevsky believed in free will whereas the art of Turgenev, the determinist, is in this sense static: people live under fate. Or rather one says again that time flows through them: they do not drive blindly forward through time.

In *The Story of Lieutenant Erguynov* a young naval officer is stripped of his money by a sly, amusing, fascinating girl who is a decoy used by thieves. Again the plot is awkward but there are some brilliant things in the tale, particularly in the account of Erguynov's state of hallucination when, his drink being doped, he sails out of consciousness to the sound of the balalaika, is robbed, knocked on the head and dumped with his skull split on the roadside. And we get pleasure from the fact that, in old age, the simple Lieutenant loves telling the whole story again and again and loves to dwell on his hallucination so that the company knows it by heart. For what we are shown is an innocent young sailor growing into a knowing old fellow, enlarging himself as he talks. He makes us feel that he is telling us something that is now more completely "true" than it was

---

when it was scattered in the fragmentary experience of real life. The point of honour crops up at the end, but comically. The thieves escape and so does the girl, but much later she writes to the sailor begging him to believe she herself was not responsible for the attempt to murder him. She had no idea they would go *that* far and she would like to see him and convince him that although she did deceive him she is not a criminal. The sailor—an honourable fellow —is rather taken by the idea, but he puts it off and does nothing. The fact that he does nothing makes the story rest delightfully in suspense—which is an aspect of life.

None of these stories approaches the power of *A Lear of the Steppes*. This is a major work. The Lear is Martin Petrovich Harlov, a hulking, rough, bear-like figure who farms 800 acres and owns serfs but who, though claiming to come of noble Russian stock "as old as Vassilievitch the Dark," is a hard-driving peasant farmer, a stern, shouting but honest man. He lives in what he calls his "mansion," a ramshackle homestead he has built with his own hands, a small manor with courtyard and a tumbledown thatched lodge. His own room in the house is unplastered. His riding whips, his horse collar, hang from nails on the wall. There is a wooden settle with a rug, flies swarm on the ceiling and the place smells as he himself does, of the forest. In the house live his two daughters: Anna, who is married to the whining and greedy son of a petty official, and Evlampia, who is being courted by a battered and broken major. Both girls are beauties.

The narrator of the story is fifteen when the events begin: the son of a wealthy landowning widow. It has, but only superficially, the tone of *A Sportsman's Sketches*, but it will go much deeper. The widow has always been Harlov's friend and adviser, so that we see Harlov through the eyes of an awed boy, as it might be Turgenev himself as a boy living with his mother at Spasskoye. If Harlov is a primitive giant he seems all the more gigantic to a boy's wondering eyes. Turgenev is careful to convey the physical force of Harlov's person by an insider's, not an outsider's metaphors that evoke the man and the working scenes of his life. The voice that came out of a small mouth was strong and resonant:

> Its sound recalled the clank of iron bars carried in a cart over a badly paved road; and when Harlov spoke it was as though someone were

shouting in a high wind across a wide ravine. . . his shoulders were like millstones. . . his ears were like twists of bread. . . he breathed like a bull but walked without a sound.

It is important to the story that the boy's mother had found a wife for Harlov, a frail girl who lasted only long enough to give him two daughters, and saw to it that they had a superior education. Times are changing: we shall see the result of this kindness. The daughters will eventually turn their father out of his own house and drive him to frenzy and death.

The wonder is that this confident, dominant and roaring man who frightens everyone—"the wood demon" as people call him—will bring about his own downfall by an act of Lear-like weakness. He is liable to fits of melancholy, during which he shuts himself up in his room, starts to hum "like a swarm of bees." The hours of humming end in singing meaningless words. He recovers. It is after one of these fits that he comes to his friend the widow and announces that Death has appeared to him in a dream in the form of a black colt that rushes into the house, dances about and finally gives him a kick in the arm. He wakes up aching in every bone. It is this terror which has driven him to a bid for power which is exorbitant and, indeed, a sign of folly: he is going to divide his property between his daughters now; willing it to them is not enough, for he wants to see their gratitude. He wants to establish his absolute rule after death *now* and before his eyes. Nothing will persuade him that this is foolish.

The story now expands. We are in the Russia of *A Sportsman's Sketches*, a crowd of characters come in, the lawyers, the police, officials, the grasping son-in-law and a spiteful, jeering figure called Souvenir, an orphan, the brother of Harlov's dead wife who is hanger-on in the landowner's house. Souvenir has a mawkish laugh that sounds like the rinsing of a bottle and whenever Harlov calls at the house he goes swaggering after him and saying "What made you kill my sister?" Souvenir has a goading, diabolical role to play. The deed of gift is signed and Souvenir tells the old man with delight that now his daughters will turn him out.

Turgenev always understands how to insert points of rest during which a story can grow of itself. The boy narrator goes away for the summer. In the autumn he goes out shooting snipe and sees a stranger riding Harlov's horse. It is the first sign of the truth of Souvenir's prophecy. Horse and carriage have been taken from Harlov by Anna and Sletkin her husband. Harlov is being starved and stripped of everything. The two sisters are at odds. Evlampia is having an affair with Sletkin—Souvenir catches them in the woods —and when he hears of this Harlov rushes in a state of madness to the big house. In his great bid for power, Harlov has exhausted his will. His terrifying force has become helpless, acquiescent and meek. This is Souvenir's moment. He mocks the old man for his fall, jeering without pity. Suddenly the old man rises to the taunts, recovers his old violence and rushes back to his manor, and in a terrible scene climbs to the roof and starts tearing down what he has built with his own hands. The peasants cannot stop him, as he rips away the rafters and knocks down chimneys. In a final triumph of strength he wrenches a gable and a cross beam off and is crushed when he falls with them to the ground.

One does not expect such a scene of violence from Turgenev. It succeeds because it is made to seem likely among the people of the steppe. The two daughters have been skilfully kept in the background where, by one small touch or another, they have aroused our apprehension. We have seen Anna's cold smile; we have seen Evlampia, silent as stone, a still, sensual beauty with a store of power in her. Of Anna, the boy remarks in a disturbing Turgenevean reflection:

> In spite of the negligence of her attire and her irritable humour, she struck me as before, as attractive and I should have been delighted to kiss the narrow hand which looked malignant too, as she twice irritably pushed back her loose tresses.

The tragedy is over and the story is restored little by little to the norms of peasant life. In studying the peasants as a group, Turgenev has gone beyond the scope of *A Sportsman's Sketches,* though the luminous quality of that early work gives the scene perspective and truth. At first the peasants stand aloof from Anna, but for Evlampia there was a kind of sympathy, except from an old man who said: "You wronged him; on your soul lies the sin." At the funeral the faces of the crowd condemn the family, but the condemnation has become impersonal. That is the next stage.

It seemed as though all those people felt that the sin into which the Harlov family had fallen—this great sin—had gone now before the presence of one righteous Judge and for that reason there was no need now for them to trouble themselves and be indignant. They prayed devoutly for the soul of the dead man whom in life they had not especially liked, whom they feared indeed.

Anna's voice, we remember, was "very pleasant, resonant and rather plaintive. . . like the note of a bird of prey," but she says nothing. Evlampia, fierce, monumental—"a free bird of the Cossack breed"—fierce in the glance of her dark blue eyes, was silent too. Sletkin tries to get a word out of her, but she treats him as she has treated the absurd Major who had wanted to marry her.

In a day or two she has sold her interest to her sister and has vanished. Years later the narrator sees her again, driving in a smart pony trap, splendidly dressed. She has become the founder, the dominant mother of a dissenting Order of Flagellant Sisters who live without priests. Whether this is a genuine order is uncertain: is her house a place of rendez-vous? For the peasants wink and say the Police Captain does well out of the Order. It is she who inherits the primitive spirit of her father, maybe is honest—but maybe not: the spirit of an extremist.

Sletkin, Anna's scheming husband, has died—the peasants say, probably untruthfully, that she poisoned him and she is now an excellent farmer, better than her father was, clever in the legal negotiations that have followed the change in the land laws after the Emancipation. The great landlords and officials respect her judgment.

In other words, after tragedy and indeed crime, a new generation rises and forgets, as Turgenev always likes to show when the present grows out of the past. Human life is short.

There is little of love in this tale, but one notices his skill in suggesting there has been an act of sexual love. The boy comes across Sletkin and Evlampia in the woods.

[Sletkin] was lying on his back with both hands under his head and with a smile of contentment gazing upwards at the sky, swinging his left leg which was crossed over his right knee. . . A few yards from him Evlampia was walking up and down the little glade, with down-cast eyes. It seemed as though she were looking for something in the grass, mushrooms perhaps: now and then she stretched out her hand. She was singing in a low voice. An old ballad.

> Hither, hither threatening storm cloud
> Slay for me the father-in-law
> Strike for me the mother-in-law
> The young wife I will kill myself.

Louder and louder she sings while Sletkin laughs to himself while she moves round and round him.

"The things that come into some people's heads," Sletkin says.
"What were those words you were singing?"
"You can't leave the words out of a song," says Evlampia.

And then they see the boy, cry out and rush away in opposite directions.

The scene tells us all, even to the fierceness of an act of lust, and what hidden fantasies it releases in the mind.

A Lear of the Steppe is, no doubt, a drama seen from the outside, but it shows Turgenev's mature power of *suggesting* the inside of his people and of concealing its documentation. The kind of documentation that obtrudes, say, in Zola's *La Terre*, or indeed in most stories of peasant life done by writers who are not peasants, is mercifully absent. In the manner of the greatest artists, he contrives to make us feel that people should be seen as self-justified themselves. The choice of a growing boy as the narrator, with some character of his own, makes this possible and evades the smoothing over of hearsay.

In defending the scene of hallucination in the story of Lieutenant Erguyvov, Turgenev wrote that he merely wanted to present the imperceptibility of the transition from reality to dream which "everyone has experienced for himself . . . I am completely indifferent to mysticism in all its forms," although one or two of the stories in the Baden period venture into this unseizable world. Turgenev is not dabbling in spiritualism, which was a mid-nineteenth century fad;

he is indulging his own morbidity. *A Strange Story* does describe a visit to a peasant medium. The narrator fortifies himself with drink, and the maniacal old medium who, in a scene excellent for its atmosphere of suggestion, makes the former think the figure of his dead tutor has possibly been evoked. But the medium is not the disturbing figure, nor is the possible ghost: it's a young girl of the gentry whom the narrator has met at a dance, a childish creature with a face of stone. She disturbs us. She has run away from her family and is obsessed with the idea of self-abasement and self-sacrifice. The narrator meets her long after trudging the roads with the medium who turns out to be a classic Russian holy fool. Her childishness has gone. She is bold, resolute and exalted. She refuses to be rescued.

> She seemed possessed by a sort of wrathful, vindictive excitement, without paying any attention to me, setting her teeth and breathing hard, she urged on the distracted vagrant in an undertone. . . To follow a half insane vagrant, to become his servant! She had lain down to be trampled underfoot.

The great talker seems to make a personal reflection in the end: "Her words were not opposed to her acts."

This is not one of Turgenev's important stories: it suffers from being too much a discussion at times, but it has the interest of being on the prevalence of wandering "holy souls" in Russia and peasant superstition and one has the impression that when he returned to Russia, even for a month, he was at once in touch with a life where the edges were less certain than they were in Europe, a life in which loneliness can make a human being take the sudden leap into frenzy or extremes. There is the slide into frenzy in two other tales of this period: *The Dog*, written at Spasskoye in one spontaneous burst; and also in the *Knock, Knock, Knock*, where a man prone to "fatality" is comically haunted by sounds that soon turn out to be hauntings of conscience and delusion which drive him to suicide. There is too much explanation here. Another story, *The Watch*, is interesting only as an ironical account of a weak youth's fear of the eye of his hero.

The chief drawback of Turgenev's happy life in Baden was perhaps not being out of Russia but of living in too cosy a milieu. The Viardot ménage was too much given to little concerts, the exchange of literary conceits, parlour games and intellectual pastimes. There was no loneliness and he could work only with part of himself. It is noticeable that he began to work on *Torrents of Spring* after the end of the Baden period. (It is called *Spring Freshets* by one or two translators, thereby losing, in my opinion, the more forcible image.) As a love-story it is Turgenev's masterpiece although some Russian critics despised it because it was a love-story and also because it was set in Germany. It is in fact very Russian if we think of inconsequence in matters of feeling and honour being Russian, though of course what the story is really about is honour and has implications far beyond the love-story itself. Comedy can only be written by serious minds and this one brims with the spontaneous and unthinking delight of youth and youth's misreading of the future:

> First love is like a revolution: the monotonous routine of life is smashed; youth takes its stand at the barricades.

Not only *first* love: the story can be felt to be true to the passion, especially to its passage from illusion to illusion, at any age. One knows that Sanin and Gemma are only twenty-two; but it is a surprise that the second implicated couple, Polozov the sleepy gourmet and Maria, the *femme fatale*, his wife, are only three years older, though the kind of young who are born old and without innocence. The story is a comedy in which the hours of the day smile at the characters as they pass over them, until passion moves them out of real time and into a state where time seems to stop. For Turgenev, love is an accident, contrived by Nature for its own purpose, and when love becomes sexual passion, honour is lost. There is something in Leonard Shapiro's suggestion—made in a valuable essay printed with his own translation—that Turgenev had been reading the fashionable and pessimistic Schopenhauer. (Tolstoy was affected by him too.) And of course there is something of Turgenev's mysterious attitude to sex in which love and sex are kept in separate compartments. Whatever conclusions we come to about this, they do not alter the fact that a story set in the 1840s in old-fashioned Frankfurt and Wiesbaden but written from the point of view of the 1870s has the tone, the directness and, above all, the economy which bring it near to ourselves. The comedy is also a crystallisation of Turgenev's sense of his personal tragedy. We are discreetly made aware, by his detachment, of a double view: he has caught the evanescence of the surface of experience—as I have said of the hours flowing through the fond yet baffled people and the scene, and yet we are aware of the moral undertow which drags at the swimmers who are living from moment to moment, drawing them out of their depth. To Turgenev the inevitable passing of youth and of its freedom was agonising and one can see his pose of premature old age or a perpetual Goodbye as a device for preserving the sense of youth untouched. The very naïveté and child-like qualities that were hidden behind his perfect manners suggest that his feeling about lost youth was more than the common nostalgia but rather a wonder always awake in his battered, personal life. Youth was a work of art in itself. The double view of love we find in the story, of middle age looking back on a folly that turns into betrayal and shame, gives the comedy of *Torrents of Spring* its moral complexities.

As in several earlier stories, notably *A Correspondence* and *Acia*, the ghost of the Turgenev-Viardot situation stands in the shadow of *Torrents of Spring*, but the characters have no resemblance to them. Sanin, the impulsive young Russian nobleman, travelling in Germany, is a sort of Turgenev without his convictions or gifts; novelists find it useful to put a derogatory half-picture of themselves into a story in order to gain perspective and to free the story from the maudlin or from the blur of introspection. The tale is said to have started in his mind from the memory of meeting a beautiful Jewish girl in Frankfurt when he was twenty-two. She had, like Gemma the Italian girl in the story, rushed out of the confectioner's shop when he was passing to ask him to save her brother who was thought to be dying inside. The young Turgenev himself went on to Russia, but the image of the beautiful girl remained in his mind: the rest of the story is invention. Most important is its frame: it opens with Sanin-Turgenev at the age of fifty-two coming back at night from a party of brilliant people in which he himself had been a brilliant talker. He is exhausted physically and spiritually and is suddenly attacked by the *taedium vitae,* the disgust with life, as a man who talks too well may easily be.

He thought of the vanity, the uselessness, the vulgar falsity of all things human . . . Everywhere was the same everlasting futility, the same ineptitude, the same kind of half-genuine, half-conscious self-delusion . . . And then all of a sudden like a bolt from the blue, old age comes upon you and with it the ever-growing corroding and undermining fear of death.

And once more he sees the familiar nightmare image of death about which Turgenev had written in *Phantoms*. He is in a boat, looking down into the transparent water, and out of the slime below he sees huge hideous fishes; one of these monsters rises to the surface as if to overturn the boat, but sinks once more. He knows that "when the appointed hour comes" it will rise up again and sink him for good. This is the classic nightmare of Turgenev's pessimism. Sanin goes to his desk to rummage among old papers in order to drive the despair away and to his surprise comes upon a garnet cross. At once he is back in his youth in Frankfurt and sees the beautiful girl rushing out of the confectioner's who has now become the Italian Gemma. The spring of youth begins to flow, Sanin loses his fifty-two years and standing over his shoulder presents the ingenuous young Sanin. This world-weary, even sentimental conventional gambit is common enough in story-telling but there is something different in Turgenev's handling of it: that opening portrait is a dramatic shadow that will run with the narrative so that the past will be seen running towards an inescapable present. Turgenev is free to mock his youth and to watch the defeat of innocence without abusing it.

He worked for two years on this story. He wrote the fifty thousand words at least three times. His art is the pursuit of truth-telling and balance; he does not allow one character to obscure another; he lets every character do what it is his nature to do. And each one delights because of the gentle but firm manner in which he makes them add unsuspected traits to themselves. All is movement.

The story also owes much of its freshness to its division into forty-three short chapters, most of them only five or six pages long and reading like variations on a deepening melody. The Italian family is delightfully drawn. There are the fond, shrewd mother, Frau Leonora with her headaches and her tears; the dramatising Panteleone, who had once been on the operatic stage but is now sunk to the state of half-servant, half-family friend; the beautiful

Gemma who is charming but has a mind of her own; her fiancé Herr
Kluber, the pompous rising shopkeeper; the rude blustering German
officer, Baron von Donhof whom Sanin challenges to a duel; the
handsome Italian son of the family who wants to be an artist and
not a shopkeeper—they are all moved into action. Sanin and
Gemma are bemused by each other, each is a wonder. In Sanin,
Gemma sees an eloquent young hero, free of the pettiness of shop-
keeping, a young man of honour, enchantingly free. Sanin sees
Gemma as a goddess and his love begins when he is jealous of Herr
Kluber and horrified to think of her becoming the wife of a stiff,
obsequious shopkeeper. Kluber, as it turns out, is afraid to stand up
to a rude German officer who shouts his drunken admiration of
Gemma across the tables at a restaurant. Kluber takes his party away,
but Sanin stays behind to challenge Von Donhof to a duel. Already
the feet of Sanin and Gemma have left the earth. What accident
will Nature trick them with to make them fall into each other's
arms? As Sanin stands near her window he and Gemma are literally
blown together.

> Suddenly, amid the dead silence and in an entirely cloudless sky, there
> arose such a violent gust of wind that the ground seemed to tremble
> underfoot, the faint starlight to quiver and shimmer and the air began
> turning round in a whirlwind. The wind, not cold but warm, almost
> burning hot, struck the trees, the roof of the house, its walls, the
> street.

The din lasts only for a minute and in that time the two have
grabbed each other for protection.

In no time the whole Italian family are in love with the lovers.
Madness seizes them all. Sanin says he will sell his estates in Russia
instantly, take a job in the diplomatic service: better still, turn
confectioner. Even Frau Leonora starts innocently working out how
she will enlarge the shop. They are all living unreal lives.

Sanin leaves the shop to find someone who will buy his estates.
Idiotic luck is on his side: he meets a Russian friend Polozov, who
had been at boarding school with him, and tells him what has
happened. Polozov says that he cannot offer any money, but says
that, very likely, if managed in the right way, his rich wife probably
will. The Polozovs are staying in nearby Wiesbaden. This prospect

seems quite normal to Sanin. We now see one kind of illusion in love, turning to a darker one.

Sanin goes with Polozov to Wiesbaden to meet his rich wife. Love is not a miracle for the Polozovs: it is a sophisticated arrangement, a tolerated enslavement which takes the form of freedom. Polozov, an idle and impotent gourmet, is married to a sexually ravenous woman, half-gypsy and possibly of serf background, apt to be vulgar in speech, intelligent, a beautiful animal, who has married in order to be free to take on any lovers she wants. The chaste Gemma has inspired the idealist in Sanin: Maria Polozov is struck by him and settles to drawing out his sensuality, promising him the money but working on him until his love for Gemma is adroitly turned into sexual desire for herself. The scenes in which she negotiates this are wonderfully done and they end with an afternoon on which Sanin and Maria go riding into the mountains and the animal exhilaration of the ride ends in her victory.

This is one of the most sustained evocations of sensual love in Turgenev's writing and may be said to be unique, for in *First Love* one has only a brief perception from an outside observer. In *Torrents of Spring* one sees the whole of the experience, except the act itself, from the growth of the intrigue, those exchanges of personal history in the theatre, those impatient yet cunning insinuations on the woman's side, the cornering of Sanin's conscience and the dissembling of the imagination as desire takes him into bewitchment. The ride into the mountains is long, constantly distracting him with the excitement of canter and gallop and yet each distraction heightening the sexual impulse as Sanin follows Maria from the road, into the woods, across the sudden light of swampy field, into darker forest and paths which she knows but he does not, to the woodman's hut where they tie their tired and shuddering horses—this detail obliquely suggesting the exhaustion and will-lessness of the mind, helpless before the act can seize them and passion come out in its full strength. Turgenev obtrudes no overt symbolism (which usually mars such episodes in other writers); indeed as an account of a healthy ride in the country, passing from sun to shade through the trees, the whole thing has a kind of innocence. What is exceptional is the sense of two people in love in hostile ways, hers a determined gamble—she has in fact a bet with her husband that she will bring off the seduction—and Sanin's love, helpless and blind. It is as if, as woman and man, they are fencing opponents yet united by intention. For both of them, despite the intention, the act of love will relieve them by seeming to come from the outside, overwhelming her fear of losing and his of succeeding. Turgenev is superior to most authors, especially of his period, in showing us this without giving us the fatal impression that he is vicariously satisfying his own erotic wishes. Above all he sees the man and the woman as separate people, as two different histories: and conveys nothing of what I have just written by his own analysis. The people exist for themselves, not for him, just as the groom whom they told to leave them half-way through the ride, exists only for himself on that day. In his way, and even like the horses, he has this day for its own sake. Turgenev, the nature lover, admired the equilibrium of nature; and this sense of balance gives the whole story a quality one can only call innocence that is a veil.

Of course, mountains and forest can be said to exist for themselves too and it is only here that Turgenev shows his own hand. The act of love, like the act of dying, is part of Nature in a different cycle. Gemma may be forgotten. Maria enslaves Sanin. But Nature enslaves even Maria who pursues power and her own freedom, regardless of others. When they leave the woodman's hut, Maria says to Sanin:

> "Where are you going, darling? To Frankfurt or to Paris?"
> He says: "I am going where you will be and I'll be with you till you drive me away."

He writes a shabby note to Gemma.

> Maria grasped his hair with her ten fingers. She slowly fingered and twisted his unresisting hair, drew herself up to her full height, her lips curled with triumph and her eyes, wide and bright, almost white, merely repressed the ruthless insensitivity and the satiety of conquest. A hawk holding a captured bird in its claw, has eyes like that.

We notice that pull of the hair: Turgenev's own initiation into sexual love came when the serf girl pulled him by the hair at Spasskoye.

Sanin hasn't the courage to travel back to Gemma's shop and collect his things. He sends Polozov's footman. He remembers every shameful detail of the life that followed: how he actually peeled a pear for the greedy, complaisant Polozov as the carriage rolled along the main street of Wiesbaden on the way to Paris, the humiliations there: the hideous tortures of the slave who is not allowed to be jealous or to complain, until in the end, he is cast off.

These late stories are profoundly Russian stories of bewitchment and of being possessed. It is a mistake to dismiss them as lesser works simply because they are not directly concerned with the Russian social question: the Russian "calypso's isle" has its own native force. Maria is an example of a contemporary Russian type: the girl who is half-peasant, half-aristocrat. Her belief in freedom is Nihilism without the politics. Sanin is uninterested in politics, but he notices for the first time that selling one's estate means selling human beings as well and that love makes him gloss over a fact which is shocking to Gemma and her family. The Italians are comical, but their young son will be a revolutionary: his honour grows, as Sanin's is lost. Such references are oblique. The epilogue which completes the frame of the story is discomforting and, on the whole, one could do without it (as we could also do without the literary references to Virgil and Hoffmann), although, since Turgenev never quite disentangles himself from the influences of shadow-autobiography, these are interesting. In his remorse before the shameful detail of his memories, Sanin at the age of fifty-two sets out to trace Gemma and her history. In Frankfurt, the old shop where in youth he had proposed to stand behind the counter selling sweets has gone. Even the street has gone. Frankfurt has been rebuilt. He does at last get a letter from Gemma. The sweet sentimental German girl was practical. She is married to a rich American businessman in New York, happy in her life. It has all turned out well, despite her tears at the time. At least the Sanin affair had made her break with Kluber who in fact went bankrupt and was sent to prison. Easily she forgives and is sorry for the wretchedness of Sanin's life.

The last we hear of Sanin is that he is talking of going to America. The cynical reader suspects that Sanin-Turgenev is going to attach himself once more to Gemma's family as in the 1860s Turgenev had re-attached himself to the Viardots. There is one sentence, buried in the story, that comes back to one with new force:

Weak people never bring anything to an end themselves: they always expect things to come to an end.

Sanin's will was weak in dealing with Maria Polozov: it was strong only in pursuing illusions.

It is said that Turgenev did not show this story to Pauline Viardot before it was published, though he may have read it to her in French afterwards. Her mind may have wandered to what was always more important to her—her own art. She was too extroverted and practical to share his pessimism and may easily have seen herself as the dark-haired Gemma, comfortably married, with her children.

Chapter 13

THE Viardots had been generous to Turgenev when he was a young man; now their fortunes had been shaken badly by the war and Pauline's singing engagements were fewer and she was obliged to take pupils who were not among the very rich. Turgenev repaid the Viardots and did so with the greatest tact. He had, as we have seen, built up a sizable dowry for Didie. They had consented to letting him have a flat in their house in the rue de Douai and, with Louis, he bought a country property near Paris, on which he built a small châlet for himself in the grounds, close to their house. After its vicissitudes, the peculiar friendship had become a sort of marriage which was taken for granted and which left them indifferent to gossip. The glow of Baden had gone and was followed by a sort of contentment. In his *Life*, David Magarshack says that for a short time in her fifties Pauline took another lover, but does not say any more about it. She was certainly fond of Turgenev's clever young friend Pietsch, a hapless borrower, who adored her in a child-like way: she used to stroke his head, but she stroked Turgenev's head also. It is true—as far as one knows—that there is a gap of a year in Turgenev's letters to Pauline when he was away in Russia.

When they first fled to London in 1870 and after he had settled them in, Turgenev went off to be honoured by Cambridge University and to shoot in Scotland. His fame in England had been founded by W.R.S. Ralston, a Cambridge don and translator. The extent of Turgenev's reading in English literature was as extraordinary as his reading in French, German and Spanish and he amused himself eagerly in translating. He even translated Burns. But he did not speak English well. He pitied the English, as Herzen had done, for their mania for work and rushing to the office; he despised English painting but he deeply admired English political institutions. And then there was the shooting and the hospitality of the great country houses. He was invited to Edinburgh to the celebrations of the birth of Sir Walter Scott—the Scottish papers called him Toogueneff, and when he mentioned Pushkin the name of the poet was spelt Tourhaine. His short speech was conventionally flattering and neat and contained one of Pushkin's excellent critical insights:

> He used to say of Scott, among other things, that if he treated with so much calmness and simplicity the Kings and heroes and other historical personages of the past, it was because he felt himself their equal before posterity—and they formed for him his natural and every day society.

Afterwards he went off to the grouse shooting at Pitlochry. He ate quantities of strawberries, but the shoot wore him out. It was a sport for the young, he said, he panted after an hour with a a young man who kept shouting "Come on" and was a dead shot, whereas Turgenev missed all the first birds and in the end only shot eleven against the young man's seventy-six. Also he injured his foot and dreaded an attack of gout would follow, but he escaped it. His host sent him a horse on the second day. Robert Browning and his son were staying there. He found Browning vain, pompous and boring. The son had a huge spot on the tip of his nose. (Turgenev had always been a collector of grotesque faces: his letters often contain caricatures. There is the woman whose nose beats time to the music she is listening to and which ends by curling up like a snail; and another, seen in the train on the way to Ghent, whose chin had a vermillion beard and who was constantly addressed as *"Mon ange"* by her husband.)

In 1874 he was fifty-six. His rooms in the rue de Douai were small and crowded with objects. The walls of the little salon were green and draped with "stuff," not papered—Henry James reported—there were few books and all signs of writing were put out of sight. There were some pictures: a Corot and one or two of the Barbizon school, for he had taken to Louis Viardot's passion for collecting in the hope that prices would rise, but his taste was uncertain and dealers found him a credulous buyer. There was a marble bust of Pauline and a model of her right hand: he followed the mid-nineteenth-century cult of the hand, for it seemed to celebrate the chaste philandering game of touch. Less effusive, Pauline would offer what she called "an English good shake-hand." It makes a difference.

Crowds of young Russians, generally would-be authors or revolutionaries of varying degrees, would climb up the stairs to show the great man their manuscripts, beg him to find publishers for them and often to borrow money, for he was known never to refuse his time, his help or his pocket. Pauline found the Russian visitors barbarous. Turgenev was usually seen lying on a divan large enough to bear his huge sleepy body, dressed in a Caucasian jacket with red lapels and talking marvellously by the hour and, when he was excited, got up and paced the little room in the manner which had maddened Tolstoy. As the years went on, worshipping Russians noted that he was always running messages for the Viardots and that the room was shabby and neglected. There was a broken window-blind, never repaired. Others of the anti-Viardot school were shocked that the master's room was not quiet, for it was immediately above the room where Pauline was giving her singing lessons, but he would point to the speaking tube he had installed in order to hear her voice more clearly and be transported into memories of times when it had put its spell upon the opera houses of Europe and upon himself, an emanation also of her will as an artist and a woman. He did not fail to be present at her fashionable Thursdays, when the distinguished guests sat in a bare simple room with its piano and its jars of cornflowers and poppies, or went to look at Louis Viardot's little gallery of pictures. Dressed in a black lace gown the stout hostess played and sang and the blood of the select audience would freeze with terror when she sang her tragic parts. She had her

Sundays, which were less austere. Charades and forfeits were played by the talented family. At a hint, Turgenev would eagerly be led into telling his fantastic stories. George Sand who loved such entertainments at Nohant watched the scene with the complacency of the one who had brought about the convenient bourgeois marriage of the young girl she had idealised in *Consuelo*.

Turgenev wrote little in Paris. He was always out and about on the affairs of the Russian Club which drained his pocket, at the Salon of the Princesse Mathilde where he met all the important French writers, Daudet, Zola, the Goncourts and, above all, Flaubert, the only one whose work he profoundly admired. Turgenev was generous in getting French writers published in Russia and, in fact, became an amateur literary agent for them. With Zola he had considerable success. He arranged for the translation of Tolstoy's *War and Peace*. He became friends with the young Maupassant, but his closest friendship was with Flaubert. He translated Flaubert's *La Légende de Saint-Julien-L'Hospitalier* into Russian. He had corresponded with him for years and went eventually to visit him at Croisset. It was a friendship of physical giants. Flaubert had the trumpeting voice and the gait of a red-faced Norman conqueror; he was the masculine figure in a kind of marriage, Daudet said, whereas Turgenev "the nervous, languid, passionate Russian yet as torpid as an Oriental" was the feminine one. But this is far from the impression we have from Turgenev's letters in which he appears as the strong, practical, compassionate figure, urging Flaubert to ignore his failure with the critics, anxious about his health. When Flaubert was ruined by the bankruptcy of his niece's husband, it was Turgenev who tried to get Gambetta to get Flaubert a pension. Turgenev used to go up to the room Flaubert kept at the end of the Faubourg Saint Honoré on Sundays if—Flaubert said—the Viardots would let him. But the two gourmets met at the Magny dinners and in other restaurants, particularly one opposite the Opéra Comique known for its bouillabaisse. Turgenev said he could talk for a week on end with his friend and laughed when Flaubert said he was liquefying like an old Camembert and called Turgenev "a soft pear."

In the summer Turgenev went with the Viardots to the small estate on a wooded hill overlooking the Seine below the Aqueduct of Marly. It was called Les Frênes. There were fountains and mossy statues in the gardens, everywhere the sound of water under the ash trees. He had his two-storey châlet there in the gardens. The rooms were large and luxuriously furnished and there he dressed in his red dressing-gown and wandered about in heavy Russian boots. Here he wrote *A Desperate Man*, his *Song of Triumphant Love, Clara Milich*, the *Poems in Prose* and *Old Portraits*.

When Henry James visited him there, he found him tall, robust, "the expression of a magnificent manhood . . . with a frame that would have made it perfectly lawful and even becoming, for him to be brutal; but there was not a grain of brutality in his composition." His intellect was beautiful. His thick hair was straight and white, so was his short beard and there was an air of "neglected strength, as if it had been part of his modesty never to remind himself that he was strong. . . His noble appearance was in itself a manner, but whatever he did he did very simply and he had not the slightest pretension to not being subject to rectification." The strongest impression was of goodness. James concluded that he was not Gallicised; the French capital was an accident for him. He had, with "that great tradition of ventilation of the Russian mind," windows open into distances which stretched far beyond the banlieue. The "ventilations" were marvellous but had their eccentric effect on his daily habits. He was one of those who breakfast at lunch-time, whose sense of time was all his own. He was beautifully late for engagements; hours would go by during which the host or guest would have to guess whether he was going to arrive or had forgotten. Clock time, despite all his watches, did not exist, indeed the watches could be said to have been a metaphysical guarantee. His life was a stream of apologies for unexpected absences and sudden appearances. This drove Pauline mad, but she could do nothing about it. The young people laughed when they heard first Turgenev and then Viardot snoring after dinner.

In the May of 1874 Turgenev was in Russia once more and stayed until July. In Petersburg he looked out of his window to see the moujiks, the Kaftans, the little carts, the pigeons flying about and the soldiers in their long coats, and felt he had never been away. Although it was spring and the sun was shining, there was no sign of leaves on the trees, there was an icy and stinging wind raising the eternal dust of Russian cities. He had a twitch of rheumatism in his shoulders. He was seeing crowds of people and went to the courts to hear a case of rape: the victim did not shout and cry as a French girl would, but was as dumb as a sheep and the awful rapist was acquitted! He was a sponge, Turgenev said of himself, mopping up every possible impression of Petersburg life for future use; the making of a new novel, *Virgin Soil*, was in his head. Russian society, he said, had changed but it was difficult to know what was going on under the surface. The young men were no longer hostile to him. He noticed that his efforts on behalf of Flaubert's *Tentation de Saint Antoine* had been a failure. There are letters to the Viardots every few days. He went to the English Club where he wonders what they thought of him; he found them all terribly aged. He visited a reformed prison: no corporal punishment, no bread and water, a kind of open prison; the governor came of an English family who had settled in Petersburg—"perhaps that explains the success of the experiment."

As always on his visits to Russia the gourmet indulges and is doubled up in a violent colic that lasts for days. He takes the train to Moscow which is ugly, dirty and stinking and stays in a palace of vast rooms and only one servant, a drunken old soldier. (His host has left for the Crimea.) Then he goes on the long drive via Mtsenk to Spasskoye and is at last under the roof of his wooden house. It has been re-painted, the ivy hangs from the verandah. He notices how sad the garden is; it seems to be filled with an ancient silence, perhaps because of the cawing of the rooks. He looks at the school he has built (the schoolmaster is a drunk but not a bad sort) and the little hospital with its old people. There is one who is ninety-one. The peasants come round begging. They embrace him and weep, not because they are pleased to see him or because they are grateful, but out of self-pity and their fear of death which brings "those little round tears to the faces of the old." He gives them 1,000 hectares of wood and six roubles worth of eau de vie.

His gout makes one of its expected attacks, as the Viardots knew it would. It flies to his knee. This is the third time he has had it in June. The only known remedy was a Dr. Joseph's pills taken in sugared water, and a hot compress with oil of arnica put on the joint. Terrible nights of agony follow; he has to send to Mtsenk for crutches. And he is burning sugar, paper and sealing wax to drive away the appalling stench of his manservant's feet.

The past comes back in the form of a visit from his old valet Porfiry, his half-brother, who had been in Germany with him when they were young. Porfiry had become a doctor and brought a dreadful son with him.

Another visitor was far more important: the Baroness Vrevskaya whose husband had been killed in the Caucasus. (Pauline Viardot became jealous of her and called her drily the *"veuve de Malabar."*) The baroness was Turgenev's neighbour and was kind enough to visit him a couple of times when she heard he was ill and spent some days with him. He had met her before in 1873 in Karlsbad where she was taking the cure and, in his way, had fallen in love with her. Baroness Vrevskaya provoked one more *épanouissement.* She was something of a beauty, she was intelligent, she was thirty-three, and her subsequent history—four years later when the Russo-Turkish war broke out she went to the Front as a nurse and died of typhus —shows she was no torpid provincial lady, but one who needed to dedicate herself to a life of action. After the neat cynicism and phrases of French society and the egotistical young Russians who came to him with their revolutionary rages and intrigues, the Baroness was a thoughtful young Russian woman well planted in her own soil, saddened but not defeated by the death of her husband. Although he protected himself by charm and self-irony, it does seem that she roused Turgenev out of the boredom of his accepted rôle at the Viardots where he had become inured to the lack of that spirit of expectation which was necessary to him as an artist. He was in the doldrums of resignation. She awakened his wavering imagination and they evidently became frank and intimate friends, not it seems in the melancholy manner of his friendship with the pious Countess Lambert and—though little is known about this—we do not hear any talk of "other bonds." Indeed, lamely as usual, saying an ever lingering Goodbye, as the friendship deepened, he wrote her in a letter which all his biographers quote, that he loved her as a friend; he "had had the desire to possess her, but it was not so uncontrollable as to make me ask you to marry me; on the other hand, you would never consent to what the French call a *passade."* One mysterious sentence is all that we are told of her reply "But some time ago, if you had wanted . . ." The fact is he had intended only a short stay in Russia and in his letters to the Viardots he explained the delay in returning by his attacks of gout and his researches, but his pleasure in the company of the Baroness seems likely to be part of the explanation. He wrote a fervent *Prose-Poem* about her when he heard of her death

> in the dirty, stinking straw under the shelter of a tumbledown barn turned in haste into a camp hospital in a ruined Bulgarian village . . . A soft tender woman and such a force, such eagerness for sacrifice . . . May her dear shade pardon this belated blossom upon which I make bold to lay upon her grave!

In Spasskoye the memories of his mother's tyranny over her serfs became vivid once more, and he wrote the long story of the two droll friends, Punin and Barburin, who were in the household when he was a boy, but the story leaps forward to the sixties and the change in the lives of a poor but intelligent man and the flighty girl who marries him. Punin, the unworldly story-teller and poet, is dead but Barburin and his wife, the man who has stood for justice and who has even been sent in his time to Siberia, are now seen enduring everything but educating themselves and the peasants. Barburin's strength never slackens. Turgenev is showing that the courage of one determined humble man who put his principles into practice can count.

The story shows him putting aside the disillusion that followed the Emancipation and turning to the hope that may lie in the influence of one man who bears all and keeps his faith in justice, outside of politics. It is a sleepy tale because he has thrown rambling reminiscence over it, but it is a preparation for the mood of the long political novel, *Virgin Soil*, where the scene is the Russia of the late seventies and the Populist movement. Solomin, the practical factory manager of that book, is another sober Barburin of a more able kind and of a new generation.

Virgin Soil is Turgenev's longest and most complex novel and it is very much written to show that he had not lost contact with the younger generation in Russia. He set out to portray the various types of educated young men and women who had thrown up the life of their class "to go to the people," live among them, dress in the clothes of workers and peasants and to work with them and even to conspire with them. A quotation from the *Notebook of a Farmer* on the title page indicates that the novel will be a piece of practical social criticism: "Virgin soil should be turned up not by a harrow skimming over the surfaces, but by a plough biting deep into the earth." The Populists were skimmers, but there were many extremists among them. To Stassyulevich, his publisher, he wrote that he expected the novel would be as violently abused in Russia as *Fathers and Sons* had been.

> Hitherto the younger generation has been presented in our literature either as a crew of crooks and scoundrels . . . or as much as possible idealised . . . I decided to chose the middle course and to get closer to the truth—to take the young people who are, for the most part, good and honest and show that despite their honesty their very course is so false and impractical that it cannot fail to lead them to complete fiasco.

Whether he succeeded or not, he said, the young would at any rate sense his sympathy if not for their aims, then for their personalities.

Turgenev feared the censor and indeed reluctantly suppressed things that might too obviously offend. The novel was published in two parts and having passed the first, the censor's Committee were in a difficulty about the more disturbing second part. One faction wanted to burn it and insist on the "correction" of the first part. The Chairman gave an embarrassed casting vote in its favour, but said if he had known the whole book in the first place he would have banned it. In the end, as Turgenev expected, the novel was damned by both sides who were swayed by party feeling. The Conservatives, the official classes, said Turgenev was a dangerous Radical who himself was personally involved with conspiracy—and indeed he did give money to the paper of the Populist leader, Lavrov, but simply because he hoped it would take the place of Herzen's *The Bell* as a forum for political discussion. He knew enough about political opinion to know that its phases do not last long. The Populists were a moral replacement of the Nihilists whose policy of rejection had soon spent itself. The Conservatives, especially, derided the idea that one of his characters, a girl called Marianna of the gentry class, would involve herself with the movement. No young woman would join it. The Radical critics ranged from those who said he was an old man libelling the young to those who said he knew nothing about the genuine revolutionaries and that, in any case, his absence from Russia made him out of date. Turgenev proved to be more accurate than either party in his diagnosis, as he had been in the case of Bazarov in *Fathers and Sons:* almost immediately after the publication of his novel 18 women out of 52 conspirators were arrested and put on trial. The world's press reported the sensation and *Virgin Soil* was translated into many languages and became a bestseller in France, Great Britain and the United States.

Turgenev was easily affected by hostile criticism. Once more he said he was finished and, once more, that he would never write again. But presently he recovered and stood by what he had written and, like many gentle men who are bullied, he had his malice and a sharp, firm pride. Indeed, the novel itself has a satirical harshness which is exceptional in his works. He repeated one or two stinging epigrammatic judgments, one particularly on the notorious Oriental love of lying which so many Westerners have complained of in Russians:

> A truthful man . . . that was the great thing! that was what touched her! It is a well known fact, though by no means easy to understand, that Russians are the greatest liars on the face of the earth and yet there is nothing they respect like the truth—nothing attracts them so much.

In its opening pages, we are pushed abruptly into a dirty attic and see a slovenly young man and a woman with coarse lips and teeth. Both are smoking and paying no attention to each other; nevertheless, we note their air of honesty, stoicism and serious commitment. From this moment we see how Turgenev's familiar world and manner has changed. The style is harder, more photographic; the grace has been replaced by the instant, the summary and the laconic. He is now attempting a larger number of characters from a wider canvas of life and is about to involve them in an elaborate plot and to grip us with a long story of imposed suspense which he had said earlier was outside his instinct and competence. We remember that Tolstoy and Dostoevsky have overtaken him, in this sense, and have given the Russian novel a density where before it had only surface and extent. We remember that what he admired in Dickens was the variety of mood—indeed he wondered, after the book was done, if he had not taken too much of the caricaturist from him. We have certainly an impression of cartoon and in that the book has something in common with, say, Dostoevsky's *The Devils*.

Both Turgenev's conspirators and his innocents who "go to the people," strike one as living in a vacuum. Conspiracy is an urban matter and Turgenev is not by nature an urban novelist, although for once he does give us a picture of a Russian town, probably Orel, for its own sake. It is well photographed:

> It was Saturday night, there were no people on the street, but the taverns were still crowded. Hoarse voices broke from them, drunken songs and the nasal notes of the concertina; from doors suddenly opened streamed the filthy warmth, the acrid smell of alcohol, the red glare of lights. Before almost every tavern were standing little peasant carts, harnessed to shaggy, pot-bellied nags; they stood with their unkempt heads hanging down submissively, and seemed asleep.

Or:

> The coach crossed a wide market place, positively stinking of rush mats and cabbages, passed the governor's house with striped sentry boxes at the gates, a private house with a turret, a promenade set with trees recently planted and already dying, a bazaar filled with the barking of dogs and the clinking of chains, and gradually reaching the boundaries of the town overtook a long long train of wagons, which had set off late for the sake of the cool of the night.

An un-Turgenevean scene, brutally observed, but it must be said, well-placed. For Nezhdanov, the young poet and idealist and, so to say, political guinea-pig of the novel, is getting a first sight of the Russia he has vowed to "go to," live with and understand. But what one suspects already is, as Richard Freeborn says in his study of Turgenev, that *Virgin Soil* is going to be a forerunner of the crude, black and white, schematic works of the Socialist Realists of our time and that:

> The distinctions Turgenev makes between the aims ot the Populists and their persons was artificial, especially for a writer who had been used to accepting both the man and his ideas.

This change is certainly felt and although one can say that Turgenev's effort of will in keeping in touch with Russian realities has
some of the guilt of the absentee in it—a matter that was, as he put
it, his fate—we know that he judged rightly when he said that the
Populist movement was a pathos, that no root and branch change
would take place for another twenty years at least. The central
characters are nevertheless representative. The aristocratic young
Nezhdanov has traits of Turgenev's character: like the young Turgenev, he is handsome and has chestnut hair (but he is an illegitimate son). He has a double nature: he is secretly a poet but ashamed
of his poetry, his real interest is political activity. He is an idealist,
passionate, chaste, timid; ashamed of these qualities, he even tries
to be coarse in his language: "Life did not come easily to him." His
feelings push him forward, but beyond his power of performance. He
is the Turgenevean mixture of Don Quixote and Hamlet, a throw-
back to "the superfluous man." When he "goes to the people" and
solemnly dresses up in workman's clothes, the workmen see through
him at once and make him drunk on raw vodka. Another time he
is "beaten up" and makes a mess of everything.

Marianna, the brusque upper-class girl whom he falls in love with
when he is tutoring in the grand house of the wordy liberal Sipyasin,
is as innocent as he, but she is the new kind of young girl. She is
a rebel who has cropped her hair and (interesting when one remembers Turgenev's old-fashioned habits), she belongs to the generation
who have also given up hand-kissing. When she boldly runs off with
Nezhdanov to "go to the people" with him, she refuses to be married
and they live together in chastity. Marianna is a rebel not a revolutionary—a rebel eager to leave her class, to be useful and to sacrifice
herself. The real revolutionary is Mashurina, the unkempt, plain and
awkward girl who silently loves Nezhdanov. She is quietly efficient
in secret work, alert for traitors, spies and mistrustful of some of the
hangers-on of the movement, for example of Palkin a cripple, a
foolish yet far-seeing man, but a danger to the cause because he is
an unstable and excitable chatterbox, easily flattered. It is Mashurina
who will disappear deeper into conspiracy when Palkin's foolishness
and swank give the group away.

The "hero" in Turgenev's eyes—although Palkin makes Turgenev's point in a prophetic speech about the dull, immovable
men who will eventually rule Russia—is Solomin. Turgenev calls

him an American type—he knew no Americans but America had provided a Utopian dream for early revolutionaries (except Herzen who called Americans "elderly children"). Turgenev rejected the traditional Russian respect for Germans as the practical race; he looked back on the Germans as the guiding philosophers of his youth; so he turned to the English and made Solomin, the son of the despised priesthood, a man who had learned his trade in the cotton factories of Manchester and his politics from the English reformers of the industrial revolution and who may have a touch of Engels in him. Solomin is sympathetic to the conspirators, protects them loyally but advises caution and gradualism to the headstrong. He is strong, healthy, hard-working, generous, sober and resourceful, a man of sense. Inevitably he strikes one as being too good to be true; as a still portrait he is well enough done, but Turgenev can't make him move except in small helpful ways. Markelov, a retired artillery officer and landowner is the dour type of cantankerous conspirator, a lonely, unhappy man who can't farm his land effectively because he tries to run everything by giving orders in a military way. He is the same in conspiracy—too aggressive, given to acting independently and openly like a fanatical officer. He is certain to be arrested and to go grimly silent and still determined to Siberia.

These figures are well enough done in the first volume of the novel which deceived the censors, for they are seen in the setting that Turgenev can always do well: the still, timeless scene of the great country house where the family and the guests dine and talk, when Sipyagin, the host, is mellifluous at the table, where his pretty wife flirts with the tutor in her boudoir, where the rebel girl gazes at Nezhdanov and sulks before her aunt, where people walk in the gardens and the carriages come and go. It is the same sort of Paradise from the past as one finds in *A Nest of Gentlefolk,* in *Fathers and Sons*—but the characters are now hardened. Turgenev shows his contempt for the gentry openly, especially for the conceited and pompous young Kammerjunker, Kallomyetsov, who is an active "Red" hunter, vain of his certainty in spotting revolutionaries. He is far cruder than Pavel in *Fathers and Sons* or the other comical Frenchified asses of earlier novels. And Sipyagin, the bland, sporting landowner with his skin-deep liberalism is also ridiculed. The drawing-room quarrels become edgy when the egregious Kallomyetsov says Sipyagin should be President of a Commission that would decide everything.

Madame Sipyagin laughed more than ever.
"You must take care: Boris Andreivitch is sometimes such a Jacobin . . . "
"Jacko, Jacko, Jacko," called the parrot.
Valentine Mihalovna shook her handkerchief at him.
"Don't prevent sensible people from talking! Marianna, tell him to be quiet."
Marianna turned to the cage and began scratching the parrot's neck which he offered her at once.
"Yes," Madame Sipyagin said, "Boris Andreivich sometimes astonishes me. He has something . . . something of the tribune."
"C'est parce qu'il est orateur," Kallomyetsov interposed hotly. "Your husband has the gift of words, as no one else has; he's accustomed to success, too . . . *ses propres paroles le grisent* . . . But he's a little off that, isn't he? *Il boude*—eh?"
"I haven't noticed it," she replied after a brief silence.
"Yes," Kallomyetsov pursued in a pensive tone, "he has been overlooked a little."

It is all drifting to a row about Marianna being a Nihilist because at this time, before she runs off with Nezhdanov, she teaches in a village school.

The things we rely on Turgenev for are here: the naturalness of all kinds of talk and the silences in it—with him it is a pianist's gift —and his ear is just as fine when we get to the drunken and confused talk of the Radicals in the second volume. His summary penetration into character does not fail. Madame Sipyagin for example, is excellent.

She was clever, not ill-natured—rather good-natured of the two, fundamentally cold and indifferent—and she could not tolerate the thought of anyone remaining indifferent to her . . . Only, these charming egoists must not be thwarted: they are fond of power and will not tolerate independence in others. Women like Sipyagina excite and work upon inexperienced and passionate natures; for themselves they like regularity and a peaceful life . . . Flirtation cost Sipyagina little; she was well aware that there was no danger for her and never could be . . . With what a happy smile she retired into herself, into the consciousness of her inaccessibility, her impregnable virtue and with what gracious condescension she submitted to the lawful embrace of her well-bred spouse.

Not until we get to the second volume does Turgenev break out of talk into dramatic scenes. Madame Sipyagin seems to be a development of Madame Odintsov in *Fathers and Sons* but done in acid. She spies on her niece, intercepts letters and exposes the girl's love for Nezhdanov to Markelov who had hoped to marry her. The point of this jealous intrigue is to show the extremes to which the apparently gracious Sipyaginas will go to preserve the unity of their class. At the moment when the defiant Markelov dashes to support a local riot of the peasants and the conspiracy is betrayed, the hypocrisy of Sipyagin's liberalism comes out. He is smoother than the violent Kallomyetsov and, in masterly fashion, Turgenev as the novelist of personal relationships shows these relationships being undermined politically. There has been an excellent scene at the end of the first part of the novel in which Markelov begins to have the force of a tragic figure. As a man of honour, reckless and incapable of spite or jealousy, indifferent to enemies, determined as an analyst and not deceived, Markelov does not spare his host:

"If we wait for the moment when everything, absolutely everything is ready, we shall never begin. If one weighs *all* the consequences beforehand, it is certain there will be some evil ones. For instance, when our predecessors organized the emancipation of the peasants, could they foresee that one result of this emancipation would be the rise of a whole class of money-lending landowners who would lend the peasant a quarter of mouldy rye for six roubles and extort them from him (here Markelov crooked one finger) first the full six roubles in labour and besides that (Markelov crooked another finger), a whole quarter of good rye and then (Markelov crooked a third), interest on top of that—in fact squeeze the peasant to the last drop. Our emancipators couldn't have foreseen that. And yet even if they had done, it was right to free the peasants and not to weigh all the consequences. And so I've made up my mind!"

And when Markelov is arrested at the end of the book he is obdurate and does not repent. It is one of Turgenev's excellences that he is true to the basic character of people. Markelov is the incurable soldier when he reflects on his betrayal:

> It is I who am to blame, I didn't understand, I didn't say the right thing, I didn't go the right way to work. I ought simply to have given orders and if anyone had tried to hinder or resist, put a bullet through his head! What's the use of explanations here. Anyone not with us has no right to live . . . spies are killed like dogs, worse than dogs.

Turgenev is hard to follow in the facts of the conspiracy: there are too many hints and shadow figures, but one is well done. This is Palkin, the vain, chattering and comic exhibitionist, the born mysterious contact-man longing to be trusted and knowing he cannot be; he is burdened by the knowledge of his own muddle-headedness. The scene in which Sipyagin flatters him, inflates his conceit, snubs him and slyly worms everything he wants out of him and dismisses him with contempt when Palkin is out to impress the Governor, is good. Into the mouth of this walking calamity, Turgenev puts shrewd prophecy. He defends Solomin to whom the intellectual revolutionaries are now cool: Russia needs sturdy, rough, dull men of the people.

> Just look at Solomin: his brain is clear as daylight, and he's as healthy as a fish . . . Isn't that a wonder! Why do we Russians always have the idea that to be a man of feeling and conscience, you've got to be an invalid?

There are two more characters to whom a complete scene is given, who on the face of it have no relevance to the theme of the novel and who in fact seem to belong to a short story thrown in for relief. Turgenev was inclined to cut them out but was persuaded to let them stay. They are an elderly, childless pair of innocent, doll-like, eccentric creatures, called Fomushka and Fimushka, the oldest inhabitants of the town, who have preserved themselves and their house as untouched models of the life of lesser gentry in the eighteenth century. They blissfully ignore everything that has happened since that time. They still drink chocolate because tea had not come in, they play duets, look at old albums and sing sweet and old-fashioned songs about hopeless love in their cracked voices. They have one unbroken rule: they have never allowed their house serfs to be flogged and if a servant turned out to be drunken and intolerable they bore with him, but after a while passed him on to a neighbour saying "Let others take their turn with him."

> But such a disaster rarely befell them, so rarely that it made an epoch in their lives and they would say for instance "That was very long ago, it happened when we had that rascal Aldoshka," or "When we had grandfather's fur cap with the fox tail stolen." They still had such caps.

The interesting thing is that this dream of an Arcadia in the past is often found in the Russian novel: in Oblomov's dream, for example; even in the talk of the senile Iudushka in Schedrin's *The Golovlyov Family*. In Turgenev, it is more than one of his "old portraits" reminiscences; it is not antiquarian; it is really an incipient fairy tale or a fable without meaning which is budding in the depths of a people's mind. It is also a relief after the vulgar scene at the merchant's house that has preceded it, a holiday of the mind from the yearning for the future which rules the whole novel—the burden of Russia which the other characters bear. Formushka and Fimushka bear no burden.

If *Virgin Soil* has not the sustained serenity of *Fathers and Sons* because the people in the right and the people in the wrong are too blatantly stated, it is an impressive attempt to have a final say. It can hardly be called an old man's book, for Turgenev was in his late fifties when he wrote it. The strain, we feel, comes from trying to pack too much into it and not without artifice. To the critics who said that he was out of touch with the new Russia, Turgenev replied that he was closely in touch with the dozens of young people who came to see him in Paris; but although they may have revealed themselves to him they did not really bring their Russia with them and were more likely to present him with arguments than with intimacy. If what we read in Anna Dostoevsky's Diary of her life with her husband and, of course, in Dostoevsky's novels, the quality that was missing in Turgenev's young visitors was the fact that at home they lived in crowds, above all in one another's lives: their very homes in whatever class, were normally crowded, public to their relations and their friends. It is in the nature of Dostoevsky's genius to show that when one of his characters appears his whole life and all his relatives seemed to be hanging out of his talking mouth. When Russians soliloquise they are never alone. Turgenev himself said that in Russia writing was easy for the novelist: the stories and people spring up around him and crowd in on him at once.

The political perspicacity of Turgenev is astonishing and now the state of our world has changed it seems closer to our political experience than it was to English admirers of Turgenev in 1900 who saw in him something close to the experience of an English country gentleman of sensitive tastes. The only thing that really shocks in *Virgin Soil* is Nezhdanov's suicide: the "superfluous man," whom Turgenev invented, seems to die as a convenience in the interests of early Romanticism and Turgenev's preoccupation with death.

Chapter 14

A T Les Frênes, his "little idol" Didie used often to sit drawing or painting in his room while he wrote: he needed the tremor of a feminine presence. He had written funny and serious letters to her since she was a little girl and he continued to do so after her marriage in 1874 and also to her husband who charmed him. Many of these letters of his have lately been discovered and published in Paris and they put his feeling for Pauline's daughter in a strange and touching light. In an introduction to them Alexandre Zviguilsky thinks there is some reason to believe that Maupassant saw those letters after Turgenev's death and that on them he built his novel *Fort Comme la Mort.* It is the story of a famous portrait-painter who falls in love with the daughter of his mistress because the girl reminds him of the mother when she had been young when he had first loved her. A parallel with Turgenev's situation is certainly there, and such transferences of feeling are not unknown, but Maupassant would not have needed Turgenev's story in order to write one of his well-known sentimental exercises in unusual love.

Turgenev's special delight in Didie was paternal in the godfatherly and innocent if faintly sexy way of old gentlemen. Although he was only fifty-six when she married, Turgenev had been posing as an old man for years and he was to go on flirting with young girls, and he had the old philanderer's harmless daring. One interesting thing about these letters is that they have the youthful tone of his early letters to her mother: he uses the similar flowery phrases in German and the second person singular (which he used only once, in a reckless moment, when writing to her mother. Of course, as one of the family, he would be entitled to continue the usage to a "goddaughter.") It is also interesting that he can permit himself to write an occasional playful sensual passage:

Je bénis ton beau corps tout entier et j'embrasse mille fois ce que tu me permets d'embrasser
Et maintenant, Madame, figurez-vous vous êtes assise sur le rebord du billard et que je me tiens devant vous, vous balancez vos pieds mignons comme cela vous arrive souvent; je les attrapes, je les baise l'un après l'autre, puis tes mains, ton visage, et tu me laisses faire, car tu sais qu'il n'y a pas d'être au monde que j'adore plus.

He wrote little fables about pee-ing and chamberpots for her babies. The letters tell us something of the family-games atmosphere of the Viardot household, some of the fantasies became scatological in the French way—or, as some psychologists might think—indicate a deep sexual repression; but one is most struck by the phrase "You see I tell you everything" which he often used in writing to her mother. And so he writes seriously about the horror of going to see the murderer Tropmann in the condemned cell and the hanging; and a great deal about art and writing. One of Didie's attractions was her talent.

I think there is something for the novelist—in regard to truthfulness —not in details and realistic description, but in describing feelings and states of soul. Even the greatest writers have done this, but according to established conventions which seem like reality but are not. It is possible to be bolder and go to the heart of things especially into double or contradictory feelings. I have these double feelings which almost cry out to meet and which disappear into one another.

In 1878 Tolstoy was fifty. Seventeen years after his violent quarrel with Turgenev he was approaching the spiritual crisis he described in his *Confessions* and, feeling that it was wrong to have an enemy, he wrote to the sixty-year-old novelist offering his friendship once more. Turgenev was in Paris and replied eagerly that Tolstoy was right in supposing he himself had no hostile feelings. On his return to Russia that year the two men met in Tula in the August and Tolstoy went to meet him there and drove him to Yasnaya Polyana. They shut themselves up and talked about religion for hours, but no troubles came from this dangerous subject and when they joined the family, Turgenev got on well with the children and was soon playing chess with Tolstoy's eldest son.

Turgenev towered in height above Tolstoy but his legs, Tolstoy's eldest son wrote, looked flabby. He was wearing wide-toed soft boots, a velvet jacket and, with his usual elegance, a silk shirt and cravat. He amused the young people with his tricks; he mimicked a chicken, one of his favourite comic turns. Tolstoy tolerated this, but afterwards said that charming though Turgenev was, "he was a fountain spouting imported water and gave one the feeling that the jet might cease playing."

The Countess, who had known Turgenev when he was young and had always liked him, enjoyed his high spirits. She made an important observation about his marvellous talk: it was not the talk of a conversationalist, she said, but of a story-teller in flow—which may in some degree account for the impression we have of a man often made invisible in the changing words that glide continually over his life. (He nearly lost the chess game with Tolstoy's son because he was carried away by a boast that in France he was known as the *Chevalier du Pion:* the bishop's knight.)

The two novelists met again in October and Tolstoy was restive; he wrote dismissively: "Turgenev is still the same and we know the degree of closeness that is possible to us," and began to suspect, as he had in the past, that Turgenev was laughing at him behind his back. It was the old suspicion that Turgenev was a patronising mocker and, of course, he did have an unguarded tongue. Tolstoy may have heard that Turgenev thought the military part of *War and Peace* was puppetry. Tolstoy seems not to have known that Turgenev had done everything to press Tolstoy's genius in France and England, and to forward translations of *War and Peace* abroad, even though he said that in *Anna Karenina,* Tolstoy was obsessed with "the Moscow swamp": "orthodoxy, nobles, slavophils, enmity to everything foreign; sour cabbage, soup and the absence of soap," but that the horse racing, the mowing scenes and the hunting were marvellous.

They met again several times in the next three years. Both enjoyed shooting. They went out to shoot woodcock one spring evening and while Turgenev was getting his gun ready, the Countess asked "Why have you not written anything for so long?" Turgenev said in his frank and touching way, "Are we out of hearing? Well, I will tell you. Whenever I have planned anything it is when I have been shaken by the fever of love. Now I am old and can neither love nor write." But later he told Tolstoy: "I had an affair the other day and I found it dull." "Ah," Tolstoy boasted, "if only I were like that."

Turgenev was speaking the truth, for he must have been referring to the young actress Savina, who had played in *A Month in the Country* when it was put on for the first time in 1872 and by whom his heart was agitated. One day Tolstoy drove over to Spasskoye and the driver of the trap lost his way and they did not arrive until after midnight. This did not prevent Tolstoy, Turgenev and Polonsky, the poet, from arguing until three in the morning. The next day Turgenev's cook got drunk and Turgenev went off to get the dinner himself, but a servant drove him out of the kitchen. Tolstoy noted in his diary afterwards: "Turgenev fears the name of God, but acknowledges Him. He is naïvely tranquil, living in luxury and idleness of life." When Turgenev read a copy of Tolstoy's *Confessions* which had been banned by the censor, he admired its sincerity, truthfulness and strength of conviction, but wrote "it is built on false premises and ultimately leads to the most sombre denial of human life. . . . This too is in its way a kind of Nihilism." (A profound insight.) Oddly, Tolstoy now admired Turgenev's *Enough* which years before he had dismissed as worthless. And he wrote: "I love (Turgenev) terribly, pity him and always read him." The most amusing visit to Yasnaya Polyana was in 1881, two years before Turgenev's death. There were amateur theatricals, the children were astonished to see Turgenev carried a watch in every pocket of his waistcoat and that he kept taking them out to check the time. There was a quadrille and suddenly the sixty-three-year-old Turgenev took off his coat, stuck his thumbs in his waistcoat and struck comic figures with his legs: he was doing the genuine old style can-can. Everyone was enchanted, except Tolstoy who wrote in his diary:

Turgenev. Cancan—sad. Meeting peasants on the road was joyful.

Another time Turgenev read his prose-poem *The Dog* after a day's shooting:

> Outside a fearful storm is howling
> The dog sits in front of me and looks me straight in the face.
> And I look into his face.
> He wants, it seems, to tell me something. He is dumb.
> He is without words, he does not understand himself—but I understand him. I understand that at this instant there is living in him and me the same feeling, that there is no difference between us. We are the same; in each of us burns and shines the same trembling spark. Death sweeps down, with a wave of its chill broad wind . . .
> And the End!
> Who can then discern what was the spark that glowed in each of us. No. We are not beast and man that glance at each other. They are the eyes of equals, those eyes rivetted on one another. And in each of these, in the beast and in the man, the same life huddles up in fear close to the other.

Neither Tolstoy nor Urusov, the Vice-Governor of the province of Tula, who was with them, agreed with Turgenev's attitude to the dog, man and death. A hot discussion about religion started and Urusov fell off his chair with excitement. There was loud laughter and relief: death was a dangerous subject with Tolstoy. Seeing that they were thirteen at table, Turgenev cried out, "Hands up those who are afraid of death." Tolstoy put his hand up and so did Turgenev, but Tolstoy asked how it was that Turgenev was not afraid to be afraid of death. When he was a very old man, Tolstoy said to Gorky:

> If a man has learned to think, no matter what he may think, he is always thinking of his own death. All philosophers were like that. And what truth can there be, if there is death?

This attack on philosophers shows no resigned spirit; the rational Turgenev was resigned; he had long seen death advancing slowly and inevitably, had no belief in religion or immortality.

In 1878 Turgenev went to England for a few days to stay with old friends, the Bullock-Halls at Six Mile Bottom, and to Didie he wrote he had fired like a pig and had brought down only eleven birds. Oxford charmed, although he found himself staying in a large cold room at Balliol where the room stank of the smoking fire—the pervading sulphurous Victorian domestic smell. He wandered in the empty streets on Sunday and heard the dogs barking behind the closed doors of the houses and went fast asleep in church where the emotional preacher unfailingly dropped his voice at the end of his sentences. The following year he was again in Oxford where the University gave him the degree of Doctor of Civil Law which bewildered him, but he loved the brilliant red gown. He said it would be useful for charades at the rue de Douai. The other honorands were Ruskin, the Governor of Fiji and Leighton, the British Ambassador in Petersburg, which gave the occasion a Pickwickian air. He was rather nervous because of anti-Russian feeling in England (because it was the time of the Turko-Bulgarian war) and he was anxious because he had lately written a skit in verse called *Croquet at Windsor* in which Queen Victoria was seen using Bulgarian heads for croquet balls. But everything passed off delightfully, he was overwhelmed by praise, though he missed the tempests that occurred at Russian literary occasions. He went on to Cambridge and was once more regaled and met George Eliot for the second time, drank her health at a dinner and sat beside her at Newmarket Races—of all entertainments—and fascinated her by talk of Russian sporting habits. An important reason for his fame in England was that he had been introduced to the best society not only as an enemy of serfdom but that, in spite of being an artist and a foreigner, he was before anything a sportsman and a gentleman.

In 1879 Turgenev went off to Russia once more. He was again very short of ready money. His daughter's marriage had broken up and she had fled to Switzerland to get away from her bankrupt husband and Turgenev was obliged to sell his Paris pictures—at a loss, as usual, when he was a seller—in order to help her. In the January his brother, Nikolai, died and left him 50,000 roubles instead of the 100,000 that he had expected. The brother had become a hermit and changed his mind and left most to the nephew of his dead wife. But these private trials were followed to Turgenev's astonishment by the enthusiastic ovations given to him by University students in Petersburg. He had thought the young hated him. Young girls rushed to kiss him, the students cheered him again and again and placed a wreath of laurel on his head: a miracle! The younger generation loved him. After the attempts on the Tsar's life by the Terrorists, the new government was repressive and Turgenev knew in his heart that he was being used as a symbol of liberal protest. Still, there was a large dinner of a hundred covers for him and, as he said, he was almost suffocated by "the flowers of eloquence." The actress Savina read a scene from his play *A Provincial Lady.* He had a terrible cold. In Moscow, a party was given for him in the enormous hall of the Noblemen's Assembly. Tickets had been sold out a week in advance. The excited speeches of the students alarmed the Rector of the University and Turgenev tried to make a speech that would preserve some sort of calm. He had to be rescued from the clamouring, cheering crowds by the police. In Petersburg at a dinner given him by writers, he made a speech saying that the breach between the generations he had described in *Fathers and Sons* was over, but he innocently added that all could now work "to crown the edifice." Crown! The word aroused the suspicions of Dostoevsky who worshipped the Tsar and understood very well that Turgenev was arguing for a constitutional monarchy. This was not the last skirmish with his enemy. That occurred at the Pushkin Memorial celebrations the following year when the pair appeared on the same platform. Turgenev's mumbled speech bored the audience by its analysis of Pushkin's art. What they wanted in these euphoric days was a "manifestation" and eloquently Dostoevsky gave it to them and they were swept off their feet. Even Turgenev approved of it, the excited Dostoevsky said. Turgenev most emphatically did not. The confirmed Westerner wrote to a friend:

> I have not yet said "Thou hast conquered, O Galilean." That clever, brilliant and crafty speech, with all its peculiarities, is based totally on deceit . . . And what is the purpose of that *universal man* whom the public so furiously applauded . . . To be original Russian is better than to be characterless universal man. The whole thing is the same old pride—disguised as humility . . . The Slavophils have not swallowed us yet.

Turgenev's triumphs had another piquancy. *A Month in the Country* was put on in Moscow and acclaimed. The young actress Savina had transformed the part of Vera, the young girl who is Natalya's rival in the play. He told her the play came from his own life and Rakitin was himself. The actress had been at first overwhelmed by attentions from so great a man and was afraid of him, but his skill in pleasing, in advising in a fatherly way—she was being divorced from her husband and had another, a railway magnate, in view—and in showing a close interest in her career, flattered her. He wrote to her often from Paris, tenderly and with the usual hand-kissing phrases and when he returned to Russia and she was travelling to Odessa, he plotted to get on her train at Mtsenk and more than half-hoped to persuade her to get off at Orel and stay with him at Spasskoye. They did travel to Orel together but she continued her journey. He dreamed of her being at Spasskoye "and kissing her little feet in ecstasy." And went on:

> I can just see the headline "Scandal at Orlov Station: An extraordinary thing happened here yesterday. The writer Turgenev (by no means a young man), was seeing off a famous actress Savina who was travelling to Odessa to fulfil a star engagement. Suddenly as the train drew out of the station he dragged Mme Savina from the window of her compartment despite her desperate objections, as if possessed by a demon . . . And yet it could have happened—it hung by a thread; so, incidentally, does everything in life.

And a week later, he wrote:

> Alas, I will never be your sin. . . . And should we meet again in two or three years I shall be quite an old man, you will have settled down at last and nothing of the past will remain. This will not affect you much for you have all your life before you and mine is behind me— and that hour in the train when I felt almost like a young man of twenty was the last flicker of the holy lamp.

He asked, as he had asked so many women, "Am I in love with you?" and said:

> I do not know—in the past such things were different. This irresistible desire to merge, possess—and to surrender—when even the urging of

the flesh loses itself in a kind of lambent flame—I am probably babbling, but I should have been immeasurably happy if only . . . if only . . .

In 1881 Savina did come to Spasskoye. The Polonsky family were staying with him and, knowing she liked swimming, Turgenev had a bath hut built for her in the deep water of the lake there. The country people came to a party for her. There was singing and dancing. He took her to his study and showed her the table at which he had written *Fathers and Sons.* By his bedside she saw the screens made by his mother's orders and the album which his mother had brought back from Sorrento. The branch of a lime tree was by the open window by the desk. Savina heard him read a *Poem in Prose* to a woman, he said, to whom his whole life had been given and who would not bring a single flower or shed a tear on his grave. He was not going to publish this poem because "It might hurt her." He was weeping as he read and Savina was very moved. On the day she left he read to her the last but one of his stories, *The Song of Triumphant Love.* She says tritely that she could not think of anything clever to say about it.

The story gushes forth and was enormously popular with the sentimental public, but the critics thought that it was trash. They could not make head nor tail of it. It is one of his fantasies, set in Italy and seems to be an attempt to convey the power of music on Turgenev's mind and may have been conceived as an attempt at an opera. Two devoted friends love the same woman. She chooses one and the rejected lover goes away to the Orient and returns years later with a dumb Malay servant to occupy a pavilion in the married couple's garden. At night from the pavilion strange music comes and appears to draw the wife from her bed to the garden: she is sleep-walking. Whether she ever reaches the rejected lover is unclear, but the suspicious husband kills the lover. The Malay injects a mysterious substance into the body and the dead lover is led away, walking: the wife is relieved of her torment and is now pregnant for the first time. The story may be put among his dream stories on the theme that love conquers death.

Pauline Viardot afterwards claimed to have worked with Turgenev on this story and it is this that inclines one to believe that it might stand as one of their *operéttes*, an attempt above all to explore the erotic power of music and the dream life it can evoke. Turgenev was tiring of realism at this time, as we have seen in one or two earlier explorations of dream and the unconscious, and he seems to be playing with the bizarre effects of surrealism, long before its time; but the stagey character of the story gives it the effect of artifice and surfeit.

Of course in his naïve way Turgenev told Pauline and Didie about Savina and they were caustic about her. He did not tell quite all: they did not hear that she had stayed with him at Spasskoye where Pauline had always refused to go. He simply said that Savina was a talented, ambitious but typically neurotic actress with a *grisette*'s common speech. But he wrote often; on his last visits to Russia he saw her and heard of her love affairs. She even came to Paris to see a doctor there and he paid her bills and back she went to get married. Turgenev was gentle, kind, paternal and was saddened by the impossibility of his love; he said it was the last flare of the "holy lamp." And it was, for he did feel something of what he felt for Pauline when he was young and, indeed not only his public triumphs but the greater importance of being in love with a young girl made him appear youthful and excited by life to his friends when he returned to France after his first meeting her. The feeling remained with him until his death.

His letters to Savina are very moving. They have an erotic note which is missing from all his known letters to Pauline Viardot and they resemble those he wrote to the Baroness Vreskaya and to Didie, but they are resigned, and show deep caring for her as a person and an artist. He had always been a teacher to the women he loved and a good one.

But as regards the tragedy in *verse*—you are not so good at reading verse. Do you know why? You read it as if you were afraid of it, and without the naturalness which is characteristic of you. You drop into a rather monotonous sort of voice—which is known as *elocution.* One should be perfectly at ease with verse (especially verse by Averkiyev) and simply observe the metre without giving unnatural emphasis to the words and so forth. You see I can even be critical of you. It seems to me I could be of some use to you. In any case, it would be very

pleasant for me to do so. But this, like many other things, must be
assigned to the realm of the impossible.

And, in another, he says::

> I won't deny that at this moment—day-dreaming and taking advan-
> tage of your permission—I am clinging to your adorable little lips, the
> touch of which can never be forgotten until the end of life.

By this time Savina had made her grand marriage, but the tone of
the letters does not change.

> You know I love you very, very much. Adieu, I kiss all of you. "All?"
> you will ask. "Yes, all," I repeat. And then I will kiss your dear hands.

He had persuaded her, as he had persuaded Pauline Viardot years
before, to let him have a cast of her hands.

In the final period of his life, after *Virgin Soil*, Turgenev wrote
a number of short Poems in Prose and although it is claimed that
they give us glimpses of his inner life, they do not match what can
be discerned in his stories and novels, or indeed in his letters. The
Poems strike one as being poetically vapid and self-conscious, if we
except things like his apostrophe to the Russian language and his
struggle with his pessimism and his ultimate assertion that in some
way "love conquers death." Each poem crystallises either a mystery
or the passing flash of a moment or a mood. But he wrote two more
remarkable stories of "possession"—*Father Alexey's Story* and *Clara
Milich*—the latter written during his last illness—and one very fine
thing, *The Relic*, which takes one back to the manner of *A Sportsman's Sketches*. *Father Alexey's Story* is about a man whose son
becomes possessed by "the devil" or "green man" of folk lore: it is
made to seem a real event troubling the common imagination of the
people of the steppe and recalls something of Hogg's *Confessions
of a Justified Sinner*.

Clara Milich is a transmuted version of a true story of theatre life.
A well-known actress, Kalmina, had committed suicide by taking
poison on the stage two years before, because of an unhappy love-
affair. From this and possibly as the result of the *épanouissement*

he experienced in Savina's company, he turned to literature for a
hint. First of all to the character of Clara Mowbray in Scott's *St.
Ronan's Well.* He had probably read this novel when he was staying
at Pitlochry and although he took only the girl's name from it and
her terror in her misuse, a man like Turgenev who had spent so much
of his life in spas and with hypochondriacs must have been amused
by a tale which comes from Scott's lyrical period and owed its feeling
to Scott's memory of an early love affair of his own. The other, and
stranger, literary tip, as Turgenev himself said, came from Edgar
Allan Poe. One often comes across such literary echoes in Turgenev:
he never ceased to be something of a *littérateur.* The story itself is
concerned with Avator, a young man who has become haughty,
timid and self-enclosed through too much reading. He abruptly
dismisses the advances made to him by a provincial actress at the
theatre, falls in love with her only when she has died on the stage
and has guilty delusions of seeing her in his room. The point of the
story is that she avenges herself by hypnotising him *after* her death,
so that he is possessed. Whenever Turgenev writes such strange
stories or fables, they become physical scrutinies; their power lies in
his habit of staring at every person or thing so that its visual exactness
is magnified and detached from normal experience; this is the habit
of the surrealists:

> in Clara's image . . .he saw her fingers, her nails, the little pores on
> her cheeks near her temples, the little mole under the left eye . . . her
> walk and how she held her head a little on the right side.

And when, in hallucination, she appears to come to his room her
lips curl: he kisses them "and even felt the moist chill of her
teeth."

Clara might very well be an exact portrait of Pauline Viardot
detached from her life:

> A half-Jewish, half-gypsy type, small black eyes under thick brows
> almost meeting in the middle, a straight slightly turned up nose,
> delicate lips with a beautiful but decided curve, an immense mass of
> black hair, heavy even in appearance, a low brow still as marble, tiny
> ears—the whole face dreamy, almost sullen. A nature passionate,
> wilful—hardly good-tempered, hardly clever, but gifted.

Avator is not in love with Clara but is possessed by her, is in her power and no longer belongs to himself and he will die as he tries to touch the vision.

The difficulty with the story is the old one: Turgenev is too elaborately careful in providing small clues that would suggest a rational basis for the hallucination—for example the lock of hair in the youth's hand when he dies as he embraces the ghost is a lock of Clara's hair left by her sister in her diary which he has been reading. The story is far too prosaically drawn out, but it has what seem to be autobiographical hints of what was passing through Turgenev's own mind as he wrote, in moments of respite, when he was dying. It is impossible not to see a direct reference in the youth's words when the vision has gone.

> Next time I will be stronger. I will master her . . . But what next. Then must I die so as to be with her? . . . Well, what then? If I must die let me die. Death has no terrors for me now. It cannot then annihilate me? On the contrary only *thus* and *then* can I be happy . . . as I have not been happy in my life, as she has not. We are both pure! Oh that kiss.

Such a kiss, he says, even Romeo and Juliet did not know—the allusion to Shakespeare is characteristic—art gives us the only immortality possible to us.

We must prefer to see Turgenev's genius in his last years in the story he wrote not long before illness destroyed all hope: *A Living Relic*, a story in which he suddenly recovered the simple feeling and transparency of *A Sportsman's Sketches*. It opens with one of those plain off-hand sentences which make us confident at once:

> For a hunter rainy weather is a veritable calamity.

The young sportsman and the glum Yermolai stand under dripping trees in the woods, a day's shooting is done for. They give up and find a hut and eventually find an old shed among the weeds of the abandoned garden of a ruined cottage. In the darkness inside they hear a voice: a sick woman is lying on some boards. The head is withered, the skin is bronze in colour, the colour of an old ikon, the nose as thin as a knife blade, the lips have almost disappeared. The only light from the face comes from the eyes and teeth; the woman's fingers move over the coverlet like a pair of sticks and over the face "a smile was striving to appear on it, to cross its metallic cheeks, was striving and could not spread." She is not an old crone. She is Lukeria, a young woman of thirty, not many years ago the most beautiful and brightest of the house serfs who used to lead the singing and dancing as it might be at Spasskoye. She had run downstairs in excitement to greet the young man she was going to marry, tripped and fell over. She is paralysed. From that moment, though doctors and hospitals had done everything for her injury, she has in seven years wasted to the condition of a mummy.

Little by little she tells her story. Kind people look after he, she says, she eats nothing, she can reach for a mug of water. She has learned to be patient. The blind and the dumb are worse off. She can hear everything—a mole digging under the ground, smell the smell of the first buckwheat and the limes or the flowers, watch the birds fly in. The priest tells her she has no sins, not even sins of the mind. She can sing to herself a little, but that brings tears, but "where could so many tears come from? For surely a woman's tears cost her nothing." She sleeps badly, but when she does she has extraordinary dreams. Death comes to her in the form of a woman and says "I am sorry I can't take you now." In another her dead father and mother appear, bow to her, because she "has lifted a great weight from their souls: she has done with her own sins and is now conquering theirs." In another, she is bitten by a dog and is whirled off to heaven and the dog has to let go. Another dream shows that, somehow, the legend of Jeanne d'Arc has travelled to Russia.

A story which might be pious, sentimental and weepy is alight with the strangeness of life and told with delicacy, sense and compassion. And one or two details—a reference, for example, to the fact that the man she was going to marry "got his passport," is enough to show the easy acceptance of serfdom. It is clear that in this story Turgenev is giving us an account of a real woman whom he certainly must have met in the circumstances he describes, for they are most clearly observed; but he has fulfilled the needs of an empathy which is at the core of his art. It is the task of the artist, as he said, to speak for a character and not simply of them. It was his belief that beauty in art seizes on that which is immortal—a matter of deep importance to a writer who himself feared death because he could rationally see no life beyond it. We are made to have a double response to this woman: the first is that, as he describes her, so exactly she was: but, also, since he cannot use her exact words when she is speaking of herself, he is so filled with her voice that he can speak *for* her and offer her as she feels her inexpressible self to be. Humility is her nature.

———

In 1881 when he was in Russia, he had an attack of neuralgia and a touch of rheumatism in his shoulder. It passed off but, always fascinated by his illnesses, he went to see the great doctor Charcot when he got back to Paris. Charcot diagnosed a mild angina and Turgenev saw himself tolerating this for many more years. He was put on a milk diet which seemed to relieve him until, after a few months, he found that he could not stand up and was henceforth completely bedridden. He had to endure a small operation for a cyst —which he called Feoktistov, the chief censor—without anaesthetic and he described to Alphonse Daudet his sensations as the surgeon's knife cut him. He said he felt as if he were a fruit being peeled; then the knife cut as if it were slicing a soft banana.

> "I studied this," he said, "so that I could tell you about it at one of our dinners."

The realists liked this kind of thing.

For Pauline Viardot the situation was terrible. Louis Viardot lay in another room, suffering from a stroke. She had to nurse the two men who were the most important in her life. It was too much for her and they had to move Turgenev to Les Frênes. Viardot and Turgenev shook hands and, soon after, Viardot died. The shock to Turgenev had to be borne and with it the agonising pain of what now turned out to be cancer of the spine. His dreams were monstrous. The gross fish images came to his mind, but in between spasms he noted down his symptoms in what he called *Journal of My Death*—for example, that he no longer had erections.

He wrote fragments of *Clara Milich* between bouts of pain. Pauline nursed him and Didie set up her easel in his room and sometimes she and her sister brought their children. There were occasional recoveries—in one he remembers the fire on the ship when he had left Russia as a youth and dictated the long and remarkable piece which appears in his *Reminiscences* and busied himself with his publisher. He even dictated a little story called *The Quail* for Countless Tolstoy's children and wrote the famous letter to Tolstoy begging him to return to his art. But frightful pain seized him; he was given morphia and he screamed in his delirium. Once he shouted that Pauline was Lady Macbeth: he was remembering her triumph in one of her greatest parts. Another time, in his madness, he threw an inkpot at her and asked her to throw him out of the window. When he came to himself, he begged her to see if she could take down a story in Russian or a mixture of languages and indeed, though it took days, she did it and put it into French for him. It is called *An End* and is obviously a violent attack on the gentry: it is about a landowner who has become a horsestealer and is lynched by his peasants. He was so pleased by achieving this that he started planning to write a long novel with Pauline's help. But he was too far gone. The huge body had wasted to nothing and by the beginning of September in 1883 he could only fitfully recognise his adoptive family. As he was dying he said of Pauline "Here's the Queen of Queens" and then went on rambling in Russian. He imagined he was a Russian peasant and is believed to have said "Goodbye my dear ones, my whitish ones."

After a funeral oration at the Gare de l'Est, the body was taken to St. Petersburg by Pauline's two sons-in-law. The Tsarist government had done what they could to prevent political demonstrations, but thousands attended the funeral in the remote Volkov cemetery where close to Gogol, he was buried.

Sources

Turgenev: The Man, His Art and His Age. Avrahm Yarmolinsky. London, Hodder & Stoughton, 1926, 1959.

Turgenev: A Life. David Magarshack. London, Faber & Faber, 1954.

The Price of Genius: The Life of Pauline Viardot. April Fitzlyon. London, Calder, 1964; New York, Appleton-Century, 1964.

The Turgenev Family. V. Zhitova. Trans. A. S. Mills. London, Harvill, 1948.

La Vie Douleureuse d'Ivan Tourguéneff. E. K. Semenov. Paris, 1930.

Turgenev in England and America. R. A. Gettman. Urbana, Ill., 1941.

Ivan Turgenev. *The Portrait Game.* Trans. and ed. Marion Mainwaring. London, Chatto & Windus, 1973; New York, Horizon Press, 1973.

Ivan Tourgéneff et les courants politiques et sociaux de son temps. Henri Granjard. Paris, 1954.

Lettres inédites à Pauline Viardot et sa famille. Trans. Henri Granjard and Alexandre Zviguilsky. Editions L'Age de l'homme. Lausanne, 1971.

Tourgenueff. Nouvelle correspondance inédite. Trans. Alexandre Zviguilsky. Librairie des Cinq Continents, Paris, 1972.

Tourgenueff, la Comtesse Lambert et le Nid des Seigneurs. Henri Granjard. Paris, 1960.

Letters to an Actress. Nora Gottlieb and Raymond Chapman. London, Allison & Busby, 1973; Ohio University Press, 1974.

Turgenev's Letters: A Selection. Edgar H. Lehrman. New York, Knopf, 1960.

Lettres à Madame Viardot. E. Halpérine-Kaminsky. Paris, 1907.

Ivan Tourguéneff d'après sa correspondance avec ses amis français. E. Halperine-Kaminsky. Paris, 1901.

Souvenirs sur Tourguéneff. Isaac Pavlovsky. Paris, 1887.

Mémoires de la vie littéraire. Edmond and Jules de Goncourt. Paris, 1887.

La Russie en 1839. Marquis de Custine. Paris, 1843.

The Marquis de Custine and His Russia in 1839. George F. Kennan. Princeton, N.J., 1971; London, Hutchinson, 1972.

My Past and Thoughts: The Memoirs of Alexander Herzen. New ed. Chatto & Windus and Knopf, 1968. One vol. ed. Chatto & Windus and Knopf, 1974.

The Romantic Exiles. E. H. Carr. London, Gollancz, 1933.

Michael Bakunin. E. H. Carr. New York, Macmillan, 1937.

The Life of Tolstoy. Aylmer Maude. Oxford University Press, 1930.

George Sand. Curtis Cate. Boston, Houghton Mifflin, 1975; London, Hamish Hamilton, 1975.

Oblomov and His Creator: The Life and Art of Ivan Goncharov. Milton Ehre. Princeton, N.J., 1974.

Dostoevsky: Reminiscences. Anna Dostoevsky. Ed. and trans. Beatrice Stillman. New York, Liveright, 1975.

Dostoevsky. Konstantin Mochulsky. Princeton, N.J., 1967.

Pushkin: A Comparative Commentary. John Bayley. London and New York, Cambridge University Press, 1971.

Letters of Anton Chekhov. Ed. and trans. Michael Henry Heim and Simon Karlinsky. New York, Harper & Row, London, Bodley Head, 1973.

Letters of Anton Chekhov. Selected and ed. Avrahm Yarmolinsky. New York, Viking, 1974; London, Cape, 1974.

History of Russian Literature. D. S. A. Mirsky. Rev. ed. London, Routledge, 1949.

Manuscrits Parisiens d'Ivan Tourguénoff. André Mazon. Paris, 1930.

Turgenev. A Study. Richard Freeborn. London and New York, Oxford University Press, 1960.

The Art of Fiction and Other Essays. Henry James. New York, Oxford University Press, 1948.

Turgenev. W. R. S. Ralston. New York, Athenaeum, 1883.

The Captain's Death Bed. Virginia Woolf. London, The Hogarth Press, 1950.

Consuelo. George Sand. Paris, 1869.

Spring Torrents. Trans. Leonard Schapiro. London, Eyre Methuen, 1972.

Fort comme la mort. Guy de Maupassant. Paris, 1889.

Fathers and Sons. Trans. Rosemary Edmonds. London, Penguin, 1965. Reissued with the *Romanes Lectures,* "Fathers and Children," by Isaiah Berlin, 1975.

First Love trans. by Isaiah Berlin. London, Hamish Hamilton, 1950 (with *Rudin*), and Panther Books, 1965.

About the Author

V. S. PRITCHETT was born in England in 1900. He is a short-story writer, novelist, critic and traveler. His short stories have appeared in collections in the United States under the titles *The Sailor and the Saint, When My Girl Comes Home, Blind Love, The Camberwell Beauty* and as individual contributions in *The New Yorker* and *Holiday.* Among his novels are *Mr. Beluncle, Dead Man Leading* and *The Key to My Heart.* Random House has also published *The Living Novel and Later Appreciations,* a collection of critical essays, most of which appeared originally in *The New Statesman,* and his Clark Lectures, *Meredith and English Comedy.* He has been a lifelong contributor to this paper and is now a director. His memoirs, *A Cab at the Door and Midnight Oil,* were published by Random House in 1968 and 1972. In 1973 he published a life of Balzac.

Mr. Pritchett's extensive sojourns in Europe, the Middle East, and South America have led to the writing of several books on travel, among them *The Offensive Traveller.* With photographs by Evelyn Hofer, Mr. Pritchett has written *London Perceived, Dublin: A Portrait* and *New York Proclaimed.*

Mr. Pritchett has visited the United States, where he gave the Christian Gauss Lectures at Princeton, was Beckman Professor at the University of California in Berkeley, and has been writer in residence at Smith College, and Zisskind Professor at Brandeis University. He is a foreign Honorary Member of the American Academy of Arts and Letters and the American Academy of Arts and Sciences.

In 1975 he received a knighthood.